COMING ALIVE!

BY: REBECKA EGGERS

©2013 REBECKA EGGERS

ALL RIGHTS RESERVED

ISBN: 978-0-9915140-0-7

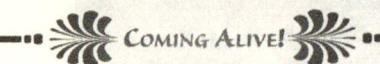

Contents

Coming Alive! ∞ The Invitation — 5

The Prologue — 9

Part 1 ∞ Disempowering Dominance — 17

Disempowering Dominance ∞ The Choice Point — 19

Disempowering Dominance ∞ Naming the Tormentor — 37

Disempowering Dominance ∞ Beyond Learning to See — 49

Disempowering Dominance ∞ The Call to Death — 59

Disempowering Dominance ∞ Confronting Evil — 85

Disempowering Dominance ∞ The Mirror of Babylon — 97

Disempowering Dominance ∞ Facing the Terrorist Within — 115

Disempowering Dominance ∞ Death — 127

Part 2 ∞ The Birth of the Passionate Warrior — 147

The Birth of the Passionate Warrior ∞ Empowering Beauty — 149

The Birth of the Passionate Warrior ∞ Present Awakening — 161

The Birth of the Passionate Warrior ∞ Liberating Passion — 175

The Birth of the Passionate Warrior ∞ Encountering The Passion Path	185
The Birth of the Passionate Warrior ∞ Rebirth	205
The Birth of the Passionate Warrior ∞ Come Into the Stillness	219
The Birth of the Passionate Warrior ∞ The Marriage of Love & War	235
The Birth of the Passionate Warrior ∞ Passion Path Activism	259
The Birth of The Passionate Warrior ∞ Passion Path Destruction	293
The Birth of The Passionate Warrior ∞ Passion Path Redemption	321
Part 3 ∞ Coming Alive	**343**
Coming Alive! ∞ The Warrior's Ma'at	345
Coming Alive! ∞ Passion	369
Epilogue	379
About the Author	389
Additional Credits	391

Coming Alive! ∞ The Invitation

I use a lot of mythology and psychology in this book. I am not a religion scholar, a psychologist, or an expert in either religion or psychology. What you are getting in this book is a cross section of many different influences that I have relied upon during the course of my life for the purpose of coming to terms with the challenges I have personally faced and that we are all facing together as a global community. I am relating my impressions and experiences with the mythology and psychology presented. This book isn't meant to be a definitive work or even my final opinion on the subject at hand. It is a journey. I invite you to take the journey with me and to relate to the material presented. Make it your own. Draw your own conclusions. Experiment!

This book is laid out in three distinct parts. The first part, *Disempowering Dominance*, is about understanding and preparing to extricate yourself from an emerging and ever growing atmosphere of global domination. The second part, *The Birth of the Passionate Warrior*, is about achieving the kind of psychological and spiritual freedom that will allow you to take up your purpose with power and passion. It is also about achieving a new vision and orientation for your life and for our collective experience together. Finally, the last section, *Coming Alive*, will provide the structural supports for the kind of new, inner consciousness that will guide and empower you as you begin to recreate your life from within the Passionate Warrior's frame of reference. It is designed to support you in resurrecting and embodying your passion from within a radically new space of freedom and power.

This book is meant to offer a point of transition from one way of being to another, from one level of consciousness to another. If you relate deeply with the material, it will affect you tremendously. I know this because writing this book forever changed me. I invite you to open yourself to the material and allow it to move you. When finally we come to the end of this book together, I hope that we will have arrived not at the end of our journey, but at the gateway to yet another adventure.

If the rather fluid nature of my invitation to a journey bothers you or if you need citations in perfect form and scholarly verification of every thought in order to feel good about what you are reading, put this book down.[1] It is not

---

[1] This feels like an appropriate place to address the capitalization of pronouns in relation to various goddesses. I have capitalized she/her as a gesture of respect, when referring to those goddesses whose energy and stories have impacted my life personally. For me they represent aspects of the collective psyche with which I have chosen to relate very deeply. To them I pay the greatest respect.

for you. If, on the other hand, you are ready to undertake the difficult, imperfect, and sometimes messy process that will allow you to stop living as a victim of circumstance who passively accepts other people's dictates, this book is for you. If you are ready to come alive as the Passionate Warrior so that you can, at last, actively create your life with passion, power, and purpose, then only the simplest of gestures is required. Turn the page!

The Prologue

> *"I daresay you haven't had much practice,' said the Queen. When I was your age I always did it for half an hour a day. Why, sometimes, I've believed as many as six impossible things before breakfast."*
> ∞ *Lewis Carroll, Through the Looking Glass*

And that ought to tell you where we are going. It ought to help you decide if you really want to come along. Whatever you decide, you should begin with the knowledge that I plan to take us to the other side of the looking glass.

My own journey through the looking glass began in a place that may be completely foreign to you. I live in the mountains of southern Mexico in the state of Chiapas. Chiapas is one of the poorest places in the world in terms of economics and one of the richest places on earth in terms of biodiversity. I live very close to the ecological transition point where the forest gives way to the lush jungle. I am surrounded by Mayan culture and ancient ruins. My home, San Cristóbal de las Casas, is also surrounded by the Zapatista rebel territories.

The Zapatistas are a mostly indigenous, Mayan force that rose up against the Mexican government in 1994. They still maintain autonomous territories within the state of Chiapas.

In the Epilogue, I have included excerpts from an article I wrote prior to penning this book. That article explains exactly how I came to live in this magical, mysterious town which some people call "El Pueblo Mágico" or The Little Town of Magic. I ask that you not skip ahead to the end, but that you read this excerpt as it was intended. It is kind of like the bow that ties all of this together. Regardless, I want you to know that the story is there and to have a little bit of history in mind about Chiapas as you read the coming chapters. This background information will be useful for you as I sometimes refer to my own experiences where relevant.

I look forward to meeting you on the other side of the looking glass. In order to hang some context around what I mean by this, I offer you the following story by Zapatista Rebel Leader, Subcomandante Insurgente Marcos:

The Glass to See to the Other Side
February-May 1995
Cut from the inverse side, a mirror ceases to be a mirror and becomes a glass. Mirrors are for looking

on this side, and glass is made to look to the other side. Mirrors are made to be etched. A glass is made to be broken…to cross to the other side…

From the Mountains of southeast Mexico

Subcomandante Insurente Marcos

P.S.

…*The image of the real or the unreal, which searches among so many mirrors for a glass to break.*

Durito

Dawn, Mexico City. Durito wanders through the streets adjoining the Zocolo. Sporting a small trench coat and a hat angled like Humphrey Bogart in Casablanca, Durito pretends to pass unnoticed. His outfit and slow crawl are unnecessary, as he sticks to the shadows that escape the bright display windows. Shadow of shadow, silent walk, angled hat, a dragging trench coat, Durito walks through dawn in Mexico City. No one notices him. They do not see him. They do not see him, not because he is well disguised or because of that tiny, quixotic detective outfit from the 1950s, or because he is barely distinguishable from the mounds of garbage. Durito walks amid papers being dragged here and there by a whisk of the unpredictable winds that populate the dawns of Mexico City. No one sees Durito, for the simple reason that in this city no one sees anyone.

"This city is sick," Durito writes to me; "It is sick from loneliness and fear. It is a great collective of solitudes. It is a collection of cities, one for each resident. It's not about sums of anguish (do you know of loneliness without anguish?), but about potency; each loneliness is multiplied by the number of lonely people that surround it. It is as though each person's solitude entered a House of Mirrors, like those you see in the country fairs. Each solitude is a mirror that reflects another solitude, and like a mirror bounces off more solitudes.

Durito has begun to discover that he is in foreign territory, that the city is not his place. In his heart and in this dawn, Durito packs his bag. He walks this road as though taking an inventory, a last caress, like a lover who knows this is good-bye. At certain moments, the sound of footsteps diminishes and the cry of sirens, which frightens outsiders, increases. And Durito is one of those outsiders, so he stops on the corner each time the red-and-blue blinking lights crisscross the street. Durito takes advantage of the complicity of a doorway in order to light a pipe gorilla-style: a tiny spark, a deep breath, and the smoke engulfing his gaze and face. Durito stops. He looks and sees. In front of him, a display window catches his eye. Durito comes near and looks through the great glass pane to what exists beyond it. Mirrors of all shapes and sizes, porcelain and glass figurines, cut crystal, tiny music box. "There are no talking boxes," Durito says to himself, without forgetting the long years spent in the jungle of the Mexican Southeast.

Durito has come to say goodbye to Mexico City and has decided to give a gift to this city, about which everyone complains and no one abandons. A gift. This is Durito, a beetle of the Lacondon Jungle in the center of Mexico City.

He makes an elegant magician's gesture. Everything stops. The lights go out like a candle extinguished by a gentle wind-lick on its face. Another gesture and a reflecting light illuminates a music box in the display window. A ballerina in a fine lilac costume holds an endless stillness, hands crossed overhead, legs held together, balanced on tiptoes. Durito tries to imitate the position but promptly gets his many arms entangled. Another magic gesture, and a piano, the size of a cigarette box appears. Durito sits in front of the piano and puts a jug of beer on the top—who knows where he got it from, but it's already half empty. He cracks and flexes his fingers, doing digital gymnastics just like the pianists in the movies. Then he turns towards the ballerina and nods his head.

The ballerina begins to stir and makes a bow. Durito hums an unknown tune, beats a rhythm with his little legs, closes his eyes, and begins to sway.

The first notes begin. Durito plays the piano with four hands. On the other side of the glass pane, the ballerina begins to twirl and gently lifts her right thigh. Durito leans on the keyboard and plays furiously. The ballerina performs her best steps within the prison of the little music box. The city disappears. There is nothing but Durito at his piano and the ballerina in her music box. Durito plays and the ballerina dances. The city is surprised; its cheeks blush as when one receives an unexpected gift, a pleasant surprise, good news. Durito gives his best gift; an unbreakable and eternal mirror, a good-bye that is harmless, that heals, that cleanses. The spectacle lasts only a few instants. The last notes fade as the cities that populate this city take shape again. The ballerina returns to her uncomfortable immobility; Durito turns up the collar on his trench coat and makes a slight bow toward the display window.

"Will you always be behind the glass pane?" Durito asks her and asks himself. "Will you always be on the other side of my over here, and will I always be on this side of your over there?"

Health to you and until always, my beloved malcontent. Happiness is like a gift; it lasts for a moment, and it is worth it.

Durito crosses the street, arranges his hat and continues to walk. Before going around the corner, he turns toward the display window. A star-shaped hole adorns the glass. The alarms are ringing uselessly. Behind the window, the ballerina is no longer in the music box...

"This city is sick. When its illness becomes a crisis, it will be cured. This collective loneliness, multiplied by millions and empowered, will end by finding itself and finding the reason for its powerlessness. Then, and only then, will this city shed its gray dress and adorn itself with the brightly colored ribbons, which are so abundant in the provinces.

"This city lives a cruel game of mirrors, but the game of the mirrors is useless and sterile if finding the transparency of glass is not the goal. It is enough to understand this and, as who-knows-who said, struggle and begin to be happy...

"I'm coming back. Prepare the tobacco and the insomnia. I have a lot to tell you, Sancho." Durito signs off.

It is morning. A few piano notes accompany the day that comes and Durito, who leaves. To the west, the sun is like a rock, shattering the glass pane of the morning…

Vale once again. Health to you, and leave surrender to the empty mirrors.

El Sup, getting up from the piano and, confused by so many mirrors, looking for the exit door…or is it the entrance?[2]

---

[2] Ponce De Leon, Juana and Subcomandante Insurgente Marcos. "The Glass to See to the Other Side." *Our Word is Our Weapon, Selected Writings*. New York. Seven Stories Press. 2002. Print. Pages 294-296. The proceeds of this book (beyond those needed to cover the cost of publishing and other related expenses) will be donated to Schools for Chiapas in sincere gratitude to the people of Chiapas for the many lessons learned and for a life of meaning plucked from the rubble of servitude. http://www.schoolsforchiapas.org

Part 1
∞
Disempowering Dominance

Can You Love Her?

After eons of neglect,
Parsed out through countless
Crimes of omission,
Not to mention outright
Hostilities,
And torture that lasted well
Beyond the night…

Now She lies dormant,
Only mostly awake.

Still.

The Lady is waiting.

But you don't get to be sure
That if you call Her
She will come
Soft and nurturing,
Divine Mother
Or
Holy Lover
Like spun silk in your hand.

NO!

She may choose not to come at all.

Or

She may come
With fire in her eyes
Demanding a sacrifice.

She may arrive
With sickle in hand
To scatter ash at your feet.

She may even call you to death
By your own hand.

And She will certainly want to know!

Can you love Her this way?

©Rebecka Eggers, 2013

Disempowering Dominance ∞ The Choice Point

"The basic difference between an ordinary man and a warrior is that a warrior takes everything as a challenge while an ordinary man takes everything as a blessing or a curse."
∞ *Carlos Castaneda*

When I was 16, I got into an abusive relationship with a much older man. He dominated and controlled me with violence. At 19, I finally left the relationship for good thinking I would never have to face that kind of exploitation again. A few years later, I made the fateful decision to become a lawyer. Just after I graduated from law school, my mother was brutally murdered. In addition to the pain of losing my mother, I was thrust into a terrifying situation of domination and power imbalance during the police investigation. My family and I were put through polygraph examinations, blood tests, and informal interrogation. I began to fear for my life at the hands of the State of Texas in addition to fearing that my mother's killer might emerge from the shadows and make me his/her next victim. I relied on my legal skills to get me through.

As soon as humanly possible, I dove headlong into my career as a lawyer, again feeling grateful that another traumatic encounter, which had left me feeling powerless and afraid, was over.

Eventually, at the age of 38, I also left law in search of something less confrontational, more cooperative, more humane…My years as a transactional tax attorney gave me a ringside seat for the game called global capitalism. When I left, I was on the run from a career, and indeed, a global financial system that felt to me like it was based on a zero sum game of exploitation and domination. I set off to start a new life in the highlands of Chiapas, Mexico. Again, I wiped my brow thinking I would never have to deal with that kind of relationship dynamic again. I am sure the gods were laughing. I may as well have moved to domination central.

Not only am I dealing with the relationship dynamics that are naturally a part of living in a foreign country where poverty is endemic, but I also live in the midst of communities that are actively in resistance. The circumstances that gave rise to the resistance in the first place are largely still in tact. In addition, the city where I live is known for intensifying whatever crisis you think you are escaping by coming here. Some of the locals have devised a nickname for the magical city of San Cristóbal: San Crisis. In short, my location changed. But my experience of being dominated and exploited moved right along with me and it intensified to the point where I could no longer do anything but face the cold hard hand of reality on my soft fleshy cheek. I managed to replicate my own servitude in professional and personal relationships alike by opening myself up to people who were more interested in getting something from me than in supporting me in my thriving. The pain and confusion were excruciating.

Suddenly one summer evening, the confusion lifted, and in a moment of intense clarity, I realized what had happened. I had made the mistake of believing I could escape my relationship and lifestyle patterns without actually understanding and fully addressing the inner dynamics created by 38 years of socialization.

On a more collective level, as I examined the various news stories rolling around in my head, I realized the old tension had returned. But this time the pattern I was noticing had become a global phenomenon. The microcosm of my own personal pain had become the macrocosm of a global system. There was no place left to run. In that moment, I realized that domination and exploitation are ubiquitous. Further, governments, large, powerful organizations, and communities are the biggest bullies on the block in many cases. The power imbalance of one individual in relation to this global circumstance is enormous.

There really is no place left unaffected by the cultural and social imperatives of domination, exploitation, and control.

By the same token, very little private space remains free from government intrusion. In many cases, and in many ways, now even our own bodies are subject to government surveillance. Escape really is not a practical option.

By way of example: Women and children are being gang raped with near impunity in places like India and the Congo (among other places) as a result of government and communal systems that support severe gender-based discrimination, exploitation, and victim blaming. Along the same lines, in many places, rape is nothing more than a weapon of war. Finally, women and children are often sold or lured into modern day slavery in the sex trade.

In the United States, government regulation of women's bodies and reproductive rights is becoming more and more common. Many U.S. states already have, and many elements of the U.S. Congress would like to enact legislation that will increase state control of women's bodies. Some U.S. states have passed legislation that forces women to have state mandated, and invasive vaginal ultrasounds before they can proceed with abortions.

Beyond the realm of women's rights, body autonomy is under attack in general. For instance, organizations like Monsanto are lobbying for the right to force feed us GMOs by restricting our alternatives and preventing GMO labeling. Government institutions like the Transportation Safety Administration routinely subject citizens to body scans that produce images of the naked body. Even killing has become a routine and largely unsupervised state function. By way of example, I cite the use of unmanned drones to kill designated terrorists. What used to be carried out in the shadows by the CIA is now being carried out in broad daylight with very little oversight.

Meanwhile, protesters, journalists, and whistle blowers alike are being labeled as terrorists which subjects them to a whole array of special government rights and reprisals. Real terrorist organizations in places like Pakistan and Afghanistan are killing ordinary citizens for defying their religious tyranny.

I could go on forever with examples of this phenomenon. I could write a whole book on the issue. But here is the linchpin: The U.S. government, through the National Security Agency spy program recently revealed by Edward Snowden, now has the ability to build (and manipulate) a pretty complete file on any and everyone in the entire modern world. It has been revealed that the NSA is now recording every telephone conversation and possibly every email that is transmitted in the U.S., and perhaps in foreign territories as well. This represents a high degree of government intrusion into our private lives. Further, the implications in terms of censorship as well as manipulation and control of the populace are staggering.

One evening last June, I sat down to reckon with all of this on both a personal and a collective basis. Initially, I had two very strong responses to the collective. First, I wanted to shout from the rooftops, insist that we all rise up and do something, start a revolution. Second, I wanted to ignore the whole thing in the blind pursuit of feeling better. I wanted to pretend it wasn't real. I was tempted to a hedonistic fantasy. In my personal and professional life, I just wanted to break free at any cost.

This is really quite normal. Generally we have 3 response to a traumatic circumstance. Fight, flight, or freeze. Freeze encompasses a range of behaviors including, submission, dissociation, and attachment.

The problem with these options is that all are dictated by the circumstance. They leave no room for a creative, conscious approach. They are automatic responses. The fight, flight, or freeze response is pure instinct. It is a survival mechanism meant to keep you alive should you meet a hungry lion in the jungle. These instincts have brought us this far. But survival really isn't enough. In fact, what I discovered, in writing this book, is that the impulse towards mere survival is part of what is holding us back.

The survival instincts aren't bad. In fact, if you have suppressed your base instincts, it is of paramount importance that you unleash them. They are necessary because they tell us when something is wrong. But these base, primal instincts are just not sufficient to move us into full thriving. In order to thrive in this complex, modern circumstance, something more is needed. Put another way, our base instincts are being activated on a fairly constant basis by the global circumstance in which we live and by those who work to stoke our fear. In order to move into our thriving, we will need to see our base instincts transformed into something more powerful.

It is my fervent hope that this book will provide a way through to our thriving. I wrote it for people who are either seasoned enough in the ways of Spirit, or innocent and open-hearted enough, to believe in miraculous change. I also wrote it for the struggling activists who are wearing themselves out trying to make a better world and for those who find the global circumstance so hopeless that it is hard for them to find joy.

I am calling those who wage peace in the Spirit to conscious activism and I am calling those who wage war in the world to a life of spiritual consciousness. I am offering those who have lost hope a road back to faith in the positive and a sense of possibility.

I am also addressing this book to those who have been affected by or are living in the midst of a severe personal trauma. I am calling these people to awareness and to life. For that matter, I am also speaking to those people who have perpetrated abuse without understanding the context of their actions. I am inviting everyone to a new way of being.

This book is meant to be a siren call to a better future. It is not an easy read. In fact, if you commit yourself to answering this call, the materials will be quite painful at times. Your commitment will require that you pass through potentially devastating psychological territory, and at times, that you risk everything in the name of freedom and wholeness. That is the nature of a siren call: "the enticing appeal of something alluring but potentially dangerous."[3] I can't tell you this will always be an enjoyable process. It will certainly not be free of risk. But having come out the other side of the journey, I can say that it will be worth it. It certainly was for me.

On that evening in June when the weight of all this came crashing down on me, I couldn't see any ready made, practical solutions to the collective or personal dilemmas I was finally finding the courage to face. On a personal level, I had already proven the recalcitrant nature of my own conditioning. My geographic change, as radical as it had been, was nothing more than a lateral move within the same patterns that had always affected my life.

The global system isn't going anywhere any time soon either. Like the patterns that were affecting my own life, it has momentum on its side. We manage to change "leadership" on a pretty routine basis, that is for sure. Some places even manage to create new forms of governance. But we often fail to move beyond rhetoric and window dressing to create the real, comprehensive changes that we seek.

Perhaps the presidency of Barrack Obama is the perfect example of this. We will never know for sure whether he sincerely meant to bring hope and change or simply to co-

---

[3] Farlex. *The Free Dictionary*. Princeton University, Farlex, Inc. 2003-2012.

opt the language that had already become so prevalent. Regardless, the expected changes have largely eluded the United States. In the place of hopeful change and the creation of a kinder, gentler, more inclusive society, what has materialized is stunning in its contrast. Hatred has bubbled to the surface of the U.S. national dialogue in a shocking fashion. Wealth has accumulated at the top while those at the bottom and in the middle of the economic spectrum have become more and more disenfranchised. Further, the president of hope and change has become the president of the largest and one of the most aggressive national security states on the planet.

I could write a whole book about Barack Obama's presidency. But that is not my purpose here. What I am suggesting is that we would be fools not to ask ourselves if Barack Obama is a wolf in sheep's clothing with a clever marketing team that sensed and exploited the zeitgeist of the times. Hope and change are practically the signature of popular New Age spirituality and the explosive personal growth industry that has swept the Western world. People were in the mood to believe in hope and change, but few had the resolve to actually create something new. They were instead, excited, if not downright desperate, for a messiah. This is instructive!

It was with all of this in mind that I took a seat on my front steps that fateful day last June. On that day, I made a commitment. I decided to find a way to come to terms with the personal and the global and to actually find a way to move from surviving to thriving. I made a commitment to transition from searching for an agent of change to being one. This book was born of that commitment and of my own search for a way through to a passionate life of real power and freedom

As I began my search, it didn't take me long to realize that the solution to the personal and global circumstances I had chosen to confront would have to emanate from changes deep within me. The same is true of us as a global community. Real solutions will only become possible when enough people are willing to undertake the hard work of changing themselves and thereby impacting the collective consciousness.

We have exhausted the old strategies. It's time for a truly original, truly revolutionary approach. This approach will not come from the strength or charisma of our external leaders, but rather from the unshakeable foundation of our own inner transformation. Anything less would be like changing the label on an old product. At best it would inspire new enthusiasm for outdated contents. At worst, it would open the door for those who would like to use and manipulate our desire for change in order to usher in their own agendas. I leave it to you to evaluate the Obama presidency for evidence that we have already been through enough of this!

In short, we are facing an intractable situation that will require nothing less than our full commitment and our unwavering participation. If we truly desire to experience something new on a personal and/or collective basis we must be willing to sacrifice who we have been for who we know we can become; we must be willing to relinquish what we have in order to make space for what we know we can create. There really are no *ready made, off the shelf* solutions to the dilemmas we are facing. In a sense, this is good news.

After years of spiritual practice, I know that whenever we come to a place that seems to have no obvious, ready made resolution, we are in the realm of magic. Our seemingly insoluble circumstance is actually calling us to a higher plane of spiritual and personal development and power. We can either respond to the situation as victims caught in predetermined responses or as a warriors (i.e., as the masters of our own destinies capable of acting creatively regardless of the circumstance). In the words of Victor Frankl, who survived the Nazi concentration camps during the second World War, "When we are no longer able to change the situation, we are challenged to change ourselves."[4]

Carlos Castaneda dealt with this transition from victim to warrior in his book, *The Fire From Within*. He described a conversation with his teacher, don Juan Matus. Don Juan was extoling the virtues of confronting self importance through an encounter with a petty tyrant. Don Juan said that, self-importance is, on the one hand, "the source of everything that is good in us, and on the other hand, the core of everything that is rotten."[5] He continued noting that, "To get rid of

---

[4] Frankl, Victor E. *Man's Search for Meaning*. Boston. Beacon Press. 1959. Print. Page 112.

[5] Castaneda, Carlos. *The Fire From Within*. Washington Square Press. New York. 1984. Print. Page 15.

the self-importance that is rotten requires a masterpiece of strategy."[6]

A petty tyrant is a key part of that masterpiece strategy because, as don Juan declared, "Self-importance can't be fought with niceties."[7] He defined the petty tyrant as "a tormenter, someone who either holds the power of life and death over warriors or simply annoys them to distraction."

When I read that line, it hit me. We are living in the age of the ubiquitous petty tyrant. Those of us who are committed to a spiritual path of awakening and/or to global or personal change, have no choice. We must stop and deal with this reality. This is what is in front of us. We must become present to it, and we must learn to deal with our circumstances, both collective and personal, effectively.

According to don Juan Matus, we have even hit the jackpot in terms of our warrior training. According to his teachings, there is no greater ally on the path of personal power and awakening than a petty tyrant. The more dangerous and tyrannical, the better.

Hard to swallow, isn't it?

Carlos Castaneda thought it was hard to swallow too. Here is a passage from the book:

---

[6] Castaneda, Carlos. *The Fire From Within*. Washington Square Press. New York. 1984. Print. Page 15.

[7] Castaneda, Carlos. *The Fire From Within*. Washington Square Press. New York. 1984. Print. Page 16.

I vociferously disagreed with him. I told him that in my opinion tyrants can only render their victims helpless or make them as brutal as they themselves are. I pointed out that countless studies had been done in the effects of physical and psychological torture on such victims.

'The difference is something you just said,' he retorted. 'They are victims, not warriors.'[8]

The term "warrior" has really gotten a bad reputation. People have come to associate it with senseless violence and the abuse of power. You might even say that the warrior, or at least, the soldier, is the star of the show in current global situation. This is not the kind of warrior to which I am referring. There are many aspects of what you might call the warrior archetype that are sorely missing in many quarters of modern society. The kind of warrior to which don Juan referred is someone who practices what he called "impeccability." He described impeccability as "nothing else but the proper us of energy." This definition provides an excellent glimpse into where this book is leading us in terms of developing the warrior archetype in us all.

The proper use of energy implies something that is crucial to warriorship, namely, an internal locus of control. The warrior archetype carries with it an element of total freedom. Despite the outside influences, a warrior is able to focus his/

---

[8] Castaneda, Carlos. *The Fire From Within*. Washington Square Press. New York. 1984. Print. Page 19.

her energy according to what s/he wants to accomplish. An internal locus of control also allows the warrior to choose his/her actions without resort to predetermined or expected courses of action. A warrior is also not bound by habitual responses. As a result, the warrior is able to use her/his inherent creative power regardless of the circumstances.

In their book, *King, Warrior, Magician, & Lover* Robert Moore and Douglas Gillette describe the warrior archetype. They conclude that "the characteristics of the Warrior in his fullness amount to a total way of life, what a samurai called do (pronounced 'dough'). These characteristics constitute the Warrior's Dharma, Ma'at, or Tao, a spiritual or psychological path through life."[9] By nature, the Warrior is aggressive. But, according to Moore and Gillette the focus is on "proper aggressiveness, in the right circumstances—circumstances strategically advantageous to the goal at hand."[10] They elaborate as follows:

> *How does the man accessing the Warrior know what aggressiveness is appropriate under the circumstances? He knows through clarity of thinking, through discernment. The warrior is always alert. He is always awake. He is never sleeping through life.*

---

[9] Moore, Robert and Douglas Gillette. *King, Warrior, Magician, Lover: Rediscovering the Archetypes of the Mature Masculine.* Harper Collins. New York. 1991. Print. Page 79.

[10] Moore, Robert and Douglas Gillette. *King, Warrior, Magician, Lover: Rediscovering the Archetypes of the Mature Masculine.* Harper Collins. New York. 1991. Print. Page 80.

> *He knows how to focus his mind and his body. He is what the samurai call "mindful."*[11]

Douglas and Gillette also note that the "Warrior's actions are never overdone, never dramatic for the sake of drama... The Warrior never spends more energy than he absolutely has to."[12] Finally, the Warrior is loyal to something beyond him/herself. The archetypal warrior lives life according to the commitment s/he has made to what Douglas and Gillette call the "transpersonal goal or cause."[13] Every action the archetypal warrior takes is filtered through this commitment, is enacted with the benefit of discernment, and is undertaken with an awareness of the appropriate use of energy and aggression.

With reference to Don Juan's teachings as described by Castaneda in Journey to Ixtlan, Douglas and Gillette conclude that,

> *...a warrior knows what he wants and he knows how to get it. As a function of his clarity of mind he is a strategist and a tactician. He can evaluate his*

---

[11] Moore, Robert and Douglas Gillette. *King, Warrior, Magician, Lover: Rediscovering the Archetypes of the Mature Masculine.* Harper Collins. New York. 1991. Print. Page 80.

[12] Moore, Robert and Douglas Gillette. *King, Warrior, Magician, Lover: Rediscovering the Archetypes of the Mature Masculine.* Harper Collins. New York. 1991. Print. Page 83.

[13] Moore, Robert and Douglas Gillette. *King, Warrior, Magician, Lover: Rediscovering the Archetypes of the Mature Masculine.* Harper Collins. New York. 1991. Print. Page 85.

> *circumstances accurately and then adapt himself to the 'situation on the ground' as we say.*[14]

Victims, on the other hand, react passively to whatever shows up in their lives. They abdicate their creative power and their autonomy as a matter of course and as a matter of habit. They see no option but to suffer the negative consequences and impact of other people's choices. Other people direct the victim's energy and his/her focus. They are, in contrast to the warrior, often sleeping. They have generally shut down their awareness as a matter of survival.

Many things are outside of our control. I am not disputing that. Many times, we are victimized by others. But it is not necessary that we respond to an experience of victimization by becoming lifelong victims. If we have gone to sleep, we can choose to wake up and to live as warriors instead.

In fact, the current global situation has brought us to an inescapable choice point. We are at the crossroads between the victim mentality and the warrior mentality.

How will you choose to see yourself? How will you choose to confront the present age of the petty tyrant and the petty tyrants in your own life? Will you take up the mantle of the warrior or will you languish as a victim of circumstance

---

[14] Moore, Robert and Douglas Gillette. *King, Warrior, Magician, Lover: Rediscovering the Archetypes of the Mature Masculine.* Harper Collins. New York. 1991. Print. Page 80.

forever caught in your habitual patterns and forever subject to an external locus of control?

If you are ready to see yourself as a warrior, go to www.rebeckaeggers.com to find out how you can get connected to Rebecka and The Passion Path. The Passion Path is the path of the Passionate Warrior and of whole-hearted, purposeful, and skillful living.

Disempowering Dominance ∞ Naming the Tormentor

> *"The perfect ingredient for the making of a superb seer is a petty tyrant with unlimited prerogatives."*
> ∞ Don Juan Matus

Before I officially launch into this matter of naming the tormenter, I want to say that it was useful, cathartic, and, as a matter of integrity, necessary for me to acknowledge my own personal and private struggles with domination and exploitation as one source of inspiration for this book. Certainly, I could not address the topic of domination as it applies to the collective unless and until I became willing to actively and aggressively confront it in my personal life and within myself. In fact, those necessary personal confrontations have greatly informed my understanding of the material presented here. But this book is not a memoir, nor is it a self help book aimed at dealing with codependent relationships. It is meant to provide something that goes beyond that.

This book is about thriving in the context of a global system that is moving farther and farther away from safeguarding freedom, prioritizing dignity, and developing human potential. So, while I will sometimes relate the collective to the personal, this book is not about me. It is about us and about cutting a path through the tangled web of domination based relating so that we can discover the delight of coming together for the purpose of bringing to fruition the most promising possibilities for the human race. It is with this vision in mind that I now turn my attention explicitly towards creating a shared understanding of exactly what we are facing and the significance that it carries. Toward this end, I ask you now to direct your attention to the quote set forth at the beginning of this chapter.

> *"The perfect ingredient for the making of a superb seer is a petty tyrant with unlimited prerogatives."*
> *Don Juan Matus*[15]

This is precisely the circumstance in which we find ourselves right now. We have met a petty tyrant with unlimited prerogatives. It isn't one person or one government or a collection of people. It is a system. Indeed, it is our collective way of being together. Walter Wink, an American biblical scholar, theologian, and activist, who taught as a professor at Auborn Theological Seminary very aptly named the system in his book called, *Engaging the Powers*,

---

[15] Castaneda, Carlos. *The Fire From Within*. Washington Square Press. New York. 1984. Print. Page 20.

Discernment and Resistance in a World of Domination. Wink coined the phrase, the "Domination System."[16]

According to Wink, the Domination System has its roots in an ancient Babylonian creation myth. Whether or not he is right about the origins of the system, his use of the myth as a framework is instructive and provides an excellent starting place.

In the myth, the Babylonian god Marduk gained ascendency and control of the gods and then created the earth through a ruthless kind of violence. He got all the gods to agree that if he murdered the mother goddess, Tiamat, they would give him total sovereignty and control of everything. At that point in the story, Tiamat was plotting revenge against the other gods for the murder of her husband, father god, Apsu. After exacting the promise of ultimate power from the other gods, Marduk brutally murdered Tiamat and used her corpse to create the cosmos.

Wink identified the Babylonian creation story as the starting point for what he called "the myth of redemptive violence."[17] He concluded that redemptive violence is the mythology that underlies the Domination System. Under this mythology, we prize the extermination of enemies, actual or metaphorical, as the best route to peace and security.

---

[16] Wink, Walter. *Engaging the Powers: Discernment and Resistance in a World of Domination.* Minneapolis. Fortress Press. 1992. Kindle

[17] Wink, Walter. *Engaging the Powers: Discernment and Resistance in a World of Domination.* Minneapolis. Fortress Press. 1992. Kindle

It is easy to see this violent ethos reflected in the Babylonian creation myth. In that myth, Marduk created order out of chaos through violence and domination. Chaos became the enemy and order became the worthiest of goals regardless of how it was accomplished. Wink also noted that it was through the violent oppression of the feminine, often associated with chaos and nature, that Marduk achieved order.

Whether or not Wink was right in his interpretation of the myth as a whole, the aspects of the myth he highlighted provide an eerie metaphor for the nature of the global situation that has emerged since the bombing of the World Trade Center on September 11, 2001. Increasingly, the citizens of the western democracies are being asked to trade greater and greater amounts of freedom and show greater and greater degrees of allegiance to a global national security state that promises to vanquish evil and terror in exchange for our fidelity and submission. Of course, other countries have been living in tyrannical circumstances for years. What is remarkable about the present circumstance is the escalation of efforts to curtail democratic rights that once seemed a foregone conclusion and a way of life for citizens of Europe, the United States and many other western democracies.

Further, the violent oppression of the feminine, and by extension, women and the earth, are part and parcel of this global system. It is impossible to deny this reality. Wink commented as follows:

> *This myth also inadvertently reveals the price men have paid for the power they have acquired over women: complete servitude to their earthly rulers and heavenly gods. Women, for their part were identified with inertia, chaos, and anarchy. Now 'Woman is to man as nature is to culture.' —the ideology that rationalizes the subordination of women in patriarchal societies by presenting their subordination as if it were a natural fate.[18]*

Finally, Wink also correctly concluded that the violent ethos of the Domination System is self perpetuating and that it has become a core part of our identity. He sees it as the key guiding principle of our relationships. Here is what he said in the first chapter of his book:

> *Violence is the ethos of our times. It is the spirituality of the modern world. It has been accorded the status of a religion, demanding from its devotees an absolute obedience to death. Its followers are not aware, however, that the devotion they pay to violence is a form of religious piety. Violence is so successful as a myth precisely because it does not appear to be mythic in the least. Violence simply appears to be the nature of things. It is what works. It is inevitable, the last, and often the first resort in conflicts.[19]*

---

[18] Wink, Walter. *Engaging the Powers: Discernment and Resistance in a World of Domination*. Minneapolis. Fortress Press. 1992. Kindle. Location 274.

[19] Wink, Walter. *Engaging the Powers: Discernment and Resistance in a World of Domination*. Minneapolis. Fortress Press. 1992. Kindle. Location 218.

Wink is squarely in the camp of non-violent resistance. Accordingly, his approach is to eschew all violence and to lump all acts of violence in with the Domination System it so often sustains. I will leave the question of non-violence for the end of this book. But for now, I will say, that what is so insidious about the approach laid out in the Babylonian mythology is not the fact that violence was marshaled to combat violence, but that the price was the surrender of freedom. Only complete allegiance and the destruction of individual rights was enough to satisfy Marduk. Only then did he rise up against the tyranny of the mother goddess.

This for me is the mirror of our own terrifying circumstance as national security increasingly supplants individual freedoms, privacy, autonomy, as well as human rights and dignity. This is an especially troubling reality in a world that is increasingly dominated by corporate actors for whom the only legal and ethical mandate imposed, at least in the United States, is the maximization of profit. In this context, human potential is lost as human beings become nothing but resources to be exploited like any other resource.

In this sense, the emergence of the current global national security apparatus has brought us to yet another crossroads. We must actually choose whether or not we are willing to continue living according to ethos of the Domination System or not. This is a crucial moment both personally and collectively. Though we might prefer to think of the Domination System as something that exists out in the world, separate and apart from us, this notion of separation is an illusion. We have all been socialized into the present mythology. With rare exceptions, whether we realize it or not, we are all agents of the Domination System. We will remain in its employment unless and until we undertake the necessary work to move beyond our socialization.

The present global situation is nothing more than the collective expression of the values contained in the Babylonian creation story. Violence is our way of being together. Exploitation is the norm. Domination is how we impose order; it is how we create the illusion of security and suppress real challenges to exploitation. As Wink said:

> *Life is combat. Any form of order is preferable to chaos according to this myth. Ours is neither a perfect nor a perfectible world; it is a theatre of perpetual conflict in which the prize goes to the strong.*

So, the first thing we have to do is accept that unless and until we address our conditioning, we are all agents of the Domination System. But our analysis cannot end with our individual participation in a system of relating. As Wink has very impressively detailed, the institutions of the Domination System have taken on a life of their own. "The Powers," as Wink calls them, are the chief enforcers of the system. [20]The Powers are the governments, corporations, religions, and other institutions that are controlled by the myth of redemptive

---

[20] Wink, Walter. *Engaging the Powers: Discernment and Resistance in a World of Domination.* Minneapolis. Fortress Press. 1992. Kindle.

violence. They maintain the status quo. These institutions are more powerful than individual human beings and they have a spirit and legacy that outlives their participants. The Powers express and carry out what is often the lowest common denominator within the collective will of society and/or institutional participants. The Powers also include relationship units such as families that function according to the ethos of the Domination System.[21]

According to Wink, this is why The New Testament says the following:

> *For our struggle is not against enemies of blood and flesh, but against the rulers, against the authorities, against the cosmic powers of the present darkness, against the spiritual forces of evil in the heavenly places. (Eph. 6:12).*[22]

Wink concluded that the author of Ephesians was talking about the Domination System and about the momentum that it has taken on through the Powers and through the collective nature of our consciousness. Wink elaborated on the nature of the Powers further in an earlier book called *Naming the Powers: The Language of Power in the New Testament.*[23]

---

[21] Wink, Walter. *Engaging the Powers: Discernment and Resistance in a World of Domination.* Minneapolis. Fortress Press. 1992. Kindle. Location 275.

[22] Quoted in: Wink, Walter. *Engaging the Powers: Discernment and Resistance in a World of Domination.* Minneapolis. Fortress Press. 1992. Kindle. Location 640.

[23] Wink, Walter. *Naming the Powers: The Language of Power in the New Testament.* Fortress Press. 1984. Kindle. Location 1191.

Wink's writing is undeniably wedded to a Christian worldview. This requires that one dig through some dogma in order to get at the heart of the perspective Wink advocated in *Naming the Powers*. Nonetheless, his perspective is extremely useful as he conceptualized of the Powers in a unique manner that recognized both their outer reality as material structures and their inner realities as manifestations of collective consciousness. In so doing, he demystified references to cosmic powers and/or demons. He challenged us to relate to the Powers on a more multifaceted level and to come to terms with an important reality: We may succeed in forcing change in the outer material expressions of the Powers on a temporary basis. But unless and until we are able to influence their inner collective consciousness or spirit, any changes we are able to make will be shallow and short lived.

He explained this concept as follows:

> *...the expression, "the Powers" should no longer be reserved for the special category of spiritual forces, but should rather be used generically for all manifestations of power, seen under dual aspect of their physical or institutional concretion on the one hand and their inner essence or spirituality on the other...What we are arguing is that the Powers are simultaneously the outer and inner aspects of one and the same indivisible concretion of power. 'Spiritual' here means the inner dimension of the material, the*

'within' of things, the subjectivity of objective entities in the world.[24]

This perspective is extremely useful in terms of specifying precisely what we are dealing with. As a matter of collective consciousness, we are living out the myth of redemptive violence on a global level. The larger than life presence of the Powers is holding us fast within that mythology and insuring the perpetuation of the Domination System. The collective consciousness of the Powers reflects clear allegiance to the principle that submission is the price of security and that violence is the primary means of creating order out of chaos.

Our struggle is not, therefore, principally against flesh and blood. It is not, in the first instance, against one another, nor is it merely against the outer reality of the Powers. But rather, our struggle is against the common ethos of the Domination System and its expression through the Powers and through our own relationship dynamics. Therefore, our challenge is to become free of the Domination System and its influence and to meet one another in a different space governed by a different mythology. From this place, we will be able to create the Powers anew or see them transformed in line with a new mythology and the accompanying shift in the collective consciousness. But, for the present moment, we struggle against the Powers and against the evil embedded in the collective consciousness of the Domination System.

---

[24] Wink, Walter. *Naming the Powers: The Language of Power in the New Testament.* Fortress Press. 1984. Kindle. Location 1210.

At this time, quite literally, the Powers are almost omnipotent and they have taken on a life of their own! In the modern global system, as a result of the vast technological developments outlined by Edward Snowden, the Powers are fast becoming omniscient as well. At the very least, they are putting on the mask of omniscience and they are exerting ever more complete control over the perceived chaos of the world. There are few remaining limits on their prerogatives!

It is easy to feel despair about all of this. It is tempting to give in to hopelessness. But if don Juan Matus can be believed, we are in the sweet spot where vision transforms. According to him, "The perfect ingredient for the making of a superb seer is a petty tyrant with unlimited prerogatives."[25]

A seer is, among other things, one who has learned the art of discernment such that she or he can see reality as it is. Seers use their circumstances to become truly aware, truly awake. Therefore, if we are willing to approach the situation as warriors and to see all that is happening as a challenge, it seems we are in luck. The Domination System we are now living under, in all of its corruption, exploitation, control, and ubiquitous power, is the perfect environment for an awakening.

Awareness is a crucial step towards actually liberating ourselves from the Domination System. Until we are able to see the system and to distinguish it from ourselves and from

---

[25] Castaneda, Carlos. *The Fire From Within*. Washington Square Press. New York. 1984. Print. Page 20.

the other people who are currently unaware of its influence, we will not be able to move beyond it. Further, the kind of vision that transforms actually goes beyond discerning what currently is to imagining what could be. It is the second kind of vision that brings the greatest degree of transformation.

If you are ready for your awakening, go to www.rebeckaeggers.com to find out how you can get connected to Rebecka and The Passion Path. The Passion Path is the path of the Passionate Warrior and of whole-hearted, purposeful, and skillful living.

Disempowering Dominance ∞ Beyond Learning to See

> *"There is a sense of danger. It is not the people. They don't seem dangerous. Out of the very air comes a sense of danger, a queer, bristling feeling of uncanny danger."*
> ∞ *D.H. Lawrence*

The Domination System is fertile ground for the lessons of seeing because we are caught in a very powerful web of delusion. The lessons we need to learn are about seeing through the delusions and about understanding our participation in the creation and maintenance of the web.

We maintain the web of delusion through a kind of willful blindness. In order to survive in, and receive the benefits of, the Domination System, we have to maintain a kind of denial. We have allowed the Domination System to tell us what to see, what to value, who we are, what we should think, and so on and so forth. Further, the major institutions of society are part of the Domination System. In a very real sense, we rely on the Powers for everything from education to economic remuneration. Even our families are among the Powers because they are collective in nature.

Like those caught in the lies of an addict, we sense something is wrong. We are aware of "the bristling feeling of uncanny danger," as D.H. Lawrence said. But we want to believe in the goodness of the system. We want to carry on with our normal lives just as the Germans wanted to carry on with their lives in the face of increasing evidence of an escalating genocide. In the quote at the beginning of this chapter, according to Walter Wink, D.H. Lawrence was describing the rise of the Nazis in Germany.[26]

To be honest, even under the most extreme circumstances, change takes effort and energy that we simply aren't sure we want to invest. So we continue to accept the messages of the system. Eventually we lose touch with ourselves. Our participation in the system makes it very difficult for us to tap into our own core of wisdom. In the words of Ann Wilson Schaef (as quoted by Wink), "We give the system the power to make the known unknown." [27] In this way, we learn to mistrust ourselves.

---

[26] Wink, Walter. *Engaging the Powers: Discernment and Resistance in a World of Domination*. Minneapolis. Fortress Press. 1992. Kindle. Location 799.

[27] Quoted in: Wink, Walter. *Engaging the Powers: Discernment and Resistance in a World of Domination*. Minneapolis. Fortress Press. 1992. Kindle. Location 821

We can begin to reverse this process if we are willing to start with ourselves and with an acknowledgment of what is really true for us. If we pay close attention, we will begin to feel that there is a knot of anxiety in the pit of our stomachs. If we allow our attention to engage this anxiety, we will begin to see that this is where we have buried the fear that is part and parcel of the Domination System. We live our lives in the midst of a low grade (and sometimes high grade) conflict. The threat of reprisals is always present. The system functions on the foundational belief that violence, actual or metaphorical, is the primary and best solution when differences arise. Beyond this emphasis on violence as the primary solution lies a foundational trust in the notion that we have the right, and even the responsibility to impose our agenda on others by sheer force of will. It is in this context that violence takes on a particularly pernicious quality because it is wedded to the concepts of domination and exploitation.

We are, in a very real sense, being threatened all the time. The threat in this context is twofold. We are threatened with harm, actual or implied. But beyond that, we face the threat of being forced to live out the dictates of someone else's agenda on an ongoing basis. In essence, we are threatened with servitude. If we look closely at our lives with this in mind, we will see the many ways that we have adjusted ourselves to the demands of the system. We will find that we have made a thousand tiny, daily adjustments that we didn't even mean to make and that, in this way, we are already being exploited; we have already accepted servitude.

But there is more. Sometimes we automatically adjust ourselves to another persons agenda in order to avoid the threatened harm and sometimes we reflexively rebel against foreign agendas with all the strength we have. At other times, we force people to accept and to live by the dictates of our own agendas. The insidious reality is that, in all of these cases, we are living our lives according to a set of options that are created by the unconscious operation of the Domination System. We swing from passivity to blind hostility/domination and back again.

In the midst of this reality, our sense of fear and danger has been with us all along. It has been something akin to the soundtrack of our lives. It has played in the background, setting the tone for every scene, yet remaining barely noticeable. Even still, it has controlled our every move. As a matter of survival, we have learned to accommodate our fear rather than risk being present to it and all that it would reveal about our circumstances. This is because the revelation contained in our fear is the kind of knowing that compels change, and up until now, we have just wanted life to go on as usual.

We have now come to the crossroads. We cannot unknow the truth of our situation, namely, that within the Domination System we are not truly free. If we want our freedom back, we must choose to break the hold of denial in our lives and we must choose to see. Our fear is wise. It knows what is true about the way we have chosen to be together in this world. We must begin to listen to it and to allow it to open our eyes. Our fear can train us to see.

As it turns out, the Domination System has been hiding in plain sight cloaked only by our willingness to remain ignorant of its presence and its influence. We have aided and abetted the system by rejecting our own sense of what is. Further the system depends on our willingness to deny reality. It fosters our denial in the same way an addict tries to hide his/her addiction from the people who would otherwise object.

Beyond all of this, we have actually internalized the ethics of the system. In a very real sense, it is inside of us. It wears the mask of normalcy. Again, the trick is to open to what is. If we are willing to hear the voice of the system that comes from within and to identify it as other than our own, we will gain our authentic sight.

Walter Wink described the process of seeing as follows:

> *The demonic spirit of the outer structure has already been internalized by the seer, along with everybody else. That is how the empire wins compliance. The seer's gift is not to be immune to invasion by the empire's spirituality, but to be able to discern that internalized spirituality, name it, and externalize it. This drives the demonic out of concealment. What is hidden is now revealed. The seer is enabled to hear her or his own voice chanting the slogans of the Powers,*

is shown that they are a lie, and is empowered to expel them. The seer locates the source of the chanting outside, and is set free from it.[28]

As already explained, by "demonic," Wink does not mean disembodied spirits floating around in space. He means the spirit that has control of the Powers. He is referring to the spirit or collective consciousness of the Domination System. In *Naming the Powers*, Wink very clearly explained what he meant by the term, "demons" as follows:

The sense is clear: demons can be manifest only through concretation in material reality. They are, in short, the name given to that real but invisible spirit of destruction and fragmentation that rends persons, communities, and nations…

In short, what Wink is saying is that we have chosen to embody the myth of redemptive violence. It has been concretized in us and within the Powers. It is expressed as the Domination System (*i.e.*, the collective living arrangements and relationships that we have created). By learning to see, we are learning to identify and expel the influence of the Domination System and to free ourselves from the myth of redemptive violence. We are choosing to stop embodying our own destruction and fragmentation on an individual and collective basis.

---

[28] Wink, Walter. *Engaging the Powers: Discernment and Resistance in a World of Domination*. Minneapolis. Fortress Press. 1992. Kindle. Location 1319.

In a very real sense, the Domination System is itself our greatest ally as we attempt to learn the art of discernment. The Domination System is reaching a point of such critical dysfunction, that we can hardly ignore it any longer. There are now significant barriers to continuing our denial because it is becoming very hard to go on with life as usual. That is why there are protests in the streets all over the world. People are beginning to sense the true nature of our circumstances and to yearn for something new.

As our eyes begin to open, anger is erupting en masse. Like our fear, our anger is telling us that something is wrong. But we must take care that we do not give in to our angry impulses. We must be on-guard for the rise of our self-importance (which expresses as pride on the one hand, and shame on the other). As a matter of strategy, we would be very wise not to follow our first impulse towards action, but to, instead, engage the situation with great curiosity and forbearance.

Seeing the nature of our circumstances is only the beginning. Feeling what we have denied and repressed is another foundational step. But we must be careful to go beyond merely uncovering the rouse and then acting reflexively against it. The Domination System is a crafty one. It has a way of replicating itself, and in this way, defeating the alternatives.

Carlos Castaneda addressed this in *The Fire From Within*. Castaneda asked don Juan Matus how you could measure a defeat at the hands of a petty tyrant. He replied that, "Anyone who joins the ranks of the petty tyrant is defeated. To act in anger, without control and discipline, to have no forbearance, is to be defeated." Castaneda asked, "What happens after warriors are defeated?" Don Juan's answer was very instructive:

> *They either regroup themselves or they abandon the quest for knowledge and join the ranks of the petty tyrants for life.*[29]

The global stakes are high at the moment. We are all faced with the question of whether or not we will truly expand beyond the Domination System or whether we will attempt to fight it through its own underlying mythology of redemptive violence. In reality, this choice can be broken down into two sub choices. First, will we choose to deal with the Domination System at its root by confronting its insistence that we must exchange our allegiance and our freedom for the protection offered by the Powers. To make such a trade is to rape the human spirit in the name of security.

Second, will we succumb to the central ethos of the Domination System that says we must rise up and impose a new order (a new outer structure) on the Powers without ever addressing the inner, collective consciousness expressed through the Powers?

---

[29] Castaneda, Carlos. *The Fire From Within*. Washington Square Press. New York. 1984. Print. Page 30.

What Don Juan said is very true. In the moment that is most pregnant with our transformation, we are in the gravest danger of falling back asleep and of joining the ranks of the petty tyrants. If we want to avoid the preset choices served up by our conditioning, the trick will be to find a way to pause and to act consciously whenever challenges arise. We will know that we are in challenging circumstances the moment we feel our fear and our anger. They will sound the alarm. Very likely, the alarm will activate the fight, flight, freeze response. These are the survival-based options served up by the false mythology of the Domination System. If we want to cultivate other options, in the words of Victor Frankl, who so heroically faced the Domination System of the Nazi concentration camps, we will have to find the "space between stimulus and response." For "in that space is our power to choose our response. In our response lies our growth and our freedom."[30]

In short, it is not enough that we see clearly. It is also not enough that we begin to feel. Real action is required, and that action must derive from our power to choose our response. Our power to choose our response, in turn, rests on our ability to see a different option and to enact it under stringent circumstances. Finally, our choice to respond differently must be rooted in something deeper than mere force of will. Effective change always comes from an inner transformation.

The transformation we are looking to make will be impossible to sustain unless we create an attractive and

---

[30] Frankl, Victor E. *Man's Search for Meaning.* Beacon Press. Boston. 1959. Print.

effective alternative to the choices served up by the myth of redemptive violence. Therefore, once we are able to see the Domination System clearly, we are tasked with three additional steps that will lay the foundation for conscious action. First, we will face a kind of death. We must die to the old mythology and to the Domination System. By logical extension, we must also fashion or discover a new mythology. That is the second task.

Our final task? To be reborn into the new mythology and to learn to live by it.

If you are ready to undertake this journey of transformation, go to www.rebeckaeggers.com to find out how you can get connected to Rebecka and The Passion Path. The Passion Path is the path of the Passionate Warrior and of whole-hearted, purposeful, and skillful living.

Disempowering Dominance ∞ The Call to Death

> *"In the power-dependence relationship, what the weak bring to the bargain is the validation of the power of the powerful: its legitimacy."* ∞ Elizabeth Janeway

The first step in designing a new mythology is to thoroughly understand the old mythology, how it has affected us, and how we can free ourselves from the effects of it.

By way of review, the Domination System is a system of power and dependence founded on the myth of redemptive violence. The Domination System maintains power over us through our perceived dependence upon it. We have accepted the premise that we need the Domination System in order to protect ourselves, individually and collectively, from being dominated by others. The myth of redemptive violence stands for the proposition that we must either dominate or be dominated (through some form of violence, actual, emotional, mental, or spiritual). In other words, dominate or be dominated are the default options. Further, the most egregious part of the myth of redemptive violence is that it insists that we must surrender our freedom and offer our allegiance to those who promise us security in exchange.

Similarly, those who perpetuate domination within the Domination System like to maintain the appearance of indispensability. This is as true of individual dominators as it is of the Powers. Domination is achieved through power over others which is maintained by force and/or by perceived dependence. It is also maintained by fear of reprisals and shame. Shame is another word for the rotten self-importance that don Juan referenced. When someone pricks our shame, it immediately triggers our instinctual fight, flight, or freeze responses. Its polar opposite is pride. Dominators project pride and legitimacy in order to maintain their position on top of the hierarchy. They also work to keep the dominated in a state of induced shame or worthlessness. Finally, sometimes exploitation is made possible not by the stick, but by the carrot. Sometimes we are sweet talked into giving up our sovereignty or giving others the benefit of our creativity and talent without fair exchange. Beware of the dominator who comes to you with sugar on his/her lips.

The Domination System is made up of both individual participants and institutions. The institutions, or Powers (including, for instance, family units), participate in the system through individuals, but nonetheless, have an ongoing presence and impact that is much greater than the sum of its individual participants. Yet, no matter how grand it sounds, the Domination System is, at it's core, nothing more, and nothing less, than our collective way of being together. The Powers are nothing more than expressions of common will.

For those who have been handily victimized by the Powers or by someone else who was trapped in the ethos of the Domination System, this is a bitter pill to swallow. The notion that this system in any way represents a collective choice is a foreign concept. Many people may even respond to the concept with anger. I am undaunted. If we are ever going to move beyond the myth of redemptive violence, we really must come to terms with the roles we play in the current system.

This is not an exercise in shifting blame from the victimizer to the victim. Blame is not even a relevant concept. Blame is, in fact, part and parcel of the Domination System because it suggests that our well being can *only* be restored if we hold someone else accountable by whatever means available. In other words, holding others accountable becomes the central focus of our well being.

Also, emotional healing can't help but take place as a part of this process, but emotional healing is not an end in and of itself. This is actually an exercise in transcending the predetermined roles of the Domination System. Our aim is to cultivate the kind of freedom that will foster meaningful change.

Again, it is tempting to fall back into the consciousness of the Domination System. This consciousness would suggest that we can achieve our freedom by simply disposing of the Powers and their agents. But, as Walter Wink has very aptly concluded, the Powers are necessary. They were meant to serve humanity. Imagine what life would be like if we never organized ourselves into institutions designed to carry out group will. The Powers are essential to our highest communal functioning. Further, the notion that we can solve our problems by destroying the Powers ignores the reality of our interdependence and of our collective choices. We are in the Domination System and it is in us. We are influencing the Domination System and it is influencing us.

In reality, because of our interdependence, it is neither enough to attempt to change the Powers nor is it sufficient for individuals within the Domination System to change their behavior towards others. A collective shift large enough to change the community ethics is the only universal way out of the Domination System. Therefore, our mandate is clear. If we want lasting and universal change, we must change ourselves, we must change our relationship to the Powers, and we must, ultimately, see the Powers transformed through a large scale shift in collective consciousness. We will accomplish this goal only if we are willing to look honestly at the dynamics of power-dependence relationships and then move past the predetermined choices established by those dynamics. Once we have done so, we can begin the process of reforming the existing Powers by shifting their inner structure/consciousness or we can create the Powers anew by creating parallel systems that offer real alternatives to the present arrangements.

Walter Wink, who wrote from a Christian perspective and Carlos Castaneda, who wrote from the perspective of a sorcerer, have both addressed the core dysfunction that arises in the kind of power-dependence relationships that stem from the Domination System. Consistent with the conclusion I reached above, neither advocated a run for the hills mentality that would allow us to avoid confronting the reality of our situation. Both urged self mastery and transformation in the face of oppression.

Wink called for the adoption of a radically different mythology based on partnership and cooperation. He also advocated the kind of personal transformation that would bring this new mythology to fruition. He anticipated that the Powers could, and indeed, must be reconfigured around this alternative system. Wink's approach is rooted in the authentic, non-violent, clever, and radically, anti-establishment teachings of Jesus (who, by the way, threw egg all over the face of the Domination System). You could say that Jesus was one of the first community organizers.

Castaneda, by contrast, was working from a paradigm of ultimate individual power and freedom. The power that Castaneda worked to develop was not the "power over" of the Domination System, but the power that comes from personal impeccability. Castaneda inspired his readers to a high degree of personal responsibility and to the cultivation of self mastery.

These two radically different traditions both have almost identical things to say about transforming ourselves, and thereby, our relationship with the Powers.

Wink very rightly noted that we must choose to be free **by dying to the control** of the Domination System. He described the issue as follows:

> *One does not become free from the Powers by defeating them in a frontal attack. Rather, one dies to their control…we are liberated, not by striking back at what enslaves us…but by dying out from under its jurisdiction and command.*[31]

Carlos Castaneda relayed very similar teachings given to him by don Juan Matus. Don Juan talked about the problem in terms of confronting self-importance. Self-importance he said,

> *is our greatest enemy. Think about it—what weakens us is feeling offended by the deeds and misdeeds of our fellow men. Our self-importance requires that we spend most of our lives offended by someone… Warriors fight self-importance as a matter of strategy…*[32]

---

[31] Wink, Walter. *Engaging the Powers: Discernment and Resistance in a World of Domination.* Minneapolis. Fortress Press. 1992. Kindle. Location 2288.

[32] Castaneda, Carlos. *The Fire From Within.* Washington Square Press. New York. 1984. Print. Page 12

Similarly, Chogyam Trungpa, a Buddhist master, spoke of coming to know our own basic goodness. He said that, "Every human being has a basic nature of goodness which is undiluted and unconfused."[33] Trungpa believed that the first step towards creating a truly enlightened society involves realizing the truth and essence of your own basic goodness.

In short, once we know the truth of our own worth and essential goodness, we also free ourselves from the sham of self-importance. When we are operating from self-importance, our actions look like evidence of self worth – we are fighting for our rights or putting someone in his/her place. But really, self-important action is just meaningless posturing. This posturing reflects the reality that our choices are not yet rooted in the genuine knowledge of our intrinsic value.

Self importance makes it easy for others to manipulate us and to drain our energy. By contrast, when we are in touch with our basic goodness, the Domination System loses its ability to define us, and thereby, to manipulate us. It can no longer prick our sense of worthlessness or our insecurity. We may still feel afraid. But fear becomes our ally, a tool for seeing rather than a means through which someone else can tap our sense of worthlessness (by bringing up the fear that something is wrong with us or that some abuse is justified). Having confronted our sense of self-importance, and having come to

---

[33] Trungpa, Chogyam. *Shambhala: The Sacred Path of the Warrior.* Shambhala Publications, Inc. Boston. 1984. Location 331.

know our own basic goodness, we are dead to the control of the Domination System.

Wink expressed this concept beautifully in terms of ego transcendence. He used the imagery of death and rebirth as symbolized by the cross in the Christian tradition (not to be confused with the perversion of the Christian tradition through organized religion). Here is what Wink had to say:

> *Why does the New Testament use the imagery of death for the process of fighting free from the Powers? Because, says Jung, the unconscious still operates on the archaic law that a psychic state cannot be changed without first being annihilated. And the annihilation must be total. 'The gift must be given as if it were being destroyed'…In the [ancient] sacrificial system the need to sacrifice the ego was projected upon an animal. When that projection is withdrawn, one faces the task of dying to the socially formed ego in order to become the self one is meant to be.*
>
> *But rebirth is not a private, inward event only. For it includes the necessity of dying to whatever in our social surroundings has shaped us inauthentically. We must die to the Domination System in order to live freely.*

We must die to the Domination System in order to live freely! Put another way, we must eradicate its influence on us and we must find another way of being together.

Wink continued with a profound explanation of what it means to die to the Domination System as follows:

> *Those born to privilege and wealth may miss life by having been installed at the center of a universe revolving around their own desires. Others, born to merciless poverty and the contempt of the ruling class, may miss life by never feeling really human at all. If the advantaged must die to their egocentricity, the underprivileged must die to their hopelessness, fatalism, and acquiescence in their own despoiling.*[34]

In other words, we must die to the influence of the Domination System no matter how it has expressed in and through us. We must destroy it's ability to shape us, define, influence, and control us.

One of the most insidious and damaging psychic states elicited by the Domination System is the victim mentality. This is, in essence, what I mean by the assertion that the Domination System is our collective way of being together. Some people are trapped in the victim role and some people have assumed the role of the victimizer.

When I say victim mentality, I am not talking about taking action in order to redress a particular wrong. I am talking about the mentality that says, for instance, "What could I do? I was only following orders." This expression of

---

[34] Wink, Walter. *Engaging the Powers: Discernment and Resistance in a World of Domination.* Minneapolis. Fortress Press. 1992. Kindle. Location 2303.

the victim mentality permits us to deny responsibility for our individual actions by affirming our own powerlessness and dependence on the system.

It is the victim mentality (among other things) that supports things like honor killings. It offers Islamic fundamentalists both an imperative and a justification for murdering their own sisters, wives, and mothers for the "crime" of besmirching the family name. Men control women under the Domination System, and the system controls men. It is the same with women who carry out genital mutilation in the name of custom. This mentality also afflicts soldiers who brutalize civilian populations under orders from headquarters.

The issues raised in the above paragraph are not meant to detract from the horror experienced by those subjected to these kind of severe traumas. Rather, they are meant to highlight the twisted logic by which those who perpetrate these atrocities are able to turn themselves into powerless victims of a much larger, systemic imperative.

The victim mentality could also be re-characterized as undue deference to authority. This phenomenon has been scientifically documented. In his book Influence, Robert B. Cialdini, PhD discussed a series of social science experiments run by Professor Stanley Milgram. In the initial Milgram experiment, one person was cast as the learner and one as the teacher. The learner was a paid actor. But the teacher was an experimental test subject. The subject was told that the purpose of the experiment was to discover the effects of punishment on learning and memory. The student was to learn a series of word pairs. Anytime an error was made, the teacher delivered an electric shock. With each error, the shock grew stronger.

Milgram's results were shocking. He found that no matter how much the learner pleaded for mercy, as long as the researcher told him to continue administering the shock, almost no one heeded the agonized cries of the actor (who was strapped to a chair and hooked up to electrodes). Not one of the 40 participants in the study quit his "job" as a teacher in protest. Even at the most severe levels of shock, only a small minority refused to administer the shocks. Here is what Dr. Cialdini had to say by way of explanation:

> *Milgram is sure he knows the answer. It has to do he says, with a deep-seated sense of duty to authority within us all. According to Milgram, the real culprit in the experiments was his subject's inability to defy the wishes of the boss of the study—the lab-coated researcher who urged and, if need be, directed the subjects to perform their duties, despite the emotional and physical mayhem they were causing.*[35]

In subsequent studies, when the researcher said "stop" and the learner asked the teacher to continue, 100 percent of the subjects cast in the role of teacher refused to give additional shocks. This confirms Milgram's theory that it was allegiance

---

[35] Cialdini, Robert B. PhD. *Influence: The Psychology of Persuasion.* New York. William Morrow & Company, Inc. 1984. Kindle. Location 3433.

to authority that prompted the test subjects to continue administering the shocks.

Cialdini relayed an anecdotal example as well. I this instance, three protestors stretched their legs across railroad tracks in an attempt to stop a train leaving the Concord, California, Naval Weapons Station. They were protesting shipments of military equipment to Nicaragua. The civilian crew had been given orders not to stop. They never even slowed the train down. One protestor, Mr. Wilson, lost his legs below the knee. He was unable to move completely out of the way. After the incident, navy medical corpsmen at the scene refused to treat Mr. Wilson or allow him to be taken to the hospital in their ambulance. Doctor Cialdini's comment on the subject follows:

> *Amazingly, Mr. Wilson, who served four years in Vietnam, does not blame either the crewmen or the corpsmen for his misfortune; he points his finger, instead, at a system that constrained their actions through pressure to obey: 'They were just doing what I did in 'Nam. They were following orders that are part of an insane policy. They're the fall guys.' Although the crew members shared Mr. Wilson's assessment of them as victims, they did not share his magnanimity. In what is perhaps the most remarkable aspect of the incident, the train crew filed suit against him, requesting punitive damages for the 'humiliation, mental anguish, and physical stress' they suffered*

because he hadn't allowed them to carry out their orders without cutting off his legs.[36]

This notion of ourselves as victims to the dictates of authority is deeply entrenched as is our almost automatic deference to it. Accordingly, we must learn to question and even subvert the directives of illegitimate authority. At the very least, we must learn to question the legitimacy of directives that we know are unjust and/or illegitimate. Of course, we must do so with caution and with the utmost respect for the risks involved. The story of Bradley Manning, who was this summer sentenced to 35 years (with the possibility of parole in 8 years) for leaking classified documents to Wikileaks, serves as an inspiration and as a cautionary tale. If he thought the bravery and nobility of his actions would save him, he made a gross miscalculation.

So, rather than suggesting blind opposition to illegitimate authority, I am challenging us all to look closely at our sense of ourselves as victims to authority bound by its dictates no matter how repugnant. It is pointless to blindly go forth in opposition to authority with absolutely no awareness of the dangers we will face and with no real plan in place for protecting our own interests in the process. The idea is to become aware, to transcend our sense of ourselves as victims, and to make conscious, strategic choices.

---

[36] Cialdini, Robert B. PhD. *Influence: The Psychology of Persuasion.* New York. William Morrow & Company, Inc. 1984. Kindle. Location 3472.

In other words, I am not suggesting that we blindly martyr ourselves anymore than I am suggesting we simply carry out atrocities in the name of duty and powerlessness. Of course, as an aside, the martyr often plays a key role in exposing corrupt authority. If chosen consciously, the person playing the role of the martyr may make a strategically valuable contribution to the public awareness and dialogue. But if someone takes on the martyr role, s/he must to be prepared to allow his/her own destruction for the sake of creating transparency.

In addition to the above manifestations of the victim mentality, the victim identity also manifests in the form of the oppressed individual who acquiesces in his or her own "despoiling." Here is an excerpt from Walter Wink's book:

> *Domination is always more than a powerful relation notes Joel Kovel. It is a spiritual state of being. The dominator exerts power by extracting being from the dominated...This domination always entails more than injustice. It wounds—and it intends to wound—the very soul itself...So, besides an unmasking of the oppressors, there must be a healing of the servile will in their victims.*[37]

Far from actually seeking real redress of wrongs, oppressed groups often trade on their victim status without ever confronting the true nature of their oppression. This is

---

[37] Wink, Walter. *Engaging the Powers: Discernment and Resistance in a World of Domination.* Minneapolis. Fortress Press. 1992. Kindle. Location 1504.

an expression of the "servile will." They beg for and accept crumbs from the dominant group without ever addressing their relationship to the Domination System. In this way, the oppressed play right into the hands of the Powers, allowing themselves to become dependent on handouts from that very system. The handouts perform a multitude of functions such as: (i) placating the oppressed; (ii) fostering dependence and submission; and (iii) inducing a sense of shame. Handouts, as such, are not a means of facilitating liberation. Handouts are part and parcel of maintaining the Domination System. Of course, handouts should not be confused with those things a society chooses to do together for the common welfare. Far from supporting community welfare, handouts quell unrest.

This is why, for instance, the Zapatista communities in Chiapas, Mexico, at least initially, refused all government aid regardless of the dire poverty in their communities. They recognized how handouts could work against them by keeping them beholden to the system and they chose to assert their personal liberties and independence instead of accepting government aid.

This servile will can also express through, for instance, individuals who do not know how to affirmatively assert themselves. They rely on being ill, weak, anguished etc. in order to carve out even the most meager portions of life for themselves. They rely on their own distress in order to prompt those around them to offer even the most basic support. Yet, these martyred individuals remain unable or unwilling to address the core relationship issues that keep them from living powerfully in their own right. The transition from victim to warrior in this case, requires that the victim begin to take responsibility for his/her own desires and for the reality that it is okay to express those desires and to see them fulfilled for their own sake rather than for the sake of need etc.

In addition, as noted in the first chapter of this book, the freeze response includes a range of actions such as submission, dissociation, and attachment. These are the most insidious habitual responses because they are the trauma responses/survival instincts of last resort. These are the things we do when the terror is in our lives to stay, for instance, when a child is being abused by a parent or a citizen is being abused by the government. These are natural and wise responses that keep us alive when our survival is threatened in a circumstance that does not permit escape or effective resistance. But they emanate from the level of survival and victimization and not from the mind of the warrior or from the level of thriving.

Submission involves doing what is asked but without actually identifying with the desires of the oppressor. When dissociation occurs, the victim simply splits off parts of his/her awareness so that denial can function effectively. When attachment occurs, the victim loses touch with her/his own desires and simply takes on the oppressor's desires. In many ways, the victim no longer knows the difference between her/his desires and the desires of the oppressor. A kind of psychic merger takes place. As a result, the attachment response is, in many ways, the most difficult to overcome because the victim completely loses touch with his/her core identity.

The way out of this maze and into the warrior mentality is for the victim to begin cultivating awareness of things like fear, anger, and her/his own desires. A deep connection with and commitment to self is required to begin overturning the psychic impact of oppression. Things that increase body awareness and physical presence are also very important. The first things a victim loses touch with are his/her own emotions and physical sensations. As the victim loses touch with him/herself, the victim often even develops considerable empathy for the victimizer. Accordingly, as the victim begins to reconnect with him/herself, it is imperative that the victim consciously shut down any empathy he/she has for the victimizer. The idea is to become deeply connected to self and to disconnect from the victimizer.

Finally, given a choice between joining the ranks of the "evil" oppressors, many people would prefer to live powerless lives. They simply abdicate their power because it is more noble to be a victim than an oppressor. This is a false dichotomy. The real solution lies in claiming a new kind of power: the power to accomplish. Seeing the victim role clearly and choosing to transcend it is the first step in cultivating this power to accomplish.

Along the path to authentic power, it is important to avoid a common pitfall that arises in the awakening period. Once the oppressed person or group truly catches on to the ruse, the first reaction is anger. The risk is a polar shift within the myth of redemptive violence. The end result is that the victim flips from victim to victimizer and then unleashes her/his fury against those who have played the dominant role in an unconscious bid for revenge or control. The transition from victim to warrior cannot take place so long as there is a mere polar shift. In fact, a polar shift may even carry deadly consequences.

By way of example, before the Zapatista rebels transitioned to more of a social movement and community building effort, the rebels rose up in an armed conflict that ended in tremendous loss of life especially on the indigenous side. They woke up to the reality of their circumstance, and tapped into their anger, but at least initially, may have failed to transcend the imperatives of the Domination System.

By initially attempting to conquer Mexico the Zapatistas appear to have woken up to their plight and then reflexively shifted into the other obvious alternative: imposing a new order of their own on Mexico through brute force rather than through affecting the consciousness of Mexican society. Then again, they may have been motivated only by a desire to reclaim sufficient land to sustain their communities or by a simple desire to be heard. In one speech, Marcos says, "We are…the voice that arms itself to be heard…"[38]

---

[38] Opening Remarks Read by Subcomandante Marcos: The First Intercontinental Meeting Against Neo-Liberalism and for Humanity, Chiapas, 1996

Either way, the Zapatistas almost immediately shifted gears and embarked on a the path of nonviolent resistance. They also advanced a PR campaign for the hearts of not only Mexican civil society, but the world. Eventually, resistance took a back seat to creativity and self governance as the Zapatistas formed autonomous Good Government Boards and embarked on a course of autonomous self rule. Now, even though they enforce the boundaries of their territories with arms, they proudly proclaim, "Our word is our weapon."

In any case, it is important to come to terms with the reality that it is the victim mentality that justifies the Domination System in the first place. In the Babylonian creation myth, the younger gods, fearing for their lives, and seeing themselves as victims unleashed Marduk's control and his murderous rampage. They also made themselves subservient to him. For this reason, the Domination System cannot be eradicated from our individual or collective consciousness until we are able to relinquish our sense of ourselves as victims. Far from identifying ourselves as victims of the Powers and thereby justifying a shift from victim to dominator (as is dictated by the myth of redemptive violence), Walter Wink has rightly asserted that we must allow the victim (along with all other domination based psychic states) to die. No. Actually, Wink's lesson is even tougher. We must sacrifice the psychic state of victimization, we must annihilate it within ourselves.

As long as we maintain the victim mentality, we will supply the system with all the energy it needs to continue. We will remain a prisoner to the belief that there are only two choices: dominate or be dominated. If we follow the script there really are only two roles to play. We can cast ourselves as oppressors or as the oppressed. In short, the limited perspective of ourselves as either oppressed or oppressors, dominated or dominators, stifles the kind of creative and strategic thought that poses a real challenge to the status quo.

In terms of sacrificing the psychic state of victimization, the approach relayed by Carlos Castaneda contains many common threads. Don Juan was a Yaqui Indian. In describing his own transformation, don Juan relayed the following:

> *I am an Indian and Indians are treated like dogs. There was nothing I could do to remedy that, so all I was left with was my sorrow. But then my good fortune spared me and someone taught me to hunt. And I realized that the way I lived was not worth living...so I changed it.*[39]

In a conversation with Castaneda, Don Juan told the story of being brutalized and eventually shot by a petty tyrant and of how his benefactor saved him, trained him as a warrior, and sent him back to his tormentor in order that he might overcome his self-importance (shame and pride). Don Juan didn't defeat his tormentor by means of a frontal attack.

---

[39] Castaneda, Carlos. *Journey to Ixtlan*. Washington Square Press. New York. 1972. Kindle. Location 1401. Page 56.

He defeated the normal functioning of the Domination System by aiding and abetting his tormentor's own self destructiveness. He was able to do so because he revoked the ability of the tormenter and the Domination System to define him or control his reactions. Here is a passage from the book:

> *What usually exhausts us in a situation like that is the wear and tear on our self-importance. Any man who has an iota of pride is ripped apart by being made to feel worthless.*
>
> *'I gladly did everything he asked of me. I was joyful and strong. And I didn't give a fig about my pride or my fear. I was there as an impeccable warrior. To tune the spirit when someone is trampling on you is called control.'*
>
> *Don Juan explained that his benefactor's strategy required that instead of feeling sorry for himself as he had done before, he immediately go to work mapping the man's strong points, his weaknesses, his quirks of behavior.*
>
> *... 'To gather all this information while they are beating you is called discipline,' don Juan said. 'The man was a regular fiend. He had no saving grace. According to the new seers, a perfect petty tyrant has no redeeming features.'*[40]

---

[40] Castaneda, Carlos. *The Fire From Within*. Washington Square Press. New York. 1984. Print. Page 26.

In other words as a matter of strategy, we are called upon to cleverly exit the polarization of victim and victimizer. If we find ourselves in the presence of someone caught in the victim mentality, we must cleverly sidestep the role of the oppressor without ourselves assuming the role of the victim. If we meet an oppressor along the way, we must be equally clever about exiting the role of the victim, again, without falling into the trap of polarization that would have us simply flip to the opposite pole.

This rather sanitized, logical presentation of the issue isn't meant to gloss over real violation. We should never lose touch with the sting of being violated as violation does, just as Walter Wink pointed out, extract being. What I am suggesting is that if we simply flip from one pole to another, we maintain the connection and the relationship dynamic of victim/victimizer. What I am also suggesting is that we can harness our sense of violation for the knowledge it provides regarding the other person and the relationship dynamic. It is not necessary that we let someone else's behavior dictate how we feel about ourselves or even the role we will play. We can let it alert us to the need for clear, conscious action.

Truthfully, once cast in one of these polarized roles, it is hard to transcend it. This is where discipline and focus comes in. This is not the discipline that emanates from shame or from a predetermined protocol. This is the discipline that emanates from wisdom, vision, and our own sense of our intrinsic worth. It is a warrior's discipline and it is a product of an internal locus of control. This kind of discipline gives rise to spontaneous, creative responses that emanate from outside the Domination System.

The outcome of don Juan's story demonstrates this perfectly. Once he knew his petty tyrant (the foreman at his job) intended to kill him, Don Juan cleverly incited his anger under circumstances he knew made it impossible for the man to kill him on the spot. He then took off running. As a matter of punishment, the tormentor had routinely shoved don Juan into the horse pens to clean up after the nervous stallions. As a result, don Juan knew how to survive in the pens. As his tormentor chased him, don Juan ran immediately to the most dangerous stallion's pen and took cover behind a board. In a blind rage, the other man ran in after him and was immediately killed by the horse.

Don Juan further explained, "We know that nothing can temper the spirit of a warrior as much as the challenges of dealing with impossible people in positions of power."[41]

In other words, the Domination System is both the poison and the antidote. It exists inside of us and all around us. By relinquishing any claim to victimhood and by eradicating our self-importance in favor of knowing our own worth and living from it, we die to the influence of the system. We expel it. We gain our freedom not by hiding from the system, or by running from it. We gain our freedom by

---

[41] Castaneda, Carlos. *The Fire From Within*. Washington Square Press. New York. 1984. Print. Page 19.

confronting the Domination System within ourselves and by learning to work effectively with the external elements of the system that would otherwise simply act upon us.

It is important to keep in mind that the people who are in the Domination System and those who act according to its dictates, are not the system. While it may appear that don Juan won a victory against his foreman. This is not entirely true. In reality, what don Juan did was to upset the functioning of the Domination System by refusing to play the usual role.

The death of the foreman was not an aim in and of itself. Don Juan was engaged in the business of fully and completely extracting himself from the influence of the Domination System. For him, the experience was about a wholesale change in his way of being. Consequently, he avoided the usual polar shift from victim to victimizer. He did not attempt to dominate the foreman or even to harm him directly. Don Juan simply allowed the natural flow of the foreman's own actions to determine his (the foreman's) fate while simultaneously transcending the routine expectations of domination-based hierarchical relationships. Most importantly, he was able to maintain contact with his own, independent self concept in an inherently humiliating circumstance and without developing an attitude of hatred towards his tormentor. In regards to the foreman, he said, "And I had not once wished the man to die."[42]

If you are ready to relinquish the victim mentality, go to www.rebeckaeggers.com to find out how you can get connected to Rebecka and The Passion Path. The Passion Path is the path of the Passionate Warrior and of wholehearted, purposeful, and skillful living.

---

[42] Castaneda, Carlos. *The Fire From Within*. Washington Square Press. New York. 1984. Print. Page 29.

Disempowering Dominance ∞ Confronting Evil

If only it were all so simple! If only there were evil people somewhere insidiously committing evil deeds, and it were necessary only to separate them from the rest of us and destroy them. But the line dividing good and evil cuts through the heart of every human being. And who is willing to destroy a piece of his own heart? ∞ Alexander Solzhenitsyn

We all sense that evil exists. Many times, in modern, Western society, we try to brush this truth to the side. In many ways, we are successful. This is even understandable. It is uncomfortable to acknowledge that evil is real. But we must come to terms with it. If you don't believe in evil, you simply haven't been to the right places. Alternatively, maybe you are simply reluctant to deal with evil because you grew up in a restrictive religious environment where you were told of your own evil in a pretty nonstop fashion. Regardless, the task is the same. We must confront evil and we must come to understand its context and its source.

In many ways, the notion of absolute evil actually helps to support the myth of redemptive violence. When we see what we believe is the commission of absolute evil, we very easily flip into what might be called the victim-hero mode. The victim-hero thinks of him or herself as absolute good locked in the battle with absolute evil, and so, is perfectly empowered to perform any act, no matter how loathsome, so long as the end goal is the eradication of absolute evil. Put another way, for the victim-hero the notion that the end of eradicating evil justifies the means, no matter how horrible, is an entrenched way of being. For this reason, among others, it is actually common place these days to shy away from the concept of absolute evil. I believe this strategy is misguided and founded on a misunderstanding of what it means to confront evil.

When I talk about confronting evil, I am talking about a considerably more nuanced circumstance than the proverbial battle between good and evil suggests. In reality, there is no battle between good and evil.

The elements of the Domination System such as rampant, unconscious violence, torture, destruction, hoarding, and environmental degradation are certainly the highest expressions of evil. But they are also the mere expression of the ethics derived from the myth of redemptive violence. The Domination System and its consequences are the expressions of our collective social agreements and mythologies. The truth is that evil is not necessarily inherent in either the Powers or individual people.

Evil is an intractable part of the Domination System.

Many people focus on healing the polarization of opposites, including good and evil, as a way through to sanity. This approach looks to integrate the poles. There is merit in working through the fantasy of rigidly constructed opposites, but not as a means of living in denial about the real expressions of evil that take place in this world every day.

We cannot afford, at this moment in history, to be swept up in the feel good notion that everything is alright. In a very real sense, everything is not alright. Just ask the people starving in Africa, or a woman who has been battered nearly to death by her husband. They will confirm for you that things are not okay.

It is true that we can use life's tragedies, and even the horrors perpetrated on us by others, as a means of fostering overall growth within ourselves and within our communities. But that growth does not come from denying that there is a problem. It comes from accepting the reality of the problem, determining to address it, and learning to use it for our own greater expansion.

The really detrimental fantasy is the fantasy that separates you from me, men from women, heaven from the earth, God from us, and so on and so forth. This fantasy gives rise to the polarization of good and evil in victim-heroes and evil villains. That fantasy is part and parcel of the Domination System. A victim-hero is not a warrior!

The unwillingness to accept the existence of true evil is, ironically, as much a part of the delusion offered up by the Domination System as is the myth of the victim-hero. These are opposite extremes of the same continuum. Both are a distraction from the reality of what afflicts us, namely, the internalized ethos of the Domination System which leads to evil outcomes and behaviors.

Walter Wink addressed this by reference to the death and rebirth of the ego as follows:

> *This process of dying and rising is menacing to those caught in the myth of redemptive violence because it means facing the evil in themselves, and they see that as the equivalent of damnation. For in that myth, salvation consists of identifying oneself as good by virtue of belonging to the right side. Psychologically, this means defining oneself as good in order to achieve a sense of well-being. The intolerable pressure of one's own inner shadow (unacknowledged hatred, anger, violence, lust, greed) can be released then only through projection onto others, against whom it can be exploded in a self-righteous fury. The myth of*

redemptive violence is mortally threatened by even the smallest amounts of self knowledge.[43]

Therefore, once we choose to die to the Domination System, we must also choose to die to the relativism that evaluates evil through the lens of justification as well as the notion that evil, in its absolute sense, is not real. We must also stop seeing evil as something that exists only in others or out in the world somewhere.

Up until now, we have largely talked about theory. But confronting evil requires genuine facts.

Just as I began writing this piece, my friend posted (on Facebook) some news from the Congo where she is actually living at the moment. 11 children were raped and tortured there this past June. One of them, a one year old, was left by the side of the road to be discovered by some passersby. This is the evil of the Domination System hitting a crescendo. This is exactly what we are dealing with. Rape is used in war for the purpose of humiliating individuals and communities, to instill fear and shame, and to destroy the very fabric of a society by making it extremely difficult for traumatized women to effectively parent the next generation. Rape is always about power over.

We have more than inner work ahead of us! Dying to the influences of the Domination System is a beginning. It is

---

[43] Wink, Walter. *Engaging the Powers: Discernment and Resistance in a World of Domination.* Minneapolis. Fortress Press. 1992. Kindle. Location 2353.

not an end in and of itself. It serves a higher purpose, namely preparing us for a new way of being together and for a new kind of positive activism that emanates from beyond the Domination System.

If the Domination System gets to define us, it wins. The system also wins if it gets to dictate our perceptions of it and our responses to it. Accordingly, we must learn to define ourselves and to hold our self concept separate from the influence and evaluation of the Domination System (and those who remain in that system). This will allow us to (i) see the system for what it is (ii) where necessary, facilitate its collapse (just as don Juan aided his tormentor in the process of his own destruction) and (iii) begin to fashion and live according to a new kind of mythology that exists beyond the confines of the current system.

Holding our self concept internally has other key benefits as well. It allows us to call a spade a spade. The Domination System and all it spawns is evil. Further, when we are in deep contact with our own sense of essential goodness, we are able to look at the ways in which we have internalized and acted out the ethics of the system.

The evil of the Domination System is, like the system itself, both the poison and the antidote. Evil, once we are able to see it objectively and to name it, becomes our ally on the spiritual path. We move into a different plane of awareness. In the light of awareness, evil is the shadow made visible. By contrast, if we are not able to name it, see it, and confront it, evil will grow ever more intense.

In other words, once we are in the Domination System, the only way out is to see it in its fullest expression and to choose something different. In fact, seeing the fullest expression of the Domination System provides tremendous incentive for us to create something different. Who, but the most afflicted among us, wants to live in a world where raping one year old girls is part of business as usual?

Evil makes the system visible and thereby subject to destruction and transcendence. In order for the evil of the Domination System to aid us, we must allow ourselves to be present to it and to accept it for what it really is. We must let it sink in. We must allow ourselves to feel the reality of babies brutalized and raped in the name of armed conflict. We must open to the anguish of the doctor who must try to save the children and of my friend who chose to go and bear witness to it all. We must allow evil to make the shadow visible so that we can finally come to terms with it.

Most importantly, we must finally see that the rape of babies in the Congo differs in degree rather than in kind from common expressions of the Domination System like intentionally violating and manipulating someone on an emotional level in order to get what you want.

Anything that disregards the basic intrinsic value and humanity of another by treating them as the means to our ends, is an expression of the Domination System. In the Domination System, people are expendable in the name of progress or profit. They are just another resource to be mined, consumed, or destroyed. When we live by the ethos of the Domination System, we express its evil in our lives. That is a bitter pill to swallow. But it certainly highlights the importance of the choice that lies in front of us.

When you consider things like the conflict in the Congo, it is easy enough to fall into the trap of the victim-hero and to adopt a brand of activism that is based on the notion of being on the right side; the side of the victim-hero. From this perspective the fantasy of opposites is hard at work aiding and abetting the Domination System itself. It tempts us to see violence and domination as the best and/or only solution to violence and domination.

But if you look deeply enough at the situation in the Congo, you will be hard pressed to point your finger at any villain greater than the Domination System itself. You will see that we could hunt down the men who raped that baby girl and we could kill them. But we would only be cutting off the head of the hydra. Ten more heads will take its place. I am not suggesting that we should not do everything in our power to stop the rampant violence in the Congo. I am not even suggesting that we should spare the men involved. They are responsible for their choices. What I am suggesting is that there is something beyond the evil actions of individual men or even armies of men at work in the Congo. There is a system of exploitation in place, and at its head are global actors far more powerful than these soldiers.

Coltan and other minerals are mined in the Congo.[44] If we look only at the evil deeds of the men involved in this one situation, we will overlook the very real role that each of us as consumers in this global marketplace played in the rape of those babies. We will get away with seeing the rapist as the true problem when ravenous, unconscious consumption; extreme poverty; and the desire of large corporate actors and Congolese mining companies alike to achieve a profit without any broader social responsibility is really at the root of war, exploitation, and domination in the Congo. None of the major participants in this fiasco has placed any emphasis on using the wealth represented in the Congolese mineral reserves to support the full development of human potential in the Congo. Everyone is focused on only one thing: getting exactly what they want without the necessity of thinking about the impact of their actions or worse yet, with an affirmative intention to externalize the costs of getting what they want such that the Congolese people bear those costs. This is perfectly reflective of the exploitative values of the Domination System at work.

Though it may seem strange to say it, the real work we have ahead of us is the work of fashioning and then choosing to live by a new vision, a vision rooted in our own sense of

---

[44] http://tribune.com.pk/story/67995/blood-coltan-is-your-cell-phone-soaked-in-congolese-blood/

our intrinsic worth and value and in the worth and value of human potential.

Coming to terms with our own intrinsic worth stands in stark contrast to identifying with the right side. When we have a sense of our own essential worth, we are able to face the shadow in ourselves, and in the collective, without the need of condemnation. We are able to call evil by its rightful name without exploding "in a self-righteous fury" and we are able to confront it in ourselves without suffering. Instead of projecting evil onto others and denying it in ourselves, we begin to work with the reality of the Domination System and its progeny. Clarity takes the place of willful blindness.

We open our eyes to the present day circumstances and we fashion a new vision for a world rooted in genuine wisdom. And when we act in response to things like the violence in the Congo, we do so from the radically different foundation of essential goodness and with real clarity about the many factors affecting the situation. We fashion our activism consciously by reference to a whole new point of origination. Whenever and wherever possible, we aid the Domination System in destroying or exposing itself. But we never lose sight of our purpose, a purpose dictated not by the mandates of the Domination System, but rather by a radically different mythology founded in human worth and our desire to see human potential brought to fruition on a mass scale.

If you are ready to confront the evil of the Domination System, go to www.rebeckaeggers.com to find out how you can get connected to Rebecka and The Passion Path. The Passion Path is the path of the Passionate Warrior and of whole-hearted, purposeful, and skillful living.

Disempowering Dominance ∞ The Mirror of Babylon

History is a relentless master. It has no present, only the past rushing into the future. To try to hold fast is to be swept aside. ∞ *John F. Kennedy Jr.*

Before we finally turn to the task of fleshing out the new mythology, let's take a closer look at the Babylonian creation myth. In the same way Walter Wink utilized it as a framework for explaining the myth of redemptive violence, I want to use it as a kind of time machine. I want to revisit Babylon and look for clues about what might have been taking place in the human psyche at that time and what might be taking place now. I believe this little side trip into antiquity will reveal a great deal about exactly the kind of mythology we might construct from outside the Domination System.

Remember that the context of the myth was ancient Mesopotamia at a time when, according to Walter Wink, floods, droughts, and storms routinely swept the Fertile Crescent and recurrent warfare commonly occurred between various city-states. These wars apparently exhausted resources and "chaos threatened every achievement of humanity." Chaos and danger lurked around every corner. People were likely trying to cope.

As reported by Wink, the Babylonian myth started with a mother and a father god who had managed to create a little family of gods. Apparently the younger gods, in all their frolicking, began making so much noise that the mother and father gods were plotting to kill them. The younger gods caught wind of the plot and struck first, killing Apsu, the father god. When the mother god, Tiamat, found out, she began plotting her revenge.

Recall that Marduk, one of the younger gods stepped up to create order. He offered to slay Tiamat, thereby bringing the chaos under control. But he exacted an extreme price. He demanded full control of everything. Once he had obtained complete dominion, he murdered the mother goddess, stretched her corpse full length, and created the cosmos from the severed parts of her body.

To me this reads like a fantasy of the human mind trying to grapple with an unstable situation. The old order, once maintained by the balance between, and the positive will of, mother goddess and father god, was breaking down. There were wars and unreliable conditions on every front. Resource shortages spurred even greater conflicts. It would have been natural to assume that mother and father had turned on their children. At the very least, the mythology needed an overhaul. Peaceful co-creation no longer reflected the earthly conditions nor did it reflect what must have seemed like the survival needs of Babylonian society.

Marduk arrived on the scene with the "perfect" solution. He agreed to restore order in exchange for perfect submission. He restored "security" at the price of freedom. The image of mother and father god co-creating the universe disappeared into a story featuring Marduk as the creator. Marduk created the universe by taking dominion over Tiamat's lifeless body not by co-creating with her. The feminine spirit left the creation process, though her body still remained as the raw material of creation.

As an aside, something similar happened in the Jewish creation myth in the sense that the creation story begins with a controversial indication of co-creation between a male and female deity. Subsequently, the feminine disappeared from the creation story altogether as Jehovah, a supreme, male god rose to supremacy in the consciousness of the people. In Genesis 1:26-27 (New International Version), the creation story reads as follows:

> *Then God said, 'Let us make mankind in our image, in our likeness, so that they may rule over the fish in the sea and the birds in the sky, over the livestock and all the wild animals, and over all the creatures that move along the ground.' So God created mankind in*

> *his own image, in the image of God he created them;*
> *male and female he created them.*

Obviously, this passage seems a bit confused. There is a reference to "our image" and then to "his own image," which is described as male and female. One could interpret this in many ways. Nonetheless, it at least suggests a co-creative function between male and female that later disappears completely. I point this out here only to suggest that the disappearance of the feminine from the world's creation myths was a common theme in and around Babylon.

The Babylonian myth continues and establishes the origins of "man." Marduk created man from the blood of another god offered in sacrifice. He cut his blood vessels and fulfilled his promise:

> *I will take blood & fashion bone.*
>
> *I will establish a savage,*
>
> *Man shall be his name.*
>
> *Truly savage-man I will create.*
>
> *He shall be charged with the service of the gods.*[45]

Thus, in this creation story, man was created to serve this new god; this god who embodies the myth of redemptive

---

[45] http://faculty.gvsu.edu/websterm/Enuma_Elish.html

violence. Man was created from violence as a savage and as a slave to the Domination System.

The conditions affecting the Fertile Crescent at the time this myth was created are so similar to our own global situation that it is actually a little eerie. For several years now, the news has been rife with stories of resource shortages and the potential conflicts this may create. From petroleum to water[46], the resources that sustain our lives are rumored to be in short supply. Food shortages and rising food prices may be to blame for the unrest in places like Tunisia and Egypt, which have been dubbed, "the Arab Spring."[47] Terror is on the rise, both actual terror, and terror in the collective psyche. Wars rage. Nothing feels secure.

For example, author Brené Brown, a sociologist and researcher who is known for her work in the realm of shame and vulnerability has likened the modern American psychological state to that of collective Post Traumatic Stress Disorder. She claims that the psychological state of at least the American public has degenerated considerably since the terror attacks that occurred on September 11, 2001. Here is an excerpt from an interview Dr. Brown gave to Salon magazine:

> **You talk about "the social climate of scarcity" — of shaming and shutting down and constantly comparing ourselves to others. Do you think**

---

[46] http://www.theguardian.com/sustainable-business/nestle-peter-brabeck-attitude-water-change-stewardship

[47] http://www.theguardian.com/lifeandstyle/2011/jul/17/bread-food-arab-spring

that it's really getting worse, as it seems, or is it something that's always been with us?

'I started my research right around 9/11, and I've seen it get progressively worse since. There's this collective PTSD from 9/11, from multiple wars, from this horrible recession that's affected everyone I know.'[48]

Hyper-vigilance is a key symptom of PTSD. It causes you to constantly scan your environment looking for the next threat. It causes you to see threats in an exaggerated fashion. When you are in a state of hyper-vigilance your whole existence can become about identifying and avoiding threats, real or imagined. You live in a state of red alert. Sound like the national security state that has now taken possession of the Western democracies?

The governments of the world have come forward in the wake of 9/11 to feed our fears, stoke our hyper-vigilance, and to act as our hyper-vigilant eyes and ears scanning the ethers for the next threat. They have also become the enforcers of our security. Just as Marduk did in the Babylonian myth, they now offer us "security" at the cost of our freedom. They offer us a Band-Aid on our collective sense of terror and our traumatized minds. In return, they are looking for more and more power over us and in our lives. Unfortunately, this time we are not talking only about the Fertile Crescent. We are talking about the potential for total world domination.

---

[48] http://www.salon.com/2012/09/18/brene_browns_campaign_against_snark/

Now is the time to take a stand. We don't have to choose to continue the Domination System. It isn't necessary that we hand our freedom over in exchange for perceived security. We don't have to listen to people who want to stoke and then leverage our fear towards gaining greater control and for the sake of advancing their own agendas. Instead, we can choose to consciously restore or even reinvent the model of cooperative co-creation reflected in the beginning of the Babylonian creation myth. To do this, we will have to deal with our collective sense of exaggerated terror. We will also have to say a clear and firm NO to those who would leverage our fear and our fragility for their own purposes. Dr. Brown addressed this perfectly in the interview cited above. Here is what she said:

> *I think we're in a [time of a] lot of fear and scarcity. And I know that that's not new. What's new is that there are groups who are willing to leverage our fear — leveraging fear to get people to do what they want. We've lost our moral courage.*

In addition to having lost our moral courage, not to mention our own internal compasses, we have also lost the balance in our own psyches between masculine and feminine values. As Walter Wink pointed out, the subjugation of the feminine goes hand in hand with and even supports the values of the Domination System. In fact, the loss of our own internal sense of direction is linked very closely with the denigration of the feminine. Feminine ways of knowing, such as intuition, play a key role in the development of inner wisdom. A system that relies on absolute control cannot function if the populace is deeply connected to its own intuitive knowing. Accordingly, we must not only reclaim our courage, we must restore the psychic balance between masculine and feminine. If we retrace our steps all the way to Babylon, this appears to be the solution, or at least a necessary and healthy beginning. It certainly does not seem possible that the new mythology we are looking to adopt can mimic the subjugation of the feminine that has been part and parcel of the Domination System. Creating a balance between and an integration of the masculine and the feminine within our individual and collective psyches strikes me as foundational.

Even though integration of the masculine and feminine is not an end in and of itself, but rather a foundational step, there is much to be learned from examining the consequences of eradicating the concept of mother and father god in harmony. In her book (co-authored with Robert Bly), *The Maiden King,* Marion Woodman talked about the loss of the natural or positive mother and father. She provided terrific insights about what we can recover if we choose to search for them, and to find them within. In regards to the natural mother, Woodman had this to say:

> *Children raised by such a mother will not spend their lives frantically searching the eyes of others for applause. They will not have to deny their own desire in order to please others just to survive. They are not*

in terror of being annihilated if they are not what they ought to be.

Woodman is not just talking about the physical mother. She is talking about the indwelling presence of the natural mother within the psyche. The internal natural mother forms within the psyche and manifests as ease, self trust, and self appreciation only when we are nurtured by someone who holds these traits within themselves.

If we look at the Babylonian myth as a story of psychic phenomenon taking place within the culture, it expresses the death of the natural, psychic mother within the Babylonian collective consciousness.

Woodmen painted an important picture of the natural mother as follows:

> *By 'natural mother' I mean a mother who lives happily in her own body, loves her femaleness, experiences her menses as her feminine relationship to the phases of the moon. In nourishing and cherishing her children, she is confident in her own feminine identity and is, therefore, able to mirror for them. They are psychically and physically fed by the unconditional love she bestows. They can look in her eyes and recognize themselves as they are, without any sense that there exists an agenda as to what they ought to be, should*

be, must be. She sees their individuality and honors its becoming into being.[49]

What happened in the Babylonian creation myth is crucial. The creation myth subjugated the feminine, and by extension, women to masculine control. The myth suggests that the cultural perspective was shifting such that women were seen as the physical raw material of creation rather than the spiritual source and nurturers of it. They became a means to an end.

In the face of this type of cultural mythology, the natural mother cannot fully manifest within individual women or within the community. It becomes very difficult for women to live happily in their own bodies and to develop the kind of self love and acceptance that would normally allow them to instill the natural mother in the minds and hearts of their offspring. The psychological costs are high for the culture as a whole.

Woodman continued her analysis along these lines noting that the subjugation of the feminine to the masculine, is a lie with terrible consequences. She says that in physical terms, this lie has

> *distanced both men and women form their first chakra, their survival chakra, the energy center in the perineum that shouts. 'I love life. I desire color, shape, texture. I desire sexuality. I desire luscious*

---

[49] Bly, Robert and Marion Woodman. *The Maiden King: The Reunion of Masculine and Feminine*. Henry Holt Company. New York. 1998. Print. Page 123.

possibilities of all life has to offer. I accept life. I accept life with its imperfections that work together toward wholeness. I love life in its constant state of flux. I accept death as a part of life, contributing to growth. I trust renewal in the abundant life of the soul.[50]

So, the loss of this psychic, natural mother as reflected in the Babylonian creation story, is the beginning of our self-importance (pride and shame). It is what separates us from our sense of essential worth and from the naturalness and health of our own desires. The loss of this mother within ourselves and within our global community is the root foundation of the Domination System. It separates us from the impulse to live passionately and openly.

And what of the loss of the positive father, which in the myth predates the murder of the mother? It is worth noting that the myth reports that mother and father god have turned on their children and thus must be killed. This suggests the relationship to the natural mother and father was already disturbed. Something was already afoot in the Babylonian collective consciousness. Marduk was the psychic response to a disturbance in the natural order, a disturbance that first became evident in the father.

I looked up the myth in full. Initially, it was Apsu, the father god who wanted to destroy the children. It was only after the murder of Apsu that Tiamat reached the same

---

[50] Bly, Robert and Marion Woodman. *The Maiden King: The Reunion of Masculine and Feminine*. Henry Holt Company. New York. 1998. Print. Page130.

conclusion. I suspect this is a very telling piece of the story. The initial disturbance was in the relationship of Babylon to its psychic father. The distortion first became visible in the masculine and the divine father was the first to be killed.

Woodman provided an explanation of this as well. She noted that for a man, "To be left without a father who can honor his soul is to be forsaken with no masculine model, no inner ordering principle. A man who has not found 'at-one-ment' with his father may fear older men, fear their authority, or remain forever a rebel against all they stand for."[51]

This is a very important point. It is the masculine that manifests in the world. The masculine brings order out of chaos, not by brute force, but by serving as the organizational principle that brings formlessness into form. It, therefore, makes perfect sense that the disturbance first became evident in the masculine. Given the conditions in and surrounding Babylon at the time, it would have appeared that the manifestation function of divinity, and by extension, humanity, had utterly failed. It would have appeared that the natural order of things had been lost. It must have even begun to seem as though the gods were angry.

Woodman continued her analysis and explained the effect of losing the ordering principle on the feminine psyche of a man. Interestingly, the story she analyzed was a Russian fairy tale. Like the Babylonian myth it is told from the perspective

---

[51] Bly, Robert and Marion Woodman. *The Maiden King: The Reunion of Masculine and Feminine.* Henry Holt Company. New York. 1998. Print. Page134.

of the masculine. Woodman noted that without a father, a man's feminine side may act like a fatherless daughter who idealizes masculinity…A woman, she concluded, "may find herself fearful of being forthright, especially with men…"[52]

It is somewhat like this in the Babylonian myth. The sons (no goddesses are mentioned in relation to the plot that kills mother and father god) turn to Marduk for help rather than confront the situation at hand. Abdicating all responsibility for understanding and confronting the situation directly, they abandon themselves to the promised security he can provide. Having somehow lost the inner ordering principle, they look for security in this exaggerated, warmongering version of masculinity. The loss of the natural father or ordering principle in the psyche is actually what causes us to lose our courage and to abdicate control of our lives to the Marduk's of the world.

With the natural divine father eliminated in the Babylonian psyche, the gods are left to fend for themselves with the shadow mother figure represented by Tiamat. She is angry, and vengeful. Woodman addresses this in *The Maiden King* as well. She explains that when the shadow mother appears in the psyche, "The masculine struggle, then becomes a struggle to break free of the devouring mother as the force that perpetually threatens manhood."[53]

---

[52] Bly, Robert and Marion Woodman. *The Maiden King: The Reunion of Masculine and Feminine*. Henry Holt Company. New York. 1998. Print. Page134.

[53] Bly, Robert and Marion Woodman. *The Maiden King: The Reunion of Masculine and Feminine*. Henry Holt Company. New York. 1998. Print. Page137.

Now we understand a bit more about why the subjugation of women is part and parcel of the Domination System. Marduk represents the distorted masculine, locked in enmity with the devouring mother. Woodman notes that many men are left with two pictures of the feminine: "dead and treacherous." If we shift the words around a little, we get a more fulsome picture. The relationship of the inner masculine to the inner feminine is represented here and the inner feminine is seen as either dead or treacherous.

And who is the "she" that is either dead or treacherous? Recall that it was chaos that existed in the fertile crescent when Marduk entered the Babylonian consciousness. It isn't a great leap for us to assume that Marduk was the psychic adaptation to the chaos of wild weather patterns and an earth that failed to bear enough fruit to sustain everyone. The divine feminine is often associated with chaos and with the earth itself. Woodman reached this conclusion as well. She noted that, "The individual relationship to the feminine has extended into the collective attitude to the planet."

In the myth, earth and humans were ultimately under the control and power of Marduk. They were his creations wrought from the dead body of mother Tiamat.

The Domination System is founded on the desire to subdue the natural, chaotic flow of life on earth. In a very real sense, it denies human creativity in favor of control and it suppresses the generative power of the feminine.

It makes sense doesn't it? As we already discovered, much like life in this modern world, life in the Fertile Crescent was, at the moment of Marduk's psychic birth, a chaotic and seemingly dangerous place of resource shortages and war. This story provides a handy mirror for all who are willing to see its reflection.

What lessons will we take from this story? Will we be content to repeat the cycle of violence and domination ad nauseum until life on earth ceases to exist? Will we go on trying to beat back the chaotic and the spontaneous in a fruitless war against death? Or will we open again to the new/old mythology of balance in the cosmos and all the richness and diversity it has to offer?

Chogyam Trungpa has described this potential new/old mythology and contrasted it to his own version of the myth of redemptive violence. He explained that we are currently living according to the "setting-sun vision." According to Trungpa, the problems of the setting sun world will be resolved when we choose to adopt what he calls the vision of the Great Eastern Sun. Trungpa contrasted the two worlds as follows:

> *The vision of the Great Eastern Sun is based on celebrating life. It is contrasted to the setting sun, the sun that is going down and dissolving into darkness. The setting-sun vision is based on trying to ward off the concept of death, trying to save ourselves from dying. The setting-sun point of view is based on fear. We are constantly afraid of ourselves. We feel that*

we can't actually hold ourselves upright. We are so ashamed of ourselves, who we are, what we are...

Great Eastern Sun vision, on the other hand, is based on appreciating ourselves and appreciating our world, so, it is a very gentle approach. Because we appreciate the world, we don't make a mess in it. We take care of our bodies, we take care of our minds, and we take care of our world. The world around us is regarded as very sacred, so we constantly serve our world and clean it up.[54]

The Great Eastern Sun vision is about redemption. Nothing is expendable. Trungpa illustrates this point in the following passage:

In the vision of the Great Eastern Sun, even criminals can be cultivated, encouraged to grow up. In the setting sun vision, criminals are hopeless, so, they are shut off; they don't have a chance. They are part of the dirt that we would rather not see. But in the vision of the Great Eastern Sun, no human being is a lost cause. We don't feel that we have to put a lid on anyone or anything. We are always willing to give things a chance to flower.

The basis of the Great Eastern Sun vision is realizing that the world is clean and pure to begin with. There

---

[54] Trungpa, Chogyam. *Shambhala: The Sacred Path of the Warrior.* Shambhala Publications, Inc. Boston. 1984. Page 666.

*is no problem cleaning things up, if we are just returning them to their natural, original state.*⁵⁵

Walter Wink took a similar approach from a Christian perspective with regards to the Powers. He said, "The Powers are good. The Powers are fallen. The Powers will be redeemed."⁵⁶

And so it is, and so it shall be.

If you are ready to clean things up, go to www.rebeckaeggers.com to find out how you can get connected to Rebecka and The Passion Path. The Passion Path is the path of the Passionate Warrior and of whole-hearted, purposeful, and skillful living.

---

⁵⁵ Trungpa, Chogyam. *Shambhala: The Sacred Path of the Warrior.* Shambhala Publications, Inc. Boston. 1984. Page 702.

⁵⁶ Wink, Walter. *Engaging the Powers: Discernment and Resistance in a World of Domination.* Minneapolis. Fortress Press. 1992. Kindle. Location 969.

Disempowering Dominance ∞ Facing the Terrorist Within

Behavior is the mirror in which everyone shows their image. ∞ Johann Wolfgang von Goethe

The Domination System is a dualistic system and it exists within each one of us. I guarantee that if you have been a victim, you have also been, at one time or another, in a position of privilege and power in relationship to someone somewhere. For instance, a peasant farmer may exercise his privilege relative to his wife and daughters. Similarly, an abused wife might still occupy a position of relative privilege in her relationship to her children. An employee in a corrupt government might be in a privileged relationship relative to the public. And so on and so forth...

It should now be clear that it is our victim identity that allows us to justify (i) flipping the poles and slipping into domination with those we believe have victimized us and

(ii) acting as the enforcers of the Domination System in various capacities such as father, soldier, mother, government employee, corporate executive etc.

In this chapter, we are going to deal with something else entirely. Now we are going to look at ourselves as dominators. We are concerned here with our role as the oppressors of people who hold less power than we do. As already acknowledged, we use the victim mentality to justify some of this. But there is more that needs to be confronted. Here we are looking at our own cruelty and our desire to control from an entirely different angle. We are relinquishing the victim mentality in order to look at our own naked aggression and desire for power in and of themselves.

I am intentionally introducing this topic here, after having painted a brief picture of the shift we need to make away from the Domination System and towards a new mythology based on intrinsic human worth and blossoming. It is important, as we go forward with this analysis, that we keep in mind the basic underpinnings of this new mythology. If we go forward with the knowledge of our intrinsic worth firmly rooted in our self concept, we can look at things through the lens of neutrality.

As Chogyam Trungpa articulated, we are here to clean things up. We are here to reveal the goodness that has been obscured by the Domination System. It is okay to look at all that is because underneath everything, there is basic goodness. We are simply revealing, through a process of rigorous honesty, the truth of what lies beneath the system and its impact on us. Put another way, our desire to uncover and to live according to our basic goodness serves a dual purpose. It both makes it palatable to and requires that we undertake this very uncomfortable task.

Note how this undertaking stands in stark opposition to the Babylonian creation myth where humans were created as savages and servants to a savage god. Under the Babylonian mythology, there isn't any work to do. In the words of Thomas Hobbes, "The condition of man...is a condition of war of everyone against everyone."

There is no way around it. If we want to create something other than a life of conflict and exploitation, we must examine the ways in which we are, ourselves, oppressors. In many ways, this is far more uncomfortable than looking at our victim mentality or even our experiences of victimization. But in reality, it is part and parcel of relinquishing our victim identity. As victims, we occupy a more noble position. People feel sorry for us. They look upon us with a kind and sympathetic eye. This is not true when we consciously acknowledge our own role as the oppressor in someone else's life. The shield of the victim provides cover and justification for many things. It is uncomfortable to give it up! Nonetheless, we must take this journey. We must open to it.

Let us then return again to Babylon.

Recall that Marduk offered his services in exchange for complete control. We can imply from his demands that he had sinister motives. It is useful to do so for the sake of this analysis. So, let's assume that Marduk did not want to share power. He was not acting as a victim-hero by identifying with the right side. The evidence we have suggests that Marduk was acting in his own self-centered interests. He was an opportunist. Later in this book, we will look at this from another angle. But for now, let's accept the evidence at face value. Marduk was motivated by power for its own sake and not by any desire to genuinely aid the younger gods in their predicament.

Are you willing to see this in yourself? Are you ready to come to terms with your own naked self interest and your ability to cruelly take what you desire?

The truth is that there is a Marduk in each one of us. Just as the people of Babylon were facing perceived resource shortages, we have been taught that we live in a world of limitation and lack. The collective belief system really functions around the notion that I can't have something unless I take it from you. We are stuck in a win-lose perspective. Through the lens of this perspective, winners are given over to their pride and the enjoyment of the spoils of war. Losers are abandoned to their shame and left to their deprivation.

From within this perspective, Marduk's actions make perfect sense. In fact, from this perspective, the only way in which we can safeguard our own interests is to actually take control, and then suppress the will and supplant the desires of everyone else. Whatever we see, we desire for ourselves and we hate people we believe have what we are lacking.

For instance, the peasant farmer might naturally admire the wealth and the power wielded by those in superior positions within the Domination System. He might naturally desire to enact such a system for himself within his own household, keeping for himself the greatest treasures the family is able to create and taking for himself the fruit of his family's labor. This is very different from the victim mentality that might urge this farmer to maintain control of his family for the sake of (i) creating for himself a safe zone free of domination at the hands of others or (ii) avoiding the scorn of other men who maintain strict control of the family. This type of domination is based on a covetous desire to be like the oppressor and/or take for yourself something that rightfully belongs to others.

I have personal experience in all of this. I grew up in a family in which my mother had little economic power relative to my father. I realized early on that the only overtly powerful role in that set-up was the role of the patriarch (although I now see that my mother wielded a lot of power through indirect means). My desire was to be like my father. I wanted to avoid being dominated by others, but more insidiously, I wanted to have the power and the control in the family.

I became a successful lawyer while my daughter's father stayed home. Rather than acknowledging his contribution as a stay-at-home father and also seeing him as an equal participant in our household, I held on to as much control as possible. I managed, and in many ways, controlled the finances. I also secretly thought I had a right to enjoy whatever purchases I wanted while also secretly harboring resentment and discouraging anything he might have wanted for himself.

My ex-husband was very much a second class citizen in my mind. Though I could not see this at the time, that is what I expected him to be. I followed in my father's footsteps as the breadwinner and I expected him to follow in my mother's footsteps by keeping the house in order and taking care of me. I wanted for myself what I imagined that my father had.

Of course, in retrospect, my father's control over the family was not nearly as complete or powerful as I had imagined. He certainly was not an oppressive person, and, in truth, my mother was no gentle subject. But through the eyes of a young girl, unschooled in the nuances of relationship, it looked to me like my father lived the life of a king and that he ran the family show. He certainly held the overt power in the family simply by virtue of the position he occupied in society, as a man and as the breadwinner of our family. I coveted his privileged position.

The truth is, looking back, I am ashamed of what I expected of my ex-husband even though I was not, at that time, fully conscious of my own expectations, or their implications. I was just imitating something I thought I understood. I saw only two positions: one up and one down. I was determined to control the high ground and that is the point of this whole discussion. My expectations and desires were not really wrong from the perspective of the Domination System. The Domination System and its imperatives create an untenable situation. From the perspective of lack, the only "safe" and "enjoyable" position is the position of power over others. Nonetheless, what I accomplished was to put my former husband in a place of natural rebellion against my sense of superiority.

Our family system ultimately failed ending in financial ruin, divorce, and ultimately, the separation of my daughter from her father. In retrospect, had my ex-husband actually fallen into line with my expectations, it would have represented a loss of his core sense of self and it would have violated his sense of himself as a man within the Domination System.

At the time, I could not understand any of this and so we lived in an environment of constant resentment. We missed out on the magic we could have created together had we been able to hold a different vision; a vision of equality founded on the notion of everyone having dignity and a chance to blossom. By way of example, my ex-husband is extremely talented in managing money and budgets. I can only imagine what would have been possible if I had given him the chance to manage our family finances. This is what the Domination

System does. It thwarts the full development of our collective and individual possibilities.

In a very real sense, the Domination System and its vision of lack creates habits of pessimism and negativity. We live in a state of being overly concerned with material well-being and with the need to maintain our power over others for the sake of our own survival, the accumulation of resources, and for our own egocentric enjoyment. We develop a jungle or dog-eat-dog mentality rooted in scarcity and fear. From within this framework, domination is the only logical choice. If we are able to dominate others, no matter how small our sphere of influence, we will naturally do so and we may even enjoy it as the spoils of victory. Our focus is not on the common welfare or on the blossoming of potential. We focus all our efforts on getting what we need and want for ourselves.

If we look carefully, however, the impulse to dominate is not actually the issue. It emanates from a part of us that knows how to survive. This is the animal instinct from which our natural fight response arises. It provides us with a wealth of information about the situation we are in. The fight response isn't bad, wrong, or unnatural. If someone comes at you from a dark alley at night, demands your money, and begins to beat you, the fight response will keep you alive. It may also help you to maintain valuable resources for yourself; resources you need in order to eat your next meal or enjoy the next week.

What we can learn from our impulse to dominate is that we have come to the place where we are living in a constant state of fear that we will not survive. Dominance insures resources and resources insure survival. Further, dominance provides safety. It allows us to escape the role of the victim. Escaping the role of the victim or the oppressed determines not just whether or not we will survive. It determines the quality of our survival experience relative to others in the hierarchy. Accordingly, a sense of scarcity is another structural support for the Domination System.

When we have a sense of scarcity, fighting appears to be synonymous with survival and the enjoyment of life. These are the group dynamics of the Domination System. They must be acknowledged. We can't continue to assume that there are neat categories of victims and villains. We must come to terms with the notion that within the Domination System we are all victims and we are all villains.

Even still, at some time or another, especially when we are waking up to the effects of the Domination System, we feel the urge to offer ourselves completely and freely. We long for greater connection and for the opportunity to share what we have openly. Yet, if we are even slightly in touch with ourselves, we also feel unable to do so. We sense that the situation we are in places very real constraints on our ability to be fully received and cared for by others. In the context of the Domination System, the idea of opening ourselves completely carries the risk that others will violate or dominate us.

The truth is, we are not really dealing with purely personal dynamics within a particular relationship or situation. We are dealing with a larger context that informs those relationships and situations. We are living in relationships and with situations that are governed by the ethos of the Domination System. It does not do us any good to pretend otherwise. The idea is not to suppress our anger, fear, resentment, or even the fight response. The idea is to alter our circumstances first through an inner shift in our vision and our way of being in the world and second, through concrete action.

Put another way, when someone who has been in the egocentric position of power either begins to wake up to the impact of their privilege on other people or simply begins to long for real connection, there is a risk that he/she will open in an unconscious way. If this happens, there will be a pole shift from dominator to dominated.

Bearing in mind this risk of a pole shift, we must still come to terms with reality. Our efforts to maintain power for its own sake and to achieve security and happiness by sheer force of will are blocking the creative flow of our lives. This way of living keeps us trapped in feelings of constant fear and dread. No matter how powerful we are, there is always a risk that someone will overtake us or some event will knock us out of the power position. The fear of this keeps us in an unstable state always waiting for the next shoe to drop. Living this way leaves us completely drained! It is a lonely and exhausting way to be.

It is absolutely clear, therefore, that something has to change. But the change cannot be a lateral shift from hoarding power and benefits (dominator) to open source living (potential victim). We must expand beyond the Domination System by seeing it for what it is, dying to its influence, and transitioning to a whole new way of being that accords with a new, more positive mythology rooted in something like Chogyam Trungpa's Great Eastern Sun vision. At the same time, we must be proactive about caring for ourselves. To put it bluntly, in the words of Thomas Hobbes, "A man cannot lay down the right of resisting them that assault him by force, to take away his life."

At this point, I have said about all that needs to be said regarding the Domination System and how it works. There is nothing left to do but die to its influence. Death is at your doorstep. Will you open the door?

Paradoxically, death is the way through to the lightness of being promised by Chogyam Trungpa's Great Eastern Sun vision.

If you are ready to accept the call of death, go to www.rebeckaeggers.com to find out how you can get connected to Rebecka and The Passion Path. The Passion Path is the path of the Passionate Warrior and of whole-hearted, purposeful, and skillful living.

Disempowering Dominance ∞ Death

A man who won't die for something is not fit to live. ∞ *Martin Luther King, Jr.*

Up until now, this book has been a bit like a "how to" manual. It has been heavy on theory and analysis. Regardless, I hope you have gotten the message that this new vision, and the conscious creative action that will bring it to life, will not come cheap. The change I am proposing will come at a steep price in personal change for those who are willing to be trend setters. That price is spiritual death, or at the very least, a burnt offering of the soul.

This book has been truly hard for me to write. I have struggled to be a container from this transformation. I have been raw, angry, afraid, shaking in my core. My own life is shifting directions rapidly and powerfully as a result of this experience. I have, in a very real sense, felt my own traumas and dilemmas of powerlessness come to the surface yet again and in the most profound way.

I have felt the powerlessness of women in Saudi Arabia who can't even drive or enter music stores and the anguish of a little 14 year old Bangladeshi girl flogged to death for the "crime" being raped. I have felt the fear of pregnant women on the verge of death being denied medically necessary abortions under draconian laws passed by arrogant men. I have felt anew the anguish of my own young self caught in domestic violence and sexual abuse. I have felt the rage well up in me and threaten to spill over and then fade to a sense of utter powerlessness and self hatred.

My own issues of domination and power center around my gender and my sexuality and around feelings of powerlessness in the face of remote or gigantic organizations with seemingly unlimited power such as the police or even the corporation that erroneously recorded a debt on my credit report while I was writing. I have lived these issues in spades during this process. I have also re-experienced the worst kind of exploitation and betrayal: the kind that comes from those who profess to love you with their lips while betraying you with their actions. I have, at times, wanted to give up, to die, to throw in the towel on humanity.

I couldn't write this book as theory. It had to have practical application. I had to be impacted and transformed by it. For this reason, over and over again, it has brought me to the brink. As I sat down to write this chapter, a part of me just wanted to quit. That part of me was screaming about the naiveté of trying to progress beyond the habitual responses that have kept me alive for this long. Still another didn't care about change anymore. That part of me just wanted revenge. It didn't care about strategy or principles. The revenge-minded part of me just wanted someone to pay.

This is exactly how the Domination System functions. Its imperatives are about anguish, defeat, fear, scarcity, powerlessness, power over others, and revenge. Since the Domination System is entrenched in us, extricating ourselves from it is an intense experience. It is a descent into the underworld of our subconscious desires and fears. It is a confrontation with our own shadows and our sense of powerlessness. Most importantly, it leads to the integration of our power and of those parts of ourselves that we have long since disowned. This journey as about reclaiming our darkness, our totality. It is not an easy thing to do. When you choose it, you are choosing to die to the personality you have carefully constructed for the sake of survival. You are agreeing to destroy your own self image and to build it anew as the full expression of your authenticity and your passion.

If you choose the descent, you will contend with your own survival reflexes as the triangle of fight, flight, or freeze rears its head again. More than that, you will encounter your own hopelessness. You will come up against your own entrenched belief that you must either dominate or be dominated. You will have to address your fundamental belief that your acquiescence to and/or your fight against the Powers, is all that is standing between you and certain annihilation. You will feel like you are giving up all of your security. In my case, because of the severe and ongoing traumas I have experienced, the habitual response that I was most afraid to let go of was actually not the fight response. It was my habitual tendency to dissociate, submit, and even empathize with those who have violated me.

At this point, it feels important to say that with severe, ongoing trauma, the natural fight, flight, and freeze responses become exaggerated. They lose the natural, instinctual quality that shows up when we confront, for instance, a one time attacker on the street or a wild animal in the woods. With severe, ongoing trauma, the survival responses become a permanent, entrenched, and distorted "normal." What is required is that you first resurrect your natural, instinctual, undistorted drives. Then you must advance beyond them to conscious, skillful action. This is, in the first instance, a confrontation with yourself. It requires that you overcome the learned self censorship that emanates from The Dominations System and that you begin to address your circumstances with clarity, conviction, and power.

Walter Wink addressed this directly. He examined the Book of Revelations as a critique of the Domination System as it manifested in Rome. He likened the imagery of the Dragon and the Beast to Marduk and the Roman emperor respectively. This is what followed:

> *The Dragon's strategy is to eviscerate opposition by a sense of induced powerlessness. To accept its*

delusional assumptions is, in effect, to worship the Dragon, to hold its values as ultimate, to stake one's life on the permanence of its sway... Obeisance to the Beast requires as its gesture a continuous shrug. 'Who is like the Beast and who can fight against it?' (shrug). 'I just carried out my orders. If I hadn't done so, someone else would have.' (shrug)...As R.D. Laing put it, 'Each person claims his own inessentiality... In this collection of reciprocal indifference, of reciprocal inessentiality and solitude, there appears to exist no freedom. There is conformity to a presence that is everywhere elsewhere...Mind and body are torn, ripped, shredded, ravaged, exhausted by these Powers and Principalities in their cosmic conflict.'

'Who is like the Beast and who can fight against it?' is the mantra whose chanting by the masses guarantees compliance... Soon one begins acting as censor to one's own mind... [57]

What I experienced during this process was the desire not just to censor my own thoughts, but to become my own executioner too. The will to live, at times during the writing of this book, slipped away so completely that I almost could not sense the warmth of my own body or the beat of my own heart. It was as though the blood had gone cold in my veins just as I was answering a deep and profound call to life.

---

[57] Wink, Walter. *Engaging the Powers: Discernment and Resistance in a World of Domination.* Minneapolis. Fortress Press. 1992. Kindle. Location 1484.

But it is death we are called to in the service of this new life we are creating, and so it is appropriate that I felt the warmth slipping away. In a very real sense, I have been leaving one world for another, moment by moment, conscious choice by conscious choice. I have been dying. According to Marion Woodman, the key is in knowing the difference between ritual death and actual death. At times the line has seemed a bit blurry! Marion Woodman described this ritual death or descent into the underworld of the psyche as follow:

> *'The Descent' is a mythological term for the period during and after a powerful event in which the ego has been overwhelmed by a wave from the unconscious. Energy that is normally available to consciousness falls into the unconscious so the person is often disoriented, exhausted, perhaps in a trance state in which creative energies are going through transformations that the unaware ego may know nothing about until big changes begin to happen in the outer world, or the studio begins to shine with totally new pictures, new music, or new sculpture… People often fall into this realm when they are about to be taken into a new phase of life and they have to die to the old order to be reborn into the new.*[58]

---

[58] Bly, Robert and Marion Woodman. *The Maiden King: The Reunion of Masculine and Feminine*. Henry Holt Company. New York. 1998. Print. Page177.

That is exactly what writing this book has been like! I have been disoriented and exhausted. I have questioned my sanity more than once.

This journey is not for everyone. It is for those who are called to play a part in the transition from a world determined by the ethos of the Domination System to a world that is inspired by a new mythology, a mythology that honors our basic goodness and fosters the blossoming of human potential.

I wrote this book for those people who take personal development seriously and for whom the global and personal state of affairs wrought by the Domination System is simply unacceptable. As I outlined at the beginning, it is for activists who are ready to incorporate spirit and it is for the spiritual who are ready to incorporate activism. It is also for those people who are dealing with trauma and for whom the recovery of their vitality is of the utmost importance as a personal matter and as a matter of changing their participation in the global system.

I intend for this book to create the ultimate union between faith and action and to serve as a healing elixir.

Thus, what I am proposing is not a rational act. If you are in the group of people I just described, I am asking you to pause at the moment when world events or your own life calls forth your fury or your acquiescence. I am encouraging you to stand when your initial impulse is to run and to run when your habit is to remain still. I am suggesting that you duck when everything in you wants punch and that you fight when you want to duck. Of course, I don't mean this to stand for trading one set of ingrained imperatives for their opposites. What I mean to say is that I want you to shake things up and to break out of your habits and routines. Experiment with new and different responses.

Ultimately, I am asking you to find the space between stimulus and response. I am inviting you to live from there, to craft a new life from the emptiness you will encounter. The space between stimulus and response is where the dying takes place. It is where you encounter the zero point of your life and it is the space in which you will be stripped of all you thought was true about your life and of who you thought you were. This commitment to death and rebirth that makes no sense without an abiding commitment to higher spirit and to a cause greater than yourself. It is not something you can undertake by sheer force of your ordinary will. This is an initiation. I am calling you out of rote reaction and onto the spirit path of power.

Walter Wink was right. The Domination System functions on induced powerlessness. Therefore, in a very real sense, the only way we can extricate ourselves from it is to claim our power. The power I am speaking of is the power to create and to act intentionally. It is rooted in wisdom. I sense it is deeply connected to the earth. It certainly demands that we get comfortable with chaos.

In order to extract our power from the clutches of the Domination System, we have to discover where it has been captured, or more to the point, where we have given it over to the system. Imagine that the Domination System is a huge mass of cables connecting each of us to the greater collective consciousness of the system. We must figure out how the cables are connected to us and then disconnect them. Again Babylon has much to teach us.

I said earlier in this book that something had already gone wrong in the Babylonian psyche by the time Marduk arrived on the scene. The story began with the junior gods frolicking in such a way that they disturbed the mother and father god. So loud was their whooping and hollering that mother and father were plotting to kill these errant boys.

If we examine this from a fresh perspective, if we consider it from the perspective of ritual death, something entirely new emerges. Every person must grow up. Indeed, at some point, our frolicking will, if we are lucky, raise the ire of mother and father. They will call us to the death of our youth and the birth of our adulthood.

Perhaps the thing that occurred in the Babylonian psyche was a refusal of the call to ritual death and to subsequent maturity. I can only speculate.

I do know that the road to seizing and ultimately wielding our creative power rests in our willingness to accept the invitation to maturity here and now.

In *The Maiden King*, Marion Woodman examined a Russian folktale. In the story, a boy named Ivan accepted the invitation of the underworld journey. He chose to face the dark side of the divine feminine. In Russian folklore, She is known as the Baba Yaga. Woodman noted that "If in our arrogant innocence we can learn from older cultures that respect the Baba Yaga, we can find some meaning in the chaos that is erupting at our very center."

There is that word again, "chaos." As I was typing that sentence, I became even more convinced about the Babylonian creation myth. Mythology is always multidimensional. It functions on many symbolic levels all at one time. I think Marduk represented, on at least one level, the ego, or personality, left unchecked by the lessons of the Baba Yaga. Marduk is the collective ego ascended, not yet willing to submit itself to the ritual death that brings new life out of chaos. Marion Woodman, I think, would agree. Here is what she says about our willingness to face the Baba Yaga:

> *Moreover, our willingness to face the Baba Yaga is our chance to grow up. Until she is encountered consciously, the values she teaches cannot be learned. We are facing her unconsciously in addictions, for example, but because we have no cultural myth to understand what we are dealing with, most of us are obliterated or obliterate ourselves through our compulsion. We come out of the experience either angry or asking, 'Why me?' We try to believe she*

does not exist, that we are miracle babies born to be happy, never to die, and prosperity is our right to life. Nothing ugly, destructive, death-dealing exists, and if it does, we dress it up to look alive.

The Death Goddess does exist. We are meeting her every day in the parts of us that need to die in order for new life to come in...So long as we are hostile to her, she is hostile to us. Our either/or thinking exacerbates our agony because we are trapped with no third possibility able to arise unless we hold the tension of opposites until they transform. Courtesy, accepting the hospitality of the Baba Yaga, eating what she offers is a third possibility.[59]

Armed with this third option, let's travel back in time again to the Fertile Crescent. From Walter Wink's description, the Fertile Crescent had descended into resource shortages and wars. These were the conditions affecting the collective consciousness of Babylon. There was chaos in the world. This outer chaos must have also given rise to the chaos within that Marion Woodman referenced. These conditions certainly must have contributed to the development of the psychological death grip represented by the Domination System.

A few chapters ago, I relayed Walter Wink's conviction that an ego sacrifice is the required means of exiting the Domination System. This assertion lines up with my theory

---

[59] Bly, Robert and Marion Woodman. *The Maiden King: The Reunion of Masculine and Feminine.* Henry Holt Company. New York. 1998. Print. Page186.

about Marduk representing the ego on a collective level. It also answers the foundational question of where the "cables" of the Domination System hook into each one of us. I believe each of us is caught in the Domination System at the level of our ascended, and as of yet, unseasoned egos. A terrified, angry juvenile god is in charge of everything! He is holding the door wide open to the energy of the broader system of domination.

In Western spiritual pop culture, it has become fashionable to blame the ego and to talk about destroying it or outgrowing it. This is not what we are talking about here. In reality, ego development is a natural and normal part of maturing. Even duality is a natural byproduct of that development. It is a natural step towards higher consciousness. Marion Woodman and Elinor Dickson, in their book, Dancing in the Flames, have elaborated on this as follows:

> *Duality belongs in the ego development stage. It is the tree of the knowledge of good and evil, which symbolizes humanity's fall up from unconscious Eden. While Eden is characterized by participation mystique, duality has to do with differentiation of energies—a necessary step in the progression toward higher consciousness. Things are identified by their parts—good or evil, black or white, strong or weak—in an either/or world. The ego world in which we live*

exercises power over against, thus perpetuating the neurotic either/or dichotomy...[60]

So, what we are talking about here is not the permanent death of the ego, but rather, it's liberation from the Domination System through a maturation process. The challenge we now face as we attempt to transcend the Domination System is not the ego itself, but its distortion. This distortion arises when development is arrested for some reason. It expresses as the exercise of power over against and as the neurotic element in the duality that is otherwise a natural part of ego development. This power over against and its accompanying neurosis is the apparent undergirding of the Domination System.

In order to understand how we might cure the neurosis and move towards greater maturity, let's look again at the Babylonian circumstance. Much like us, the Babylonians faced perilous times. In addition to the wars and resource shortages, recall that the weather patterns were undergoing significant upheavals. The Death Goddess was afoot in ancient Babylon. Marduk, it seems, arose as an unwillingness or lack of readiness in the Babylonian consciousness, to, in Marion Woodman's words, eat what the goddess was offering. Rather than face the weather disturbances and resource shortages, Marduk arose as a solution. Subdue nature and one another;

---

[60] Woodman, Marion and Elinor Dickson. *Dancing in the Flames: The Dark Goddess in the Transformation of Consciousness.* Shambhala Publications. Boston. 1997. Print. Page 49.

address the competition for resources with an iron fist. To the victors go the spoils.

This eat what you kill mentality is exactly what manifests when, for whatever reason, the ego fails to progress towards higher consciousness. In fact, Woodman and Dickson have described this precise phenomenon. They have explained it by analyzing the transformation of energy into consciousness and secondarily, the chakra system of Eastern religions. In the Chakra system, the ego is associated with the lower chakras. They elaborated on this point as follows:

> *If, however, the ego becomes the basis for a split in the evolution of energy on its rise to consciousness, we are likely to develop a heart of stone rather than a heart of flesh. If the ego consciousness, in its will to power, represses the lower levels of energy, they become distorted. Then, the root chakra, symbolized in kundalini by the coiled serpent, becomes, seemingly evil. What is repressed becomes negative when the energy of the root chakra is blocked; the "I desire" withdraws because it knows it will not be fulfilled. Unconsciously, that withdrawal can become a withdrawal from a desire to live consciously. It may appear as a fierce possessiveness—holding on to an idea, a project, a person. But the possessiveness is based on the terror of annihilation. Out of it arises rage, jealousy, greed, clinging, codependency, parasitic feeding on others, as an infant is forced to feed.*

Beneath these seeming passions lies dread—dread of life, dread of chaos, dread of the fundamental feminine cycle (i.e., dying to be reborn). Beneath that dread is frozen despair that lies at the core of the negative mother complex...It is also the archetypal darkness that lies at the core of much of our daily news, even our daily addictions...

...If the energy of the root chakra is fundamentally afraid of life itself, transforming this energy into the very basis of life and further evolution is a daunting task. If we remain in the ego world, the externalized world of concrete reality, death in any form is unthinkable...

...We have not seen death for what it really is—a transformation—and we are, therefore, unable to enter into a process wherein that transformation can be experienced consciously at each level of growth. We may, consequently, be very fearful of our ultimate encounter with the Great Goddess. Without experiencing the light energy within us, either we see death as final and meaningless, or we surround ourselves with rituals, talismans, or plenary indulgences, which assure us a place in heaven through our power, rather than through our own transformation.[61]

---

[61] Woodman, Marion and Elinor Dickson. *Dancing in the Flames: The Dark Goddess in the Transformation of Consciousness.* Shambhala Publications. Boston. 1997. Print. Page 60.

In essence, the root chakra is the seat of desire and of passion and when the energies of the lower chakras become blocked or repressed by fear, something very like the Domination System emerges: parasitic, possessive, greedy, controlling, dominating. Rather than supporting the full enlightenment of the soul, the root chakra becomes the seat of our effort to avoid death and to create security at the expense of free expression. In our arrogance, we askew the death of each cycle, expecting to storm the gates of heaven with hubris and brute force. What we are really eschewing are the experiences that would otherwise usher us through the dying process and into the transformation that death offers; we reject that which would open the very space between stimulus and response.

It strikes me that the ultimate solution rests in our ability to loosen the grip of the ego-based dread of death and allow the energies of the root and other lower chakras to flow freely. In a very real sense, our life force energy and the seed of our enlightenment, is trapped in the Domination System. It is trapped in the grips of immature ego and in the mind poison of the victim mentality (the induced powerlessness of the Domination System).

So, this chaos we have been working overtime to control is actually the way through. It is the wrench that will unhook the sinister connective cables of the Domination System. We are, therefore, tasked with embracing the inner and outer chaos.

Right now the world is in the grips of some of the most intense, widespread, interconnected chaos ever. Likewise, the capacity of the global Domination System to assert control in Marduk-like fashion is growing every day. In fact, the chaos, rather than being liberating, if not properly engaged, will provide the justification for full out global control by the Powers. If we attempt to opt out of chaos in favor of promised security, in a very real sense, we, like "man" in the Babylonian creation myth, could **ALL** become the servants of the existing Powers (our collective expression of the immature ego) permanently. As I said at the beginning of this book, there really is no place left on earth that remains beyond the grasp of the Powers. We are nearing the point at which the Powers will have the full capacity to monitor our every word, deed, action…

And so, we have come full circle. We are indeed facing a petty tyrant with almost unlimited prerogatives. We have come to the global crossroads. Each one of us must determine whether or not to answer the call of chaos and its mistress, the Dark Goddess. Will we choose the painful, messy descent that has the potential to liberate our passion, our desire, our power to affect the world, and our soft fleshy hearts. Or will we be content with the heart of stone?

Will we remain trapped in the entrenched patterns of self-importance and ego ascendency? Or will we embrace basic goodness and the lessons of chaos that will allow us to finally know it's truth?

These questions can be distilled to their essence as follows:

Are we willing to eat what the Baba Yaga is serving and hence cast off the illusions of the Domination System so that we might emerge as Passionate Warriors: : alive with life force energy, powerfully creative, disciplined by inner wisdom, and dynamically active in service of purpose and of the new mythology of intrinsic worth and human potential?

If so, then we are faced with the task of finally growing up. Growing up entails liberating the ego from its fearful spasm and bringing it into alignment with the wisdom we gain in the grips of the Baba Yaga. Marion Woodman has described what it means to grow up very aptly as follows:

> *Growing up is accepting the darkness within us, as it is in everyone. Until we can accept the responsibility, we will go on blaming the other sex, our parents, other countries, other religions, the environment, the dog.*
>
> *In our story [The Maiden King]…the Baba Yaga threatens [Ivan] in his head, heart, body. At this threshold in life, people trained in patriarchy who idealize intellectual order, controlled passion, physical hygiene are thrown into terrifying chaos. People like Ivan, women and men who idealize the perfection of feminine are faced with its opposite. The archetype has two sides, and if we blind ourselves to the side we*

> *do not wish to see, it paradoxically appears before us in compensating horror and beauty.* [62]

As I said earlier in the book, the evil of the Domination System is both the poison and its antidote. We are healed and released when we finally choose to look at it and to deal with it. Is the Dark Goddess evil? No. Evil is born when we refuse to accept her lessons, when we refuse to heed the call of ritual death. Evil is the horror born of and multiplied by our refusal to look, and by our refusal to eat what the Baba Yaga is serving.

I don't know the outcome for the world. But I do know what the call of the Divine is. We are being called to maturity. The time to answer is NOW! I scarcely think we can afford another escalation!

If you are ready to accept the call of maturity, go to <u>www.rebeckaeggers.com</u> *to find out how you can get connected to Rebecka and The Passion Path. The Passion Path is the path of the Passionate Warrior and of wholehearted, purposeful, and skillful living.*

---

[62] Bly, Robert and Marion Woodman. The Maiden King: The Reunion of Masculine and Feminine. Henry Holt Company. New York. 1998. Print. Page 191.

Part 2
∞
The Birth of the Passionate Warrior

Laughter is the Only Thing Left

Take a moment to enter the secret places,
Where you have stored,
And almost forgotten,
The dreams
You once knew so intimately,
Like the beat of your own heart.

Take a moment to listen,
For the sound of your rhythm,
The one that inspired you
To dance,
Naked,
Sun beams streaming,

In the hours before the cold light of reason
Pierced everything you own.

Now dance
Until you know
What is asking to be born,
What
Is crying out
To pass through,

YOU.

©Rebecka Eggers, 2011

The Birth of the Passionate Warrior ∞ Empowering Beauty

Life is a mirror and will reflect back to the thinker what he thinks into it. ∞ *Ernest Holmes*

Beauty is eternity gazing at itself in a mirror. ∞ *Khalil Gibran*

I sat down to write this book, in part, because there is an enormous personal growth industry in the developed world that seems to me to be largely divorced from the global circumstances we face. I wondered what value there is in personal fulfillment in and of itself when we are faced with terrifying global circumstances such as climate change, pending resource shortages, the possible build up to war in the Middle East, government treachery and surveillance, grinding poverty, severe infant mortality, starvation, oppression of women etc. I wondered if there can truly be such a thing as meaningful individual happiness in this context.

Put another way, our interdependence is so blatantly obvious these days, that I wondered if there is any meaning in individual happiness that has no awareness of, or concern for, the cost of that happiness in real human terms. If you look around the world, it is obvious that certain populations thrive at the expense of others. For instance, U.S. retailers routinely purchase very cheap garments from Bangladesh. But recently, when a factory there collapsed killing thousands of people, those same retailers refused to sign off on mandatory safety improvements citing pricing pressures. One consumer interviewed said she would still shop at, H&M, one of the retailers, because, even though they needed to make improvements, "It is so cheap." This woman's cheap readymade garments were another person's death, literally![63]

With all of this in mind, I journeyed to Isla Mujeres on the Atlantic coast of Mexico. I arrived there with the intention of completing the second part of the book, *The Birth of the Passionate Warrior*. Isla Mujeres seemed an appropriate location to invoke a new vision that is oriented to the rising

---

[63] Greenhouse, Steven and Stephanie Clifford. "U.S. Retailers Offer Plan for Safety at Factories." New York Times. July 10, 2013
    http://www.nytimes.com/2013/07/11/business/global/us-retailers-offer-safety-plan-for-bangladeshi-factories.html?ref=business&_r=0
    Khazan, Olga. "Better Safety in Bangladesh Could Raise Clothing Prices by About 25 Cents." The Atlantic. May 10, 2013.
    http://www.theatlantic.com/international/archive/2013/05/better-safety-in-bangladesh-could-raise-clothing-prices-by-about-25-cents/275765/

sun and all it stands for. There is a Mayan Temple on the island. The temple sits on the easternmost point in all of Mexico. Just below the temple is the Cliff of the Dawn. It bears this name because the sun rises at the temple ruins before it touches land anywhere else in Mexico.

Just as I began working on the transition, I went in for a little pampering at my friend's spa. As I sat receiving a luscious foot rub, I put down the book I was reading and began gazing out at the ocean. Suddenly I realized that, given the global circumstances in which we live, I have not felt entitled to my own happiness, joy, and passion for years.

I have wanted to create something larger than my own well-being for a long time now. I have not wanted to contribute to factory collapses in places like Bangladesh so that I can have the "joy" of cheap clothing. I have not wanted children to be raped in the Congo over minerals needed to make the phone that allows me to be constantly available. I can see through the ordinary objects of my life to the consequences for real people who live a world away from me, or maybe in a hovel a few blocks from my own home.

This is all part of why I have chosen to live in Chiapas, Mexico among the poverty and the constant reminders of the Domination System and its consequences. I have never wanted to allow myself to forget, not even for a little while. I have been in search of happiness amidst the misery that walks beside me on every street in town.

So many times, my willingness to have a meal in a sidewalk café while starving children peddled their little animals and begged for money in the street beside me has struck me as the height of garishness and gall. I have not actually enjoyed one of these meals in a long time. By the same token, I have learned a great deal about the system that puts these children on the street in a kind of indentured servitude. I no longer find joy in sharing my food with them either. It feels like a perpetuation of a system that is truly broken. There is a safe house in town that provides food and educational opportunities to the street children. I think the best thing I could do is actually support the safe house in its mission. If you would like to donate, the information is set forth in this footnote.[64]

On the flip side, many a night, I have just wanted to eat in peace and silence without the guilt and the constant interruption. I have grown to despise the kind of entitlement (passed down from generation to generation) that causes someone to walk up to me and demand (without even so much as a hello), that I buy something, give the person money, or hand over the food from my plate. My generosity has been buried beneath my sense that there are no human beings in this kind of exchange. None of the people I pass on the street remember me from day to day. The same ones approach me in a kind of daze and repeat the same process over and over again.

---

[64] If you would like to donate, here is the information: http://www.casaflores.org/donate.html

No attempt on my part to connect, to move beyond pre-constructed roles, to humanize myself in their eyes or to humanize the exchange, makes any difference at all. I am just a wallet walking. As long as money or resources are going from my hand to theirs, nothing changes.

If this perspective sounds harsh, you are mistaken. I sometimes buy food for a little 8 year old girl. I realized one day that she was only nice when I had money to spend. It broke my heart because I could see the next logical step in her life might entail. She may already have learned to trade affection for the things she wants. Sometimes help isn't help at all.

By the same token, I have known Mexicans and Americans alike who have tried to help the street children. Some have taken in a street child only to wake up the next morning to find all their valuables missing. Others have taken a child home for a meal only to have the child's "parent" demand a cash payment for alleged molestation. Sometimes "helping" is a dangerous game.

What does seem to at least break the momentum is humor. I have seen people turn the tables and ask for something from the beggars or pretend to steal a wooden animal from a child. It diffuses the situation. It is a clever step outside the normal exchange that allows both people to recall their humanity and the absurdity of the situation. It is effective because nothing but human interaction passes between the two people. Equality is restored in that moment.

The daze is lifted temporarily. This is the clever sidestep out of the polarization that I described earlier in the book. It does nothing to assuage the hunger, of course. But it does seem to lift the spirits!

In any case, what I am trying to say is that I am not grappling with the Domination System as a matter of theory. I am grappling with it as a matter of intense personal sorrow. In the midst of it all, I am trying to recall how to be joyful. I am trying to understand the meaning of joy in this context. It reflects our global circumstance: wealth in the midst of poverty. To the starving children, someone enjoying a chai latte at a well appointed café must seem like a queen in her castle! This is an ugly and perplexing reality. It is hard to look at. It is harder still to ignore.

At the end of the last chapter, I quoted Marion Woodman. The last sentence of the quote said this: "The archetype [of the feminine] has two sides, and if we blind ourselves to the side we do not wish to see, it paradoxically appears before us in compensating horror and beauty."

I have spent years now making myself willing to see the horror. I have made myself live in the midst of it. Until now, I can't say I fully understood it as something operating separate and apart from individual actors, in other words, as a system that has taken on a life of its own. I read Walter Wink's book years ago. I could not fully absorb its meaning.

Truthfully, I have been tempted by the false dichotomy between victim-heroes and villains. It has been my endeavor to identify with the noble side of the conflict. As a result, I have been unconsciously trapped in the victim identity that allows me to feel as though I have chosen the right side. Paradoxically, this has meant that, on a very personal level, it has not been okay for me to thrive even if my thriving does not happen at the expense of anyone and/or if I minimize the impact of my choices on places like Bangladesh and the Congo. This would be the case even if I use my choices to force change, for instance, by supporting initiatives that would require cell phone manufacturers to buy "safe" minerals from the Congo, or put pressure on retailers to enter into real safety accords with the garment industries in third world nations. Something deeper is going on.

As I concluded the last chapter, I noticed that there is a second word in the Woodman quote: "beauty." There is a side of the feminine archetype that is not about chaos or destruction. There is a Dark Goddess, but there is also a Light Goddess. It is this side of the divine feminine that I believe we are, in many ways, most afraid to look at. But if Marion Woodman is right, it must be appearing before us in equal proportions to the horror. In fact, the world thrives on horror now. The horror often lacks real context, and so, serves only to deepen the false dichotomies of the Domination System. Nonetheless, we are at least willing to gaze upon it. I would even say we are addicted to it.

Beauty on the other hand is in short supply in our worldview. When it does show up, it too is lacking in the kind of context that would give it real meaning. Regardless, I imagine that if we went looking for it, we would see that the beauty far exceeds the horrors of the world. I imagine it has been growing exponentially while our gaze was fixed elsewhere.

For example, in San Cristóbal, there is certainly tragedy amongst the high dollar tourist hotels and fancy restaurants of the tourist strip. But there is more than tragedy. There is love thriving in places you could never imagine. Many nights as I make my way home, I come across a mother and her children. It rains a lot in Chiapas in the summertime. It is cold. As I pass her by, I notice her little wooden box full of candy and cigarettes for sale. I also notice her children sleeping on the hard rocky sidewalk, tucked beneath blankets and plastic drapes to keep out the rain. She is often nursing her baby as she dozes against the side of the building. This scene is extraordinary in its contrast to the stark environment all around her and the upscale tourist restaurants that populate the street. It is exceptional only in the sense that I am given a nightly glimpse into the quiet family life of this woman who has found the courage to nurture her barefoot babies in the wet, cold, dirty streets of the rainy summer.

The truth is that this scene is multiplied by millions night after night in city after city from the south pole to the north. The world is full of nursing mothers nurturing young life in the midst of lavish apartments on 5th Avenue in Manhattan U.S.A. and in welfare projects in Chicago, and in average, every day homes in Europe, and in the midst of the war torn Congo. The question is, will we turn our eyes from the manufactured beauty of Madison Avenue and from the manufactured horror of the 24 hour news services. Will we turn instead to the truth of what ails us and then to the truth of what lies beyond it: our capacity to nourish life and to live together with joy and passion? Will we choose to develop our power and our resolve as the gateways to a new way of being together?

We can continue our steady diet of horror and never integrate or act on its message. By the same token, we can refuse to turn our attention to real beauty. We can choose not to empower it or to integrate it. We can choose to remain lost in Baba Yaga's crucible of destruction and chaos until it becomes nothing more than a cruel bastardization of the descent. Should we choose it, we can die with the Baba Yaga by failing to grasp the purpose of our time with Her.

I have felt the truth of this over the last few months as I have worked so hard to describe the Domination System and to articulate the means by which we can become conscious and choose a different option. It was the pressure of this choice that caused me to feel so close to death. I wasn't sure I could turn my eyes from the horror. I was not sure I had a right to do it. But beyond that, to claim my own power and thriving felt like a betrayal of someone or something I could not quite specify.

As an aside, this is, I am sure, what happens to activists who have never stopped to imagine that a global activism that does not claim the power of the individual activist's own happiness is as meaningless as so-called personal growth that has no broader context. What I have described is the fate of activists that must idealize and side with the world's victims. Despite their desire to make the world a better place, it becomes very hard for them to give themselves or anyone else full permission to thrive. Thriving is mistakenly identified with egocentricity and corrupt power.

What I have actually discovered is that beauty is the purpose of the descent. There is no sense in coming to terms with the darkness and the chaos if we cannot bring beauty to life in the swirling eddies of its potential. All will have been for naught if we cannot bring that beauty into our own lives and allow it to nourish us. Further, we cannot actually make real, sustained contact with the beauty until we have done our time with Baba Yaga. Otherwise, the beauty will remain idealized somehow like so many fashion commercials or the endless depictions of the so-called goddess that do little more than slap a label on the same old images of idealized female sexuality.

We take the underworld journey so that we can return with the boon of wisdom and so that we can use that wisdom to create real joy in ourselves and the world around us. The journey into darkness is what wipes away our illusion so that we make sustained contact with our basic goodness and with our power. Yet, it is also our first glimpse of what Chogyam Trungpa called "basic goodness" that allows us to face the illusion in the first place. Beauty is just another way of talking about basic goodness. The day we can see basic goodness as the root of beauty, we will know we have finished our time with Baba Yaga. We can then turn our eyes toward the sky and await the moment or our rebirth as the Passionate Warriors we are destined to become if only we will choose it.

The darkness is real. It is black like the night. But there is a sun that rises each day in the east. It beckons us to rise with it and to choose its vision of life blossoming and of lives truly celebrated. In fact, the darkness is not the antithesis of our thriving, it is its genesis. The things we have hidden in the darkness, once consciously owned and cultivated, are the very things we most need in order to claim a new experience.

And so, let us all wipe away the last, and perhaps the greatest illusions of the Domination System and then let us choose to rise.

If you are ready to empower beauty in your own life, go to www.rebeckaeggers.com to find out how you can get connected to Rebecka and The Passion Path. The Passion Path is the path of the Passionate Warrior and of wholehearted, purposeful, and skillful living.

The Birth of the Passionate Warrior ∞ Present Awakening

Reality is merely an illusion albeit a very persistent one. ∞ Albert Einstein

One of the greatest illusions of the Domination System is the notion that it is the only game in town. One of the ways it proliferates is to maintain our focus on it. Our lives are a constant barrage of negative messages designed to keep us in fear of one another and of the Powers. In this way, we maintain our sense of dependence on the Domination System. We expend all of our energy fighting to protect ourselves from the perceived threats, real and imagined rather than investing our energy in actively creating what we desire.

The reality is that the Domination System wasn't even the only game in town in Babylon. Ishtar stood in stark contrast to the myth of redemptive violence. She integrated love and war. If you put these two things together, you get something very different from the myth of redemptive violence. You get compassionate, disciplined, skillful, passionate action. Further, the Babylonian fertility rights that revolved around Ishtar were creative in nature. They represented the joining of masculine and feminine in service of life.

Jesus is another example. To this day, the actual teachings of Jesus stand in stark contrast to the modern church and to its history of denigrating the feminine and spreading the "faith" by brute force.

Chogyam Trungpa has brilliantly expressed the ethos of this parallel mythology of love and war. He described the Shambala Warrior's path as one of renunciation.

> *In order to be a good warrior, one has to feel this sad and tender heart. If a person does not feel alone and sad, he cannot be a warrior at all. The warrior is sensitive to every aspect of phenomena—sight, smell, sound, feelings. He appreciates everything that goes on in this world as an artist does. His experience is full and extremely vivid…*
>
> *…What the warrior renounces is anything in his experience that is a barrier between himself and others. In other words, renunciation is making yourself more available, more gentle and open with others. Any hesitation about opening yourself to others is removed.*[65]

---

[65] Trungpa, Chogyam. *Shambhala: The Sacred Path of the Warrior.* Shambhala Publications, Inc. Boston. 1984. Location 794.

What an intense contrast! In the Domination System, we are armored against everything that we perceive as a threat. We are closed off and we are fighting. Mostly we are on guard against our own shadows and against the loss of our victim-hero status. It is our job to ward off evil and we must, therefore, locate evil outside of ourselves.

As long as we are in the Domination System and held hostage to the myth of redemptive violence, we feel the need to maintain a traditional warrior's stance. We feel as though we must remain forever on guard, prepared to exert our will through physical power and the domination of our "enemies." Our sword's must remain forever at the ready.

In Chogyam Trungpa's Great Eastern Sun world, we are focused on blossoming. Everyone is given the chance to grow and to prosper. We are open. We are able to experience everything as it is, including the Domination System and its effects on us. There is no shame. We clean up what needs to be cleaned up while holding the truth of our basic goodness. This is not the same as a polar shift from being closed and withholding to unconsciously open. This kind of openness is rooted in our sense of intrinsic worth. We are able to open because nothing anyone does has any personal significance for us anymore. By the same token, just because we open does not mean we must become completely accessible for use and exploitation by others. It does not mean we have to accept violation as a way of life. We can be tender and open without being doormats to those who are still in the Domination System.

Therefore, the Great Eastern Sun world opens up the possibility that we can relax. Its mythology of basic goodness and its orientation towards maximizing human potential call for something new. It asks us to allow our libido, our life force energy to flow. It asks us to open to ourselves and to each other. The Great Eastern Sun vision is inviting us to live tenderly and fearlessly, right here, right now. Chogyam Trungpa captured this concept beautifully as follows:

> ***Real fearlessness is the product of tenderness. It comes from letting the world tickle your heart, your raw and beautiful heart. You are willing to open up, without resistance or shyness, and face the world. You are willing to share your heart with others.***[66]

From within the Domination System, it seems that such an opening must always wait for some more perfect day. Thus, the other grand lie of the Domination System is perfectionism. We imagine that some utopian version of the world is going to suddenly materialize in front of us. We tell ourselves that when the new world order arrives we will change ourselves to meet it. Worse yet, we tell ourselves that we are already ready and are merely waiting for the world to change too. These may be the greatest lies of all. They seal off the present forever delaying the moment of our

---

[66] Trungpa, Chogyam. Shambhala: The Sacred Path of the Warrior. Shambhala Publications, Inc. Boston. 1984. Page 541.

awakening for some more perfect day. These lies lull us into a terrible complacency that destroys our incentive to create and to change ourselves and our lives right here and now. Redemption happens in the present moment or it does not happen at all. The real secret is overcoming self-importance (pride and shame) and integrating our sense of intrinsic worth. Once we have done so, opening does not seem like such a terrifying prospect, nor does enforcing our boundaries seem like an impossibility.

The real question does not concern whether to open, but, rather, how to open while also protecting ourselves. When Trungpa talked about opening and sharing our hearts with others, to me it appears that he was talking about presence. As is reflected in the earlier quote, what we are opening to is an experience of the world in all its vivid forms. What Trungpa does not appear to be saying is that we are to open our lives and let everything, in all of its manifestations, become an intimate part of our worlds. Presence is about accepting the reality of how someone or something is expressing in actuality. We can open our hearts to a serial killer if we choose to do so. But we do not have to get in the car with him! Part of opening our hearts is discerning what is and treating it appropriately.

The truth is that we don't have control over the Domination System because it is made up of people with agency and free will just as powerful as our own. We cannot gain more control of it by trying to drag the world, kicking and screaming, into loving space. But once we have dared to identify the Domination System and name it according to what it is, it becomes possible for us to reap the benefits of what can only be described as a potent psychological breakthrough.

This breakthrough, which is rooted in basic goodness, allows us to live in the midst of the system without being in the system. It also allows us to open our hearts to others because, even if they are stuck in the Domination System, we are able to see our own humanity and basic goodness as well as theirs. Whatever happens, we know the truth of who and what we all are and we see the truth of how we are presently expressing. Further, our sense of basic goodness allows us to open without taking on the role of the victim because, though we offer an alternative to domination based relating, we do not attempt to impose it on others or to control their realizations. We do not tell ourselves lies about what other people's intentions are. Once we are oriented towards our basic goodness, we know how to open and to be spontaneous while also caring for ourselves. In fact, part of spontaneity is allowing ourselves to respond to the world around us in an authentic manner. If and when we sense we are in danger, we heed the message contained in that feeling. We take it into the space between stimulus and response, and we find our power to choose; we find our power to move beyond our habitual responses.

Walter Wink addressed the import of this psychological breakthrough beautifully.

> *When anyone steps out of the system and tells the truth, lives the truth, that person enables everyone else to peer behind the curtain too. That person has shown everyone that it is possible to live within the truth, despite the repercussions. 'Living within the lie can constitute the system only if it is universal.' Anyone who steps out of line therefore 'denies it in principle and threatens it in its entirety...If the main pillar of the system is living a lie, then it is not surprising that the fundamental threat to it is living the truth.*[67]

Right now, this breakthrough of truth regarding the Domination System and its impact is happening in epic proportions all over the world: in the streets of Turkey and Brazil; in the groups of Indian women who have come together to refuse the unwanted advances of men; in Wendy Davis' courageous stand for women's reproductive health; in the world wide outcry in response to Monsanto's attempts to force feed us GMOs; in the willingness of American activists to stand up and shed light on the injustice of Obama's drone strikes; and in the willingness of people like Edward Snowden and Bradley Manning to expose the truth about government abuses and the national security surveillance state.

---

[67] Wink, Walter. *Engaging the Powers: Discernment and Resistance in a World of Domination.* Minneapolis. Fortress Press. 1992. Kindle. Location 1465.

You might say that the breakthrough that is happening now is the first wave breakthrough. We have come alive to what is. The impact of the first wave breakthrough will be tempered, however, if we allow the emergence of truth to draw us back into the myth of redemptive violence; if we experience a pole shift from dominated to dominator.

We can and we must have a second wave breakthrough regarding the truth of basic goodness. We must consciously choose the ethos of the Great Eastern Sun right here and right now. It is time for us to open to life and orient all of our choices around our openness. It is essential that we place our focus immediately on the blossoming of human potential and that we bypass the potential foot fault into the victim-hero stance. If you were to relate this to Buddhist notions of reincarnation, you could say, we must not allow ourselves to be pulled into another round of karmic birth, death, and rebirth whereby the rebirth places us again at the place where we started. We must finally burn up the karma (the cause and effect) of the Domination System.

Right now there is immense tension in the international collective psyche as people all over the world are coming to terms with what is happening. After the experience of writing about the Domination System, there is an intense amount of tension in my own body, and very likely in yours as a result of reading all of this. But if you put your ear to the ground, you will also hear something stirring at the core of the earth. You may even feel a quickening in your own root chakra. The life force is being stirred and awakened like never before. We are ripe for a second wave breakthrough; we are ripe for an awakening and a cosmic rebirth into a new way of being together.

This stirring is our creative potential welling up and seeking expression. Just as the body needs a certain amount of tension to generate an orgasm, the tension in the collective consciousness is a necessary build up to the expression of our full human creativity. But just as in the case of an orgasm, the full expression of that creativity will only become sustainable if we can let the tension morph into a state of profound relaxation. It will flow freely and abundantly in the moment when we are finally able to honestly embrace our tender-hearted openness and the blossoming of our full potential.

And so, in this moment, I call us to a collective time out in the space between stimulus and response. Let's relax into the tranquility and peace that comes from our willingness to release the mythology of the Domination System.

Pause for a moment. Breathe deeply and slowly. Feel the passionate energy of life stirring in your root and in the earth. Allow this life force energy to well up inside of you and to blossom in your body. Allow yourself to taste the sweetness, the nectar of life. It is here, accessible to you in this very moment. It has always been here. The difference? You have chosen to see. You have looked evil in the face, you have confronted it within yourself and within the Domination System, and now you can see that which is greater than the

Domination System: Your unlimited human potential and your love for yourself and this world. As Chogyam Trungpa said:

> *You have looked and you have seen, and you don't have to apologize for being born on this earth.*
>
> *This discovery is the first glimpse of what is called the Great Eastern Sun. When we say sun here, we mean human dignity, the sun of human dignity, the sun of human power. The Great Eastern Sun is the rising sun rather than the setting sun, so it represents the dawning, or awakening of human dignity—the rising of human warriorship.*[68]

Don't be surprised if later today or maybe tomorrow, you lose this sense of your own dignity and of the potential in the rising sun. Be comforted by the knowledge that you can always return to this place. Remember, it was there in Babylon, in Ishtar, and it has been here all along. In order to return to it, you need only make your eyes available again to see.

Honestly, losing the feeling is all part of the process. As you go through it, you will meet what Marion Woodman called the natural law of "action/reaction" in the psyche. At first you may feel the exuberance of freedom. But soon the resistance will come. Woodman describes it like this:

---

[68] Trungpa, Chogyam. *Shambhala: The Sacred Path of the Warrior.* Shambhala Publications, Inc. Boston. 1984. Location 650.

> *Think of an energy pendulum swinging back and forth. We can feel it swinging further into trust, hope, faith, but as it swings further on one side, it balances that new reach with a corresponding reach on the other side into fear and vulnerability. The psyche that has protected itself from annihilation all its life will feel totally unprotected in this new free swinging trust.*[69]

Here again, we must avoid the trap of perfectionism. Just as Woodman described, it is not likely that the Domination System is going to blow apart in one giant orgasm of cosmic bliss, well, at least not until it does. What we are looking for is a tipping point. We are looking to create such a wellspring of celebratory energy that the old system simply grows, moment by moment, more and more obsolete, first within ourselves, and then in everyone around us. The important thing is that there is movement. It is also important that we understand: the free swinging trust we are developing is for ourselves. We are learning to trust ourselves to discern and to act according to our discernments. We are placing our faith and our hope in our ability to transcend the ethos of the Domination System and to create a viable alternative.

In other words, we must participate! The joy and vitality of the rising sun world is something we must choose over and over again until the momentum of the choice takes over.

---

[69] Bly, Robert and Marion Woodman. *The Maiden King: The Reunion of Masculine and Feminine.* Henry Holt Company. New York. 1998. Print. Page 178.

We can only do this if we relinquish our judgment of the Domination System, and then continue to relate openly to what truly is within ourselves and in the world around us. The Domination System is not wrong from within the perspective that gave rise to it. It will simply cease to function once we are able to shift into a new way of being and into a new perspective.

The true antidote to the Domination System is openness, expansiveness, and presence. And so, when you feel the peace and the joy slipping away, when you are tempted to take up the sword of justification and domination, and especially, when you are feeling vulnerable, breathe, expand, open, come into the present moment, and allow your creativity to flow. It is that simple.

Does that mean we can immediately enter into a relaxed state of sharing with everyone and in all circumstances? No it does not. I hope by now I have made this clear! Regardless it bears repeating. There are people who are deeply wedded to the use of domination and power over others for the purpose of exploitation. Further, there are those who will take up the language of human dignity and love of humanity for the sake of manipulation. They will elicit a false trust for the purpose of advancing the Domination System and/or their own interests. We must be wise in our discernment of these people and we must deal with them according to how they are expressing and according to the world in which they live. Otherwise, we will suffer greatly at their hands. In point of fact, a huge part of opening to the present moment is opening to what is and dealing with it appropriately rather than constructing an illusion around what we hope will be. What I am saying is that you cannot create something that is outside the Domination System with a person who is wedded to the ethics of that system. Be present to what is and look for people who want the alternative.

If you are ready to choose presence and the celebration of life, go to www.rebeckaeggers.com to find out how you can get connected to Rebecka and The Passion Path. The Passion Path is the path of the Passionate Warrior and of whole-hearted, purposeful, and skillful living.

The Birth of the Passionate Warrior ∞ Liberating Passion

Haven't you noticed that passion is contagious? ∞ *Barbara De Angelis*

As the pendulum swings ever higher, what we are rising into is a new way of being. We are becoming Passionate Warriors. When we were in the Domination System we were clenched tight, fearing life, dreading death, dreading one another, and even dreading the truth about ourselves. Now we have faced our dread. We have faced death and seen it for what it is – a doorway into transformation. Now we are free of our dread.

The Passionate Warrior, by contrast, lives with life force flowing, embracing life, cultivating joy and human potential, safe guarding his/her life and desires with wisdom and skillful action. The Passionate Warrior is literally alive and overflowing with passion and desire. Where the Domination System had us deny the potential for the fulfillment of our natural desires, the Passionate Warrior is in touch with Spirit-generated desires and knows that these desires are naturally fulfilled whenever we commit to the path dictated by wisdom.

The Passionate Warrior is committed to a warrior's way of life. But it is not the way followed by the "warriors" of the Domination System who deployed at the behest of the system in order to enforce its hierarchy and externally generated social mores. These old so-called, warriors are really just soldiers and they are charged with subjugating anything that threatens the system. Their discipline comes from the sheer force of will and the threat of annihilation by the Powers.

This Passionate Warrior is a sacred warrior. Her/His discipline is founded in inner wisdom. Whenever and wherever possible, the Passionate Warrior aids the Domination System along its way to self destruction. But this is not the Passionate Warrior's focus.

The Passionate Warrior's focus is on developing human potential in himself/herself and others. The Passionate Warrior stands outside the Domination System. S/He lives the truth of basic goodness so completely that his/her very existence begins to unravel the old Domination System. The Passionate Warrior is the one who denies the system in principle, and thereby, threatens it in its entirety simply by standing in stark contrast to it. S/He does not stand in opposition to the Domination System. The Passionate Warrior stands free of it. The Passionate Warrior is the seer who has heard his/her own voice shouting the slogans of the Powers, recognized them as false, and expelled them.

But there is more to the Passionate Warrior than even this. There is a reason I have not simply used the term "warrior." Alone, this word is not sufficient to indicate the fullness of our rebirth. I have deliberately chosen the term "Passionate Warrior" so that it stands in stark contrast to the Powers and their mercenary soldiers, and so that it stands apart from our own, now discredited, egoic warriors.

The word "Passionate" is essential to describing our new way of being. In the Domination System, the ego has a death grip on the energy of life. Literally, it is passion that is trapped in the system, unable to flow freely. The following quote from Walter Wink's book bears repeating:

> *Domination is always more than a powerful relation, notes Joel Kovel. It is a **spiritual state of being**. The dominator exerts power by extracting being from the dominated…This domination always entails more than injustice. It wounds—and it intends to wound—the very soul itself…So, besides an unmasking of the oppressors, there must be a **healing of the servile will in their victims**.*[70]

The extraction of being referred to in this quote is really the extraction of passion. Passion is life force energy.

---

[70] Wink, Walter. *Engaging the Powers: Discernment and Resistance in a World of Domination*. Minneapolis. Fortress Press. 1992. Kindle. Location 1530.

According to author Barbara De Angelis, "When we encounter a person who is passionate about the part they play in the world, we are witnessing the life force as it expresses itself fully through this individual."[71]

When we choose the ritual death of the ego, we are not really killing off part of ourselves. We are liberating ourselves from the death grip of the undeveloped ego and its self-importance. We are freeing the life force energy from the control of the Domination System.

Recall the cable analogy I used earlier. The energetic cables of the Domination System connect in through the immature ego and syphon off the energy of life. Creativity and life force energy are taken over by the Domination System and applied according to its ethos. The healing of the servile will is really the liberation of passion. The development of the sacred warrior is about carrying out the dictates of this liberated passion. This passion is radically different from the seeming passion of the Domination System which is intense, but is not alive. The imitation passion of the Domination System is not life affirming. By contrast, the passion we are liberating has its foundations in inner wisdom. It is rooted in the joy of living.

This passion I am talking about is the red hot passion of life. It brings to mind the color of blood. It speaks to me of the life force coursing through our veins. It reminds me of the

---

[71] De Angelis, Barbara. *Passion*. Dell Publishing. New York. 1999. Kindle. Location 136. Page 11.

richness and sweetness of strawberries. This passion is soul desire made manifest in our actions and the way we choose to live our lives.

Barbara De Angelis, in her book, Passion, articulated this process of allowing our passion beautifully:

> *...because passion is what happens when you let go of control.*
>
> *Control is really the antithesis of passion. Control approaches situations with rigidity; it likes to confine things to boundaries; it seeks certainty, lack of movement; it resists change.*
>
> *Passion, on the other hand, overflows the boundaries and seeks no limit, no end. It thrives on the unknown; it feeds off movement and transformation; it adores the uninhibited.*
>
> *Passion is not necessarily logical, or appropriate—words which are favorites of those who love control. It manifests simply because it wants to. It expresses itself for its own sake. **Its purpose is none other than the celebration of life, of love, of God's creation.***[72]

If this sounds familiar, that is because it is. This is similar to how Chogyam Trungpa described the Great Eastern Sun vision, though, admittedly, it has more heat. Trungpa said

---

[72] De Angelis, Barbara. *Passion*. Dell Publishing. New York. 1999. Kindle. Location 237. Page 124.

that the Great Eastern Sun vision is about "celebrating life" rather than warding off death. He explained that in the Great Eastern Sun vision, all are given a chance to blossom. The warrior, in the Great Eastern Sun vision uses discipline to cultivate tenderness, joy, and blossoming.

Walter Wink put forth something very similar from the Christian perspective. He called it God's "domination-free order" which he described as follows:

> *[the domination-free order] is characterized by partnership, interdependence, equality of opportunity and mutual respect between men and women that cuts across all distinctions between people. This egalitarian realm repudiates violence, domination, hierarchies, patriarchy, racism, and authoritarianism: a total system detrimental to human life...*[73]

In other words, God's domination-free order eschews everything that is not supportive of human life and embraces everything that is supportive of our blossoming.

Walter Wink has correctly noted that in order to arrive at this point, the sacrifice of the ego must be given as though the ego will truly be destroyed. But in the end, the ego is not really killed so much as it is brought into right relationship with something deeper: our sense of our own intrinsic worth

---

[73] Wink, Walter. *Engaging the Powers: Discernment and Resistance in a World of Domination.* Minneapolis. Fortress Press. 1992. Kindle. Location 1563.

and the dictates of our own inner wisdom (reflected in our connection to our joy and fulfillment on the one hand and our willingness to be present to our fear and anger on the other).

Ultimately, our feelings begin to foster curiosity and curiosity furthers our connection to wisdom. When we are curious, we do not know. We do not need to follow our first instinct into action. We can allow the world to communicate with us and we can allow our feelings to alert us, to awaken our curiosity. Chogyam Trungpa spoke to this phenomenon as follows:

> *You want to look at every situation and examine it, so that you are not fooling yourself by relying on belief alone. Instead, you want to make a personal discovery of reality, through your own intelligence and ability...If you take steps to accomplish something, that action will have a result—either failure or success. When you shoot your arrow, either it will hit the target or it will miss. Trust is knowing that there will be a message.*[74]

In other words, the ego or personality begins to express according to the dictates of higher self rather than through the automatic, survival-based reactions associated with the myth of redemptive violence. We become curious instead of reactive, wise instead of purely instinctual.

---

[74] Trungpa, Chogyam. *Shambhala: The Sacred Path of the Warrior.* Shambhala Publications, Inc. Boston. 1984. Location 907.

As self-importance fades, so does our need to feel offended and to react. We can receive what comes as a message. In this way, our instincts, like fear and anger, which give rise to the fight, flight, or freeze reactions, are refined such that they cease to be mandates. They become indicators of things that need our attention and communicators of wisdom. Our instincts alert us to the need to open to what truly is so that we can unleash our creativity in the service of a joyful, fulfilling life. Finally, freed from its own dread of life and staunch need to control, the ego, now transformed, becomes the vehicle for expressing our passionate life force energy.

For the Passionate Warrior, everything gets reconfigured in service of passionate expression. Rather than acting to block the ego, the Passionate Warrior is the champion of passion.

What we are rising into then, isn't somewhere in the sky in some far off place called heaven. We are rising into a passionate way of being that celebrates life and supports the unfolding of its potential and its passion through wisdom, discipline, and authentic freedom right here and right now.

This new, passionate way of being includes all the elements and ethics of Chogyam Trungpa's Great Eastern Sun vision that I have already articulated: blossoming potential, tenderness, basic goodness, human dignity, and the warrior's discipline that is rooted in wisdom. It incorporates what Walter Wink described as God's domination free order, which is supportive of life and partnership. But it also expressly incorporates the red hot element of passion and the deep rouge color of blood pumping through our hearts. This passion bespeaks the satisfaction of juicy ripe fruit. It delights the palate.

This new way of being is the power of Spirit embodied and expressed in a life lived passionately and purposefully right here on earth. We are not just talking here about the golden orb of the morning peeking over the horizon. What we are experiencing is the red hot lava from the hot, dark core bursting forth to meet the intense light of the dawn.

For those who choose to come this way, what we are rising into is The World of the Red Sun Morning. In the words of the Gnostic Mass:

> *And our Lady Sophia answers: Ye shall dance, sing, feast, make music and love, all in my praise. For mine is the ecstasy of the spirit, and mine also joy on earth. Let my worship be in the heart that rejoiceth. Wherefore let there be beauty and strength, power and compassion, honor and humility, mirth and reverence within you, now and evermore. Amen.*[75]

---

[75] Quoted in: Beak, Sera. *Red Hot & Holy*. Sounds True. Boulder. 2013. Kindle. Page 155. Location 5352.

If you are ready to rise into The World of the Red Sun Morning, go to www.rebeckaeggers.com to find out how you can get connected to Rebecka and The Passion Path. The Passion Path is the path of the Passionate Warrior and of whole-hearted, purposeful, and skillful living.

The Birth of the Passionate Warrior ∞ Encountering The Passion Path

> *Revolution doesn't have to do with smashing something; it has to do with bringing something forth.* ∞ *Joseph Campbell*

Recall that early on in this book, I said I was inviting you to find the place between stimulus and response and to live there. When I wrote that, I didn't fully understand all that it symbolized. But just as I concluded the last chapter, I very clearly saw this space not so much as the bridge or place to pause between what happens and how we respond, but as a path that opens up in the in-between space. It isn't so much about responding differently to the things of the Domination System, although that will surely happen. This space is a gateway into, what Walter Wink described as God's domination-free order and what Chogyam Trungpa has called the vision of the Great Eastern Sun. Carlos Castaneda described this path as choosing "total consciousness, total freedom."

At the beginning of this book, I said that when no readily apparent option presents itself, we are in the realm or magic. And so we are. When we pause in the space between stimulus and response, if we are paying attention, a new path unfolds. This new path appears like magic in the gap. It offers itself up as the way out of the dilemma presented by the Domination System and as the path into a whole new kind of living. This new path that opens up in the space between stimulus and response is The Passion Path. Like an emissary, it extends itself to us from within The World of the Red Sun Morning. It beckons us to accept its brilliant, red, sparkling invitation to a rich and powerful life.

The Domination System runs lengthwise between stimulus and unconscious response. It constantly beckons us to repeat the same old outcomes over and over again. It is the path of struggle where, as Carlos Castaneda said, everything that happens is either a blessing or a curse. The Domination System is the path of suffering and of resistance.

The Passion Path, by contrast, does not run along any ordinary, earthly trajectory. The moment you step onto it, The Passion Path takes a very sudden downward turn, not south, but down into the darkness and the chaos and the fiery core of the earth where we encounter the Baba Yaga and the lessons of death. And then, just as suddenly as it went down, the path rises again. When we emerge from the darkness, we find we are in the east. It is morning. We have risen with the sun. Far from fearing the moment when the sun will set, we welcome it with all of its own color and its bright red brilliance. We also welcome the darkness that reveals itself as the light slowly withdraws and we hold the promise of the light that will again pierce the darkness when morning arrives. By now, we have learned to accept and to engage the cycles of darkness and light and of life and death.

There are no blessings or curses on the Passion Path, only messages that offer feedback and obstacles that present themselves as challenges. Challenges help us progress along the path. They are teachers who bring us new skills.

On the Passion Path, we are blazing a trail in The World of the Red Sun Morning. We are blazing a trail towards intrinsic joy and authentic happiness. We are, in the words of Castaneda, choosing total consciousness and total freedom.

The simple act of rising into The World of the Red Sun Morning is a radical act. Like Walter Wink said, "Anyone who steps out of line therefore *'denies [the system] in principle and threatens it in its entirety.'* "

Similarly, in the words of Subcomandante Insurgente Marcos, "To the west, the sun is like a rock, shattering the pane of the morning…" When I first read those words years ago, they meant nothing to me. They seemed nonsensical. But upon further reflection and with the passage of time, I realized, you could say it like this: For the Domination System, for the setting-sun world, the red sun rising is like a rock shattering the pane of the morning.

We have found our glass to break. When we rise, the mirror ceases to be a mirror and becomes a looking glass. We are poised to cross to the other side.

Recall this quote from the Prologue, from Marcos' story *The Glass to See to the Other Side:*

> *Cut from the inverse side, a mirror ceases to be a mirror and becomes a glass. Mirrors are for looking on this side, a glass is made to look to the other side. Mirrors are made to be etched. A glass is made to be broken…to cross to the other side…The image of the real or the unreal, which searches among so many mirrors, for a glass to break.*[76]

The Passion Path is the way of the Passionate Warrior. It is not the path of resistance for its own sake, but the path of a new kind of passionate revolution. This revolution is not about what we are against, but rather, it is about what we are for. In the words of Joseph Campbell, "Revolution doesn't have to do with smashing something; it has to do with bringing something forth."

What we are bringing forth is ourselves, our human potential, and the divine gifts that will allow us to make our contribution to The World of the Red Sun Morning. The moment we rise into The World of the Red Sun Morning, we

---

[76] Ponce De Leon, Juana and Subcomandante Insurgente Marcos. "The Glass to See to the Other Side." *Our Word is Our Weapon, Selected Writings.* New York. Seven Stories Press. 2002. Print. Pages 294-296.

break the glass. We shatter the pane of the morning, and with it, the Domination System.

Another way of saying this, is that from the intrinsic knowledge of our own basic goodness extends our ability to pull back all of our projections and to finally leave behind the mirror in favor of the looking glass; in favor of the transparency that allows us to see one another as we are with full awareness of both our potential and the current manner in which we are able to express. We can only ever hope to come together in a new space for the purpose of creating something new once we have seen and accepted both (i) the potential that has not yet come to fruition, and (ii) the sometimes, mangled, distorted way of being we have taken on in order to survive. Once we are able to find the glass to break it becomes possible to separate from the energy of the Domination System with all of its fear mongering and hate and to truly choose to bring our potential to full fruition together.

This is the purpose of choosing The Passion Path. When you get on The Passion Path, you are choosing to finally move beyond the fun house mirrors and into real, intimate relating with yourself and the world around you. This is a huge part of what it means to be a Passionate Warrior. You are willing and able to see yourself and others clearly. You can be present to what is and what is possible. But there is more. You also learn to refuse other people's projections. You know who you are and what you are about.

As a result of facing him/herself and the world, the Passionate Warrior begins to live like the Rebel described in the *Osho Zen Tarot*:

> *Whether he is wealthy or poor, the Rebel is really an emperor because he has broken the chains of society's repressive conditioning and opinions. He has formed himself by embracing all the colors of the rainbow, emerging from the dark and formless roots of his unconscious past and growing wings to fly into the sky. His very way of being is rebellious – not because he is fighting against anybody or anything, but because he has discovered his own true nature and is determined to live in accordance with it.*

The Passion Path is, in the first instance, about having the courage to face ourselves so that we can finally grow up. It is the place where we learn to accept what the Baba Yaga is serving.

The second part of The Passion Path consists of bringing forth new life. It is a rebirth and the adoption of a new mythology. Part 2 of the Passion Path is shattering the pane of the morning.

The third part of The Passion Path is skillful living. This is where we actually begin living into our maturity and fulfilling our Spirit given purpose by living according to the ethics of our new mythology. Part 3 of The Passion Path is about cultivating joy and fulfillment. In Part 3, we begin *Trailblazing*

The Passion Path in earnest. We have faced ourselves, given voice to our sorrow, grown up into The World of the Red Sun Morning, and now we are opening up a new path; we are inspiring others to do the same. From here we will walk The Passion Path together. In the light of The Red Sun Morning, the old isolation and fear of the Domination System begins to feel like nothing more than a bad dream.

Growing up begins the moment we choose to descend and to submit to the lessons of the Baba Yaga. The process will ultimately take us from victim to Passionate Warrior, from being trapped in our habitual patterns and subject to the imperatives of the Domination System to free people who are capable of actively creating our lives no matter the circumstance.

The transformative descent into Baba Yaga's world is a feminine process. When we descend, we meet the many fragmented parts of ourselves, we heal them, and we draw them together. I am not talking about a **female** process or a womanly process. I am talking about the **feminine** process that heals our neurotic egoic duality and ultimately allows duality to serve its purpose. Recall that duality is meant to aid the process of enlightenment.

Once we get to the surface, we move into the masculine process of learning skillful action. Skillful action brings the wisdom from the deep into the world.

Ultimately, what we are doing is healing the rift between the masculine and feminine as expressed in the violent death of Tiamat, reunifying the fractured feminine represented by Tiamat's body, and then restoring the ordering and protective functions we lost with the death of Apsu. If this were a linear function, you could say we are going back in time in order to go forward again. We will ultimately arrive at the original unity of masculine and feminine otherwise known as androgynous totality. But keep in mind, nothing magical and/or feminine is actually linear. This is an iterative process.

If we look again at the Babylonian myth, we will find support for what I have said. Marduk's world was created out of feminine duality. Here is an excerpt of The Babylonian Creation Story (*Enuma elish*):

> *Marduk encircles Tiamat with his net, blows her up with his winds, and shoots "an arrow which pierced her belly, / Split her down the middle and slit her heart" (Dalley 253). After standing on Tiamat's corpse, he easily defeats the rebel gods, capturing most of them and smashing their weapons. He ties the arms of the monsters and leads them away with nose-ropes. He grabs the Tablet of Destiny away from Kingu and fastens it to his own breast. Marduk then proceeds to create the universe from Tiamat's body:*
>
> > *He sliced her in half like a fish for drying:*
> > *Half of her he put up to roof the sky,*

> Drew a bolt across and made a guard to hold it.
> Her waters he arranged so they could not escape. (Dalley 255)

> ...From two ribs of Tiamat, Marduk creates east and west, and with her liver, he creates the pole star. He also creates the sun and moon and organizes their daily and monthly cycles. From Tiamat's spittle, he forms clouds, rain, and fog. Heaping a mountain over Tiamat's head, he pierces her eyes, from which spring the sources for the Tigris and Euphrates rivers. (In Akkadian, inu means both "eyes" and "springs.") In a similar way, he heaps mountains over her udder, piercing it "to make the rivers from the eastern mountains which flow into the Tigris. Her tail he bent up to the sky to make the Milky Way, and her crotch he used to support the sky" (Jacobsen 179).[77]

My interpretation, right or wrong, is consistent with Tibetan Buddhist practices. In her book, *Dakini's Warm Breath, The Feminist Principle in Tibetan Buddhism,* Judith Simmer-Brown explained that, in the Tibetan Tantric tradition, the Dakini (or female principle) is emptiness, potentiality, and wisdom. The masculine is skillful action.

Specifically, Simmer-Brown said, "Sacred outlook requires that both feminine and masculine be revered in ritual space.

---

[77] http://faculty.gvsu.edu/websterm/Enuma_Elish.html.

But spiritually in Vajrayana the realization of the feminine must come first; one needs wisdom in order to enact skillful means."[78] Simmer-Brown explains that ultimately this is not about men and women or male and female. "The gendered symbols associated with the Mother communicate truths that are not directly related to gender." She further explained as follows:

> *In Vajrayana the Mother is said to be powerful because of her unique abilities to express the vast, awesome, limitless (and genderless) nature of emptiness. And dakinis are the transmitters of the radical realization of emptiness in all levels of manifestation.*
>
> *This interpretation favors the feminine without denigrating the masculine, which is also important in the world of duality.*[79]

If we relate the masculine to the ego and the feminine to the higher wisdom developed in Baba Yaga's presence (or in the context of Tibetan Buddhism, the charnel grounds inhabited by the dakinis), the end result is a masculine ego, aligned with feminine wisdom. What we are aiming for is the marriage of wisdom and skillful means. Again, the symbolism used in Tibetan Buddhism is informative. According to Simmer-Brown:

---

[78] Simmer-Brown, Judith. *Dakini's Warm Breath: The Feminine Principle in Tibetan Buddhism*. Shambhala Publications. Boston & London. 2001. Print. Page 115

[79] Simmer-Brown, Judith. *Dakini's Warm Breath: The Feminine Principle in Tibetan Buddhism*. Shambhala Publications. Boston & London. 2001. Print. Page 115

> *The feminine wisdom dakini, signifying emptiness and space, cannot be fully realized unless she is joined with the masculine principle of skillful means, compassion, and great bliss. This is called the union of bliss and emptiness, and it is represented iconographically as the sexual union of male and female consorts. Together they form an inseparable pair, 'not one, not two.' They can never truly be apart, for penetrating insight and skillful means are interdependent and complete in a Vajrayana world.*[80]

From this union of wisdom and skillful means comes forth the Passionate Warrior in his/her fullest expression: alive with life force energy, powerfully creative, disciplined by inner wisdom, and dynamically active in service of purpose and of the new mythology of intrinsic worth and human potential.

What I am trying to convey, is that the split we are initially seeking to heal is in the feminine. All life springs from the feminine womb of emptiness and unbounded potential. When the feminine is non-dual, it contains the totality, the unity of all things. Marion Woodman said this very clearly and very much in alignment with the lessons of tantric Buddhism set forth above. Here is what she said:

---

[80] Simmer-Brown, Judith. *Dakini's Warm Breath: The Feminine Principle in Tibetan Buddhism*. Shambhala Publications. Boston & London. 2001. Print. Page 154.

> *Patriarchy flourished on a crippled masculinity rooted in split femininity.*[81]

This same perspective is contained within the Judeo-Christian creation myth. In that story as set forth in Genesis 3, Eve ate of the apple from the Tree of the Knowledge of Good and Evil – the tree of the knowledge of duality. But nothing actually happened in the world. It was Adam's bite that actually brought about the shift in the worldly circumstances. In the words of my very dear friends, Nathan Martin and Aline Van Meer, "the woman (feminine) ate of the fruit first, experienced a shift in her being, and Adam (masculine) followed by manifesting the earthly reality by also eating of the forbidden fruit."

In other words, when the feminine is in duality, the masculine which has as its function, doing/manifesting, will reflect that duality. The myth of redemptive violence flourished based upon a crippled version of masculinity rooted in the divided femininity of mother Tiamat, murdered, split into pieces, and used as the raw material of the universe. In the Babylonian myth, "man" was created as a savage. His home, the cosmos, is Tiamut's fractured, lifeless body.

Put another way, when duality is our way of being, our way of doing will reflect that duality. Therefore, what we are aiming to do as an initial matter, is to heal the warped duality that thinks in terms of *either/or and power over against*. In this

---

[81] Bly, Robert and Marion Woodman. *The Maiden King: The Reunion of Masculine and Feminine.* Henry Holt Company. New York. 1998. Print.

way we will allow duality to serve its intended purpose: the individuation that ultimately progresses towards conscious integration.

We are looking to replace duality consciousness with a new kind of unity consciousness that begins in the feminine; in the integration of, for instance, darkness and light; the maiden and the whore.

In unity consciousness, all opposites are integrated in a kind of harmony rather than existing in unconscious, undifferentiated unity. Undifferentiated unity might visually look like a puddle of motor oil, whereas, conscious integration might look more like a passionate tango. You can see the opposites, but they have gained the ability to come together in harmonious creativity. Duality functions within a greater unity revealed and integrated. Inner harmony fosters authentic human creative power and passionate expression as it empowers the masculine principle to bring order to the swirling pool of feminine potential. It allows masculine skillful action to bring the fruits of feminine wisdom to the world.

The story of the Maiden Tsar, the Russian folktale relayed in the book, *The Maiden King*, by Marion Woodman and Robert Bly, offers and interesting perspective on this process. The story is about the journey of Ivan, a young man, into the feminine process of the underworld and back out again. The story is interesting because Ivan starts off in a situation very similar to the one set forth in the Babylonian creation myth. He begins the story in the care of his stepmother and his tutor. The stepmother, according to Woodman represents the shadow mother and the tutor represents the shadow father.

At the beginning of the story, the tutor took Ivan fishing and during his fishing trip, Ivan encountered the Maiden Tsar. After their initial meeting, the Maiden Tsar proposed that Ivan return the next day prepared to leave with her as her husband. Ivan accepted. What a fascinating proposal!

As Robert Bly pointed out in the book, the first thing to notice is that this woman is not a Maiden Queen. She is a king in her own right. This bespeaks an awe inspiring degree of inner wholeness. When I imagine the Maiden Tsar, I do not imagine the Divine Feminine, but the androgynous Divine. Androgynous Divinity is totality. The Maiden Tsar is total.

I do not see the Maiden Tsar as separate and apart from Ivan. I believe that on that first fishing trip, Ivan glimpsed his own basic goodness, the beloved, non-dual feminine in him and the kingly man he will be at the end of his journey. Unbeknownst to Ivan, he caught a glimpse of how he will emerge at the end of the story. He will emerge as the fully integrated Divine Feminine in harmonious union with the Divine Masculine. Whether he knows it or not, at the beginning of the story, Ivan is on his way to discovering that he is the Maiden Tsar.

Of course, Ivan was enticed to take the journey by what appeared to be a idyllically beautiful young woman. Ivan became infatuated with her beauty. But we get the strong sense that something more than mere infatuation is taking place. The stepmother, who represents the fractured feminine in Ivan's consciousness, immediately began plotting against the union. The stepmother had no maternal instincts. She meant, for self interested reasons, to keep Ivan for herself. She meant nothing good for Ivan.

The stepmother instructed the tutor to place a pin in Ivan's neck when he next met the Maiden Tsar. He did, and the pin caused Ivan to fall asleep. The tutor did not possess the ordering function of a healthy, mature masculine. The stepmother's commands did not come from wisdom.

According to his orders, the tutor put Ivan to sleep just as the Maiden Tsar was approaching with her armada. This happened for several days running. Here is what transpired on the third day:

> *On the third day he again went fishing with his tutor. They came to the same old place, and beheld the ships sailing in the distance, and the tutor straightaway stuck in his pin, and Ivan fell sound asleep. The ships sailed close and dropped anchor; the Maiden Tsar sent for her betrothed to come aboard her ship. The servants tried in every possible way to rouse him, but no matter what they did, they could not waken him.*
>
> *The ships had no sooner set sail and put out to sea than the tutor pulled the pin from Ivan's garment; he*

awoke and began to bemoan his loss of the Maiden Tsar; but she was far away and could not hear him.

The Maiden Tsar learned of the stepmother's ruse and the tutor's treason, and wrote to Ivan telling him to cut off the tutor's head, and if he loved his betrothed, to come find her beyond the thrice nine lands in the thrice tenth kingdom.

Ivan read it, drew out his sharp saber, and cut off the wicked tutor's head. Then he sailed hurriedly to the shore, went home, said farewell to his father, and set out to find the thrice tenth kingdom.[82]

How radically different this is from the Babylonian creation myth. There is violence in this story. This suggests there are times when violence is needed. There is certainly a time when destruction supports creation. But the important question is not whether or not there is ever a time for violence in the new mythology, but rather, whether or not there is a difference between the two stories.

In this instance, Ivan did not murder the tutor for his own grandiose plans of self promotion. He did not offer to bring order from chaos. Rather, he brought chaos to order. He cut himself loose from that which had forced him into sleep and kept him bound to the intentions of the stepmother. Ivan also didn't murder the stepmother in order to use her body

---

[82] Quoted in: Bly, Robert and Marion Woodman. *The Maiden King: The Reunion of Masculine and Feminine*. Henry Holt Company. New York. 1998. Print.

as the raw material of creation. Ivan never even approached his stepmother. The story said he went home to tell his father goodbye. Ivan did only what was necessary and he left in search of the Maiden Tsar. He left in search of the new vision of beauty and unity promised in the moment the two were betrothed.

Upon making contact with the authentic wholeness of the Maiden Tsar, Ivan simply found his stepmother had become irrelevant. Something else was driving the process! Though Ivan still had a long road ahead of him, he had come in contact with wholeness. His stepmother lost her influence.

Here is what Robert Bly had to say on this subject:

> *The matter of cutting off the tutor's head is disturbing to some people. Isn't that violence? On the other hand, if the tutor is inside you, no one will be harmed but you. Ivan's brusque motion with the sword is a kind of healthy animal act. The animal knows how to survive; the animal in us will, when hungry in the desert, catch and eat a rabbit and it is the right thing to do. Ivan never would have been taught to cut off the tutor's head at school. It's a question of survival…*
>
> *So, if you take all events in a story literally, I suppose you would say that Ivan has become a killer. But that does not describe it quite rightly. He offered the old animal in him—secretly set in his soul through*

> *millions of years of life before this—a chance to act. The act was not sneaky but clear.*
>
> *If you prefer to imagine all the persons in the story as parts of one person, then you remember that some people achieve their proper work by cutting off the academic's head...*
>
> *The beheading has taken place now, and the tutor is out of the story; and that is good.*[83]

Without taking up the question of whether violence ever has a place in the new vision of basic goodness and blossoming of human potential, I love the distinction Bly makes: "The act was not sneaky but clear."

This is precisely what I was getting at. There is a difference here. There is nothing corrupt in what Ivan did. Though it is animalistic, it is not among the rote options served up by the Domination System. It is not a replication of that system either. This is not the **exaggerated** fight, flight, or freeze response that finds its source in trauma. This is something entirely conscious. Ivan knows what he is doing and why he is doing it and it has nothing to do with control. Ivan has something to accomplish. He has to find the Maiden Tsar in the thrice tenth kingdom.

---

[83] Bly, Robert and Marion Woodman. The Maiden King: The Reunion of Masculine and Feminine. Henry Holt Company. New York. 1998. Print. Page 33.

The tutor kept Ivan asleep, locked in convention, a prisoner to his stepmothers ill intentions. As he cut off the tutor's head, Ivan was about to begin the journey that would take him into his full maturity and integration. The tutor had to go one way or the other.

There are things in all of our lives like the tutor, things that serve to keep us caught in the slumber of depression, addiction, misery, and immaturity. These things are agents and indicators of the old Domination System. They alert us to the syphoning off of our life force energy. It's time to cut off the tutor's head! No need to be sneaky. Pick up the sword and be done with it!

Marion Woodman summarized the moment with the tutor in a very instructive way:

Ivan's masculinity springs into action to defend the new life his femininity is offering. Suddenly in touch with his own life force, he acts from his own desire. Whereas he was lost, now he is found.

If you substitute the word wisdom for femininity, you get a much clearer picture. In this scene, Ivan glimpses his own inner wisdom, his own integrated wholeness. He is listening to the dictates of his own Spirit. Ivan is now in contact with his own primal, undivided center. It is this initial contact with wildness and wisdom that inspires him to act and it is this glimpse of wholeness and of basic goodness that inspires him to begin his search.

At the moment when Ivan first caught a glimpse of the Maiden Tsar, he came to the choice point I originally articulated in the fist chapter of this book. The choice came to fruition with the Maiden Tsar's instruction to cut off the tutor's head. This was Ivan's first encounter with The Passion Path. It was the moment he chose to show up in the world as the Passionate Warrior instead of remaining bound to the dictates of his fractured femininity as embodied in the stepmother and imposed by the tutor. The moment Ivan picked up his sword and cut away that which had held him in bondage, he took his first step onto The Passion Path.

If you are ready for your Encounter with The Passion Path, go to www.rebeckaeggers.com to find out how you can get connected to Rebecka and The Passion Path. The Passion Path is the path of the Passionate Warrior and of whole-hearted, purposeful, and skillful living.

The Birth of the Passionate Warrior ∞ Rebirth

"Very truly I tell you, no one can enter the kingdom of God unless they are born of water and the Spirit. Flesh gives birth to flesh, but the Spirit gives birth to spirit." ∞ *John 3:5-7 New International Version*

Ivan began his journey with Baba Yaga. We won't backtrack through the analysis about the Dark Goddess. I feel I have said enough about Baba Yaga and about embracing Her chaos. There is but one lesson left that I feel merits coverage here: The old, neurotic, either/or duality of the distorted ego will not serve you in Baba Yaga's crucible.

The journey to Baba Yaga is about integration. It is a *both/and* journey. Marion Woodman addressed this lesson beautifully as follows:

> *He knows better than to speak from a polarized either/or when he is talking to the feminine, which abhors polarity. Both/and is her vision. He lets go of the tutor's philosophy before he arrives at her hut.*[84]

To be clear, the split we are trying to address here is the split in our own consciousness. The Divine Feminine and the Divine Masculine exist in wholeness at a higher, more integrated level of consciousness. The time Ivan spent with Baba Yaga was about practicing this new experience and philosophy of non-duality under the pressure of ritual death. With the Dark Goddess, Ivan began to see the unity of death and rebirth; he began to see the unity of Baba Yaga's horror and the beauty of the Maiden who appeared to him initially.

Essentially, this is a story about growing up. All along the way, Ivan is growing up and into unity consciousness. His journey began in the fiery root, in the subterranean space where Baba Yaga lives. He had to go down to rise up! Or more to the point, he had to descend in order to realize the truth of that old alchemical reality: so above, so below. His journey will no doubt end in the arms of a radically different kind of beauty.

In the story, when it was time to ascend from the underworld, Ivan borrowed three horns from Baba Yaga herself. He blew each one in turn. When he blew the last horn, a Firebird appeared to carry him up. Marion Woodman

---

[84] Bly, Robert and Marion Woodman. *The Maiden King: The Reunion of Masculine and Feminine.* Henry Holt Company. New York. 1998. Print. Page192.

has likened this to the opening of the fifth or throat chakra. This is fascinating to me. It is Ivan's own breath that called the Firebird. He had to be the one to blow the trumpets.

Recall what I revealed earlier: We can choose to die in the realm of the Baba Yaga. We can choose to remain there long past the time necessary to learn Her lessons. It is our choice. By our own agency, we call upon the Firebird. Baba Yaga is not going to do it for us! She will loan us Her horns.

Marion Woodman talks about this in terms of finally giving voice to our grief and our pain and thereby unlocking the creativity of the second chakra. This is precisely the moment the undeveloped ego was guarding against. This is what it was dreading. The death grip was about never having to acknowledge the painful things in life. But it is the verbal acknowledgment that finally takes us from the underworld. Once the grief is out, the sacrifice is complete. Here is what Marion Woodman had to say about this:

> *Like Ivan without the grounding, people in body workshop have no idea what is going to come through their open throat when the pin is out. All they never said, the grief of their body, jealousy, anger, and shame, plus the grief of generations and the planet's grief may be in there—everything the Baba Yaga symbolizes. More than that, when the throat chakra opens, the sexual chakra opens. If too much is released too fast, psychosis is a real danger. The breath of life reaching deep into the body opens the closed-down*

resonators, bringing the bodysoul back to life. The soul is in the anguished cries. The feminine side of God is crying.[85]

It is the soul cry that brings the Firebird.

There is a myth older than Babylon that embodies this same truth. The Descent of Inanna[86] tells of this same journey to maturity taken by the idealized feminine. In this story, Inanna, Queen of Heaven & Earth took the journey to the underworld to meet Her dark sister, Ershkigal. When Inanna finally arrived, She had surrendered even Her clothing. She was naked. In all Her naked vulnerability, She encountered an enraged Erishkigal. Her sister struck Her dead and hung Her upside down on a hook for 3 days.

Inanna suspected something might happen to Her in the underworld. So, She left Her instructions with Her servant Ninshubur. If She was not back in three days, Ninshubur was to go to various gods and beg for assistance. When She did, only the god Enki, the God of Wisdom, agreed to help. He fashioned two asexual beings from dirt and sent them to the underworld. He instructed them to appease Erishkigal. When they arrived, the Dark Goddess was in the agony of birth.

---

[85] Bly, Robert and Marion Woodman. *The Maiden King: The Reunion of Masculine and Feminine.* Henry Holt Company. New York. 1998. Print. Page198.

[86] The details regarding the descent of Inanna are from my study of the following source: Wolkstein, Diane and Samual Noah Kramer. *Inanna: Queen of Heaven and Earth.* Harper & Row. New York. 1983. Print.

I like to imagine that Erishkigal is Inanna's own shadow – the part of Herself that holds Her grief, Her unacknowledged pain, and Her discarded power. I think of Her as Inanna grieving and laboring to bring about Her own rebirth. This fits. Erishkigal hung Inanna upside down. The image of the Goddess hanging upside down brings to mind the image of a baby in the birth canal. Erishkigal is the goddess of darkness and of death. Take this in. The Goddess of death is wailing and straining in the birthing process. Life and death have been transposed at the very least. More likely their unity has been revealed.

This is very different from Ivan's encounter with the Baba Yaga. The story clearly portrayed Baba Yaga as separate from Ivan. The "divisions" are less clear to me in the Inanna story.

In any case, the asexual beings comforted Erishkigal helping to relieve Her agony. In compensation, She allowed Inanna to be reborn, and ultimately, allowed Her to leave. There is a catch though, which will become relevant later in the analysis. No one who once enters the underworld is allowed to leave. In this case, Erishkigal allowed Inanna to go, but with the stipulation that She must send a replacement.

In this story, like the story of Ivan's descent, it is the expression of grief and agony that precedes the rise. Likewise, it is Inanna's own forethought, Her own conscious decision to rise again, that ultimately set Her free. Had She not forewarned Her servant, She would have remained in the underworld. She presumably would have died with the Baba Yaga.

The descent of Inanna involves the descent of the feminine. This is where the feminine comes home to herself. In this case, it is Erishkigal who cries out. The Baba Yaga herself gives voice to the feminine agony. As Marion Woodman said, the feminine side of God is crying. If we relate this back to Ivan, it is also the feminine side of God that is crying. But She must cry through Ivan, not for him. The masculine must, apparently, grieve for himself. More to the point, he must come to know the grief that surfaces in Baba Yaga's presence as his own.

Regardless, what seems clear is that one way or another, the agony must be expressed, and in both stories, it has been; and this is a good thing.

Can you hear Ivan as he blows the last of the horns? Can you see the Firebird?

What a magnificent image!

The Firebird like the phoenix is the symbol of rebirth. The contractions have begun.

The story literally reads as follows:

> *Suddenly birds of all kinds swarmed about him, among them, the Firebird. 'Sit upon me quickly,' said the Firebird, 'and we shall fly wherever you want; if*

you don't come with me, the Baba Yaga will devour you.[87]

Again, Ivan has come to a choice point. No one is forcing him to rise. But should he choose to remain, ritual death will become actual death. Either way, Ivan isn't out of the woods yet. Birth is a messy process!

Marion Woodman referred us back to the notion of a pendulum swinging as follows:

> *Like the pendulum swinging, the Firebird is going to carry Ivan further into the positive side than ever before, and therefore, open him to a greater possibility of despair. So long as he holds his connection to his body, he can find a place midway on the swing where he remains still and allows the pendulum to swing through. Then he may say to himself, 'Despair is in me. I am not despair. This shall pass.' or 'I am in love, madly in love. But I am not love. This too shall pass.*[88]

This is not full maturity. This is only the ascent. But notice what is happening here. Ivan is beginning to see what is in him, but not him. If he is to survive his herky jerky ride to the surface, Ivan must begin to discern what belongs to him and what is merely in him. Ivan must become a seer!

---

[87] Quoted in: Bly, Robert and Marion Woodman. *The Maiden King: The Reunion of Masculine and Feminine.* Henry Holt Company. New York. 1998. Print.

[88] Woodman, Marion and Elinor Dickson. *Dancing in the Flames: The Dark Goddess in the Transformation of Consciousness.* Shambhala Publications. Boston. 1997. Print. Page 200.

But there is more. Ivan is literally choosing between life and death when he chooses to take this ride. During the ride, he must choose over and over again. If his initial infatuation with the Maiden Tsar was enough to sustain him through his time with Baba Yaga, surely it will not be enough to sustain him now.

This is where the notion of personal growth takes on a whole new meaning. If it is detached from reality, if our desire for personal growth is founded on nothing more than our desire for a superficially beautiful life, we might survive our meeting with Baba Yaga. But we won't survive our time with the Firebird. Here we are going to meet our shadow side again but with more intensity than we ever could have imagined. In the rising, we meet the part of us that does not know how to live a meaningful, integrated, purposeful, full life.

I can vouch for this. In the days when I was attempting to construct the transition from the section of this book that dealt with disempowering the Domination System to the Birth of the Passionate Warrior, I met my fear and my anguish again. I met them at even deeper levels. I wasn't at all sure I could go on. But then something shifted. As I sat there in the nail salon, another key piece fell into place for me (in regards to my unwillingness to thrive). I was able to externalize it and release it. Only then was I able to find the still point in the middle of the birth pangs and simply rest there. Only then did I feel my initial desire to create something beautiful in the world transform into something more profound, something that could and would sustain me and my new vision. In that moment, I felt new life preparing to move through me.

Over and over again, I have been called to the stillness in the midst of an unsteady rise. Over an over again, the intensity of the integration has pushed me to the brink and then called me back again to this still point where all external realities lose their significance. It is in the still point that we learn who we are separate and apart from what we are experiencing. In the still point, we are finally able to access what is needed in order for us to finally integrate the Baba Yaga and our original glimpse of the beauty in our own basic goodness. Here infatuation stabilizes. The spiritual journey moves beyond the pink cloud that drew us in and beyond the anguish of the descent.

Again, Marion Woodman has captured the psychological phenomenon of the Firebird perfectly as follows:

> *As the newly released form of pent-up energy, the flaming bird is the transformation of 'I desire' as instinctual energy into 'I desire' as spiritual energy. The coming of the bird is comparable to the first time the explosive energy locked up in the atom was unleashed, an event that permanently transformed our understanding of matter, and our relationship to life on the planet.*

The transformation of instinctual energy into spiritual energy does not involve the sacrifice of instinct, but rather a refinement of instinct.[89]

Yes. This is very much like splitting the atom. What has happened is that Ivan has met pure spirit in the Firebird. The experience has split the atom of his psyche. If Ivan cannot, as Woodman noted in the earlier quote, maintain his connection to his body and to the earth, if he cannot find the in between space where heaven and earth meet, he will simply evaporate into madness.

Baba Yaga prepares us for this splitting of the psychological atom. She puts us in such deep contact with ourselves, that we can sustain the full integration of Spirit without losing our connection to earth and to our bodies. Along the way, our instincts toward fighting, fleeing, or freezing are transformed from the base material of survival into the refined material of thriving. In essence, we are now able to wield our instinctual knowing as the sword of discriminating wisdom and in service of something higher than mere existence.

Note that it is different for Inanna. She had already been to heaven. She is the Queen of Heaven and Earth. It was the descent into earth, into death, that left Her in perilous condition. Interestingly, Inanna's descent is not so much, upon

---

[89] Woodman, Marion and Elinor Dickson. *Dancing in the Flames: The Dark Goddess in the Transformation of Consciousness.* Shambhala Publications. Boston. 1997. Print. Page 199.

first impression at least, about transcending duality. It is about annihilation. During Inanna's descent She gave up everything external that had previously defined Her. Everything was stripped away until Inanna was forced to reckon with Her own annihilation, and in a sense, with the realities of life.

Inanna literally had to be revived before She could rise. She had to find that place where pure spirit meets the belly of the earth and connect the two. It was in the incorporation of death and in the stripping away of status that Inanna experienced the splitting of the psychological atom. This is what happens to those who have spent a lifetime in the New Age world of the ethers. It is also what happens, incidentally, to the egocentric, dominator side of us that has never had to deal with the ugly and the uncomfortable. In fact, this makes sense. Inanna's descent was about surrendering privilege and the image of idealized beauty. The trick in this kind of descent is not to integrate pure Spirit without losing the body, but to integrate pure body without losing the Spirit.

Ivan's rise more closely resembles what activists and the oppressed will face when they attempt to integrate the miraculous and the spiritual. In a sense, walking with Baba Yaga is more comfortable for them. Horror is already part of how they understand the world. Encountering the horror in themselves and voicing their own grief is somewhat natural. Mustering the courage to mount the Firebird is where the real challenge lies. It means turning from what they have, up until now, experienced as concrete reality, namely, the ubiquitous nature of horror and the pervasiveness of evil. But the turning away is very necessary, at least momentarily. The experience of beauty and Spirit is a necessary part of the integration. The time comes when the earthbound must fly into the ethers.

Inanna's time in the underworld more accurately reflects what must occur for those who have eschewed reality for the heavenly realms. They must open their eyes to the horror and the anguish and know it as real and somehow beyond their control. Up until their encounter with death, the New Age spiritualist and the privileged have been able to keep horror and anguish out of their experience of reality by simply flying too high for it to touch them.

Erishkigal's sudden, merciless blow is a shock to the system of the privileged and the star clad. There is nothing subjective about dear Erishkigal. She is death, and death is impartial. It teaches us that no matter how powerful we are, no matter how high we fly or how many angels we channel, the final say does not belong to us. We cannot escape death. When it comes for us, we must heed its call. Once the privileged and the New Age spiritualists have regained their consciousness and made peace with death, the rise comes easily. They already know where they are going.

Either way, we are called to embody the alchemical truth: so above, so below. In fact, we are called to take both of these journeys. Recall that everyone is both a victim and a villain; everyone is privileged and underprivileged in relative terms. Put another way, everyone is Inanna and everyone is Ivan.

One path brings us to wholeness through integration and one through annihilation. In reality there is only one path. The stripping away is itself an integration. It is in the stripping away that we come to integrate death and the realities of life. Status, privilege, and disconnected meanderings in heaven are a huge part of our denial.

If you are ready for your integration, go to <u>www.rebeckaeggers.com</u> to find out how you can get connected to Rebecka and The Passion Path. The Passion Path is the path of the Passionate Warrior and of whole-hearted, purposeful, and skillful living.

The Birth of the Passionate Warrior ∞ Come Into the Stillness

> *Except for the point, the still point, there would be no dance, and there is only the dance.* ∞ *T.S. Eliot*

Fascinating things happen once we break the surface. These two stories tell us a lot about what is coming. In Ivan's case, he meets the Crone. With her, he begins to practice the discipline of stillness at a deeper level. But he adds a new component. Ivan must now incorporate the practice of neutrality.

The Crone has a message for Ivan. The Maiden Tsar no longer loves him. What a startling message! Ivan must learn to work with the message rather than allowing it to destroy him.

In Inanna's case, She rises to find that only one person has failed to grieve Her absence: Her husband, Dumuzi. She finds him sitting on the throne She gave to him. Far from mourning Her, he has, in Her absence, used Her power and the position She gave to him to increase his earthly prestige. Inanna immediately recognizes him as the perfect replacement to carry out Her underworld death sentence. It is Dumuzi who must now complete his time in the underworld. It is his turn to meet death and to reckon with it.

Again, there are useful distinctions between these two stories that inform our journey in critical ways. We have no sense from Ivan's story what his relationship is to activism or whether or not he is stuck in the victim mentality. We only know he is the merchant's son. He comes from a conventional family of relative privilege and yet he has been mistreated in critical ways. We also know that his father, as many fathers do today, placed him in the hands of his stepmother (shadow feminine) and that the stepmother controlled the only masculine authority in his life, his tutor. Finally, we know that the stepmother wanted to keep possession of Ivan for her own purposes. When you add all of this up, Ivan's life does not sound too far off from the set up of the Domination System. The masculine ordering principle was not present. The feminine was void of wisdom.

Regardless, Ivan's story contains the lessons we must learn when we have taken things very personally in the past; when everything has served to confront our sense of worth and to disturb our sense of security; when we have learned to fight our way through life; when we have placed undue focus on the horrors of the world; and when we have historically fallen into a deep sleep at just the moment when our full presence was needed. If we are to progress along the spiritual path to maturity, sooner or later we have to learn a different way. One day, we will be tasked with learning to receive the messages of life from a place of neutrality while also maintaining our vision. We will have to learn a kind of wakeful stillness.

Ivan is on a mission to find his betrothed. He can't allow himself to be distracted by hurt feelings, that is for sure! Otherwise, he may just fall back asleep.

On the flip side, those of us who have preferred to keep our hands clean and to fly high above the messiness of life have often neglected to address key components of our lives. We have not been rooted in our bodies and their wisdom.

Inanna's story begins with the idealism of romance and budding sexuality as She weds Her beloved Dumuzi. She is innocent, as yet, unschooled in sorrow and hardship. Her domain has been limited to heaven and earth. Love has been Her focus. Like the New Age spiritualists who begin to awaken to life here on earth and/or the privileged who become conscious of their status and its consequences, Inanna began to feel the call of the underworld. By the time of Her descent, Inanna knew there were gaps in Her experience. It had tilted too far towards the heavenly. Some key truths were missing from Her awareness.

Just as happened to Inanna, when anyone who has been largely insulated from the realities of life finds the courage to descend, important bits of awareness come through. When these individuals rise with their discernment intact and their vision healed, they often find someone has usurped their position and is sitting comfortably on the throne of their lives. They find that their lives are populated with mirror images of who they once were and with opportunists who slipped in to take advantage of the old gaps in their understanding. When these formerly insulated people break the surface, clarity breaks across the dawn. There is generally a moment of reckoning dead ahead.

Ivan's story represents the neutrality we must learn to cultivate in order to maintain a vision centered life. Inanna's story reminds me, at this point, of the moment when the Maiden Tsar instructed Ivan to cut off the tutor's head. Now that Inanna has met and incorporated the lessons of Her dark sister, She has encountered Her own wholeness. She must also similarly reclaim Her power. Like the tutor, one way or the other, Dumuzi had to come down off the throne. Now he is down; and that is a good thing.

Let's return now to Ivan's story.

When Ivan rocketed to the surface of earth on his flaming bird, he learned that the journey was not over. The Firebird told him where the thrice tenth kingdom was, but informed Ivan that he couldn't accompany him there. Here is how the story unfolded:

> *The Firebird flew with Ivan on its back; for a long time it soared in the skies, till finally it came to the broad sea. 'Now, Ivan, merchant's son, the thrice tenth land lies beyond this sea. I am not strong enough to carry you to the other shore; get there as best you can.' Ivan climbed down from the Firebird, thanked it, and walked along the shore.*[90]

Both Robert Bly and Marion Woodman noted that this means Ivan has work left to do. He is not yet ready for the wedding with the beloved Maiden Tsar. In fact, as I already mentioned, Ivan will soon meet the Crone, and she has a message for him.

> *'Ah,' said the old woman, 'she no longer loves you; if she gets hold of you, she will tear you to shreds; her love is stored away in a remote place.'*[91]

Things are indeed looking pretty bleak for Ivan. Not only does the beloved not love him, she will tear him to shreds. Imagine the despair! What can Ivan do? As it turns out, all he can do is wait. Here is how the story progresses:

> *'Then how can I get it?' Wait a bit! My daughter lives at the Maiden Tsar's palace and she is coming to visit me today; we may learn something from her.' Then*

---

[90] Quoted in: Bly, Robert and Marion Woodman. *The Maiden King: The Reunion of Masculine and Feminine.* Henry Holt Company. New York. 1998. Print.

[91] Quoted in: Bly, Robert and Marion Woodman. *The Maiden King: The Reunion of Masculine and Feminine.* Henry Holt Company. New York. 1998. Print.

the old woman turned Ivan into a pin and stuck him into the wall; at night her daughter flew in. Her mother asked her whether she knew where the Maiden Tsar's love was stored away. 'I do not know,' said the daughter, and promised to find out from the Maiden Tsar herself.[92]

Ivan has come full circle. He started with a pin in his neck and now he is a pin in the wall. How fascinating. Marion Woodman explained the Crone's actions as follows:

> *This action is characteristic of crone energy… With no sentimentality and great love, she takes the dreamer into a cave, a tunnel, or a grove and points her finger at the scene that makes the core issue nakedly clear. The dreamer is forced to look at it. Running away is no longer possible. In being turned into a pin, Ivan is reduced to the negative essence that is his sleeping self at the beginning of the fairy tale. Why does the crone do this to him? Before Ivan can find and unite with the Maiden Tsar, he needs to stay still and silent and confront fully his own absence from his true self. He will then be able to assume full responsibility for his growing presence.*
>
> *This is a pregnant moment. Will Ivan be able to remain still? Will he be able to listen, to sacrifice his illusions so that he will be able to comprehend*

---

[92] Quoted in: Bly, Robert and Marion Woodman. *The Maiden King: The Reunion of Masculine and Feminine*. Henry Holt Company. New York. 1998. Print.

and follow through to his next task? This is the real growing up—moving beyond narcissistic adolescence and polarization. This is the holding of paradox. This is the move beyond the gender wars.

Speaking of this point in **Four Quartets***, T.S. Eliot writes, 'Except for the point, the still point, there would be no dance, and there is only the dance.'*

This is the still point of soul. The psychic pendulum will continue to swing in its inevitable rhythm, but the 'I desire' is now coming from a different place. Soul watches the ego swinging without becoming identified with its yearnings. The first 'I desire' is for physical survival; this 'I desire' is for soul survival. Here is the holding of the tension of the opposites in the still point.[93]

I think what we are getting at here is really the practice of meditation. Ivan must become still long enough to hear the wisdom of the old Crone in his belly. He must learn to let his thoughts go galloping by and to let his emotions unravel without actually getting caught up in them. Shit happens. Ivan's task now is to let it and to listen for the message that lies beyond his egoic reactions.

---

[93] Woodman, Marion and Elinor Dickson. *Dancing in the Flames: The Dark Goddess in the Transformation of Consciousness.* Shambhala Publications. Boston. 1997. Print.

If you recall, this is a key part of how both Chogyam Trunpa and Carlos Castaneda talked about the warrior's way. Trungpa mentioned inquisitiveness and talked about receiving the messages of success and failure. He said that "Trust is knowing that there will always be a message." He continued:

> *When you trust in those messages, the reflections of the phenomenal world, the world begins to seem like a bank, a reservoir, of richness. You feel that you are living in a rich world, one that never runs out of messages. A problem arises only if you attempt to manipulate the situation to your advantage or ignore it. Then you are violating your relationship of trust with the phenomenal world, so then the reservoir might dry up. But usually you will get a message first. If you are being too arrogant, you will find yourself being pushed down by heaven, and if you are being too timid, you will find yourself being raised up by earth.*[94]

So Ivan has become a still point, a pin in the wall. His job is to hear the messages.

This is a matter of being in right relationship with the world. It is also about freedom. Ivan wants to find his betrothed. But more than that, he wants to know where her love is stored so that he can restore it and finally achieve his marriage to the Maiden Tsar. Ivan doesn't have time to cry

---

[94] Trungpa, Chogyam. *Shambhala: The Sacred Path of the Warrior.* Shambhala Publications, Inc. Boston. 1984. Location 910.

about the loss of her love. He can't afford to be a prisoner to his conditioning or his old habitual responses. Ivan must claim his freedom from these things so he can rise to the occasion.

What is called for here is ultimate neutrality towards the messages we receive. Castaneda confirms this. As relayed in *The Fire From Within*, don Juan explained it this way, 'A nagual is someone who is flexible enough to be anything. To be a nagual, among other things, means to have no points to defend."[95] This is very similar to the quote I included at the beginning of the first chapter in this book:

> *"The basic difference between an ordinary man and a warrior is that a warrior takes everything as a challenge while an ordinary man takes everything as a blessing or a curse."* ∞ Carlos Castaneda

Ivan is becoming a warrior. He is on his way to having no points to defend and to living in harmony with the messages he receives. The question is, can Ivan embrace the still point. Can he surrender to what is and to this process which is rooted in something greater than Ivan's limited perspective?

The still point is where the drama collapses. It is not the excitement of falling in love nor is it the horror of Baba Yaga's hut. This is not the life and death matter of finding the eye of the storm as the Firebird ascends. The flaming, flashy colors of the Firebird have departed. Ivan is in a most interesting

---

[95] Castaneda, Carlos. *The Fire From Within*. Washington Square Press. New York. 1984. Print. Page 16.

position. He must simply be present to what is happening and wait for further instruction. This is where many people collapse under the pressure of losing their stories. In this place, there is no one left to fight. There are no absolute truths about anything in the presence of the Crone. There is only information. Do I cross the lake in search of my beloved or do I go off on some other path in search of her love?

Chogyam Trungpa has explained this place with brilliance as follows:

> *Ordinarily trusting your world means that you expect to be taken care of or to be saved. You think that the world will give you what you want—or at least what you expect. But as a warrior, you are willing to take a chance; you are willing to expose yourself to the phenomenal world, and you trust that it will give you a message, either of success or failure. Those messages are regarded neither as punishment nor as congratulation. You trust not in success, but in reality. You begin to realize that you usually fail when action and intellect are undisciplined, unsynchronized, and that you usually succeed when intelligence and action are fully joined. But whatever the result that comes from your action, that result is not an end in itself. You can always go beyond the result; it is the seed for a further journey.[96]*

---

[96] Trungpa, Chogyam. *Shambhala: The Sacred Path of the Warrior.* Shambhala Publications, Inc. Boston. 1984. Location 921.

In the Crone energy only receptivity and vision will serve us. The only "weapon" we have left is our willingness to take up the simplest and most demanding of tasks: surrendering to what is. If we have not encountered our own sense of basic goodness along the way, if we are still clinging to our self-importance (pride and shame), the surrender will be excruciating. It will be nigh impossible. Remember, we have been through this entire, arduous, soul rending journey because we wanted to find our beloved and now she does not love us. This is the point of extremity. We will be tempted to give up the vision in this place. But, in the light of basic goodness, we can choose to allow this moment to become the seed of something more. With even a fledgling understanding of basic goodness, we can harness the power of the required surrender. It is surrender itself that will allow the flow of this process to carry us on to the arms of the Beloved.

Barbara De Angelis has spoken to this kind of surrender in her book Passion. Here is what she said:

> *To surrender means to get your limited ego out of the way and align yourself with a force more powerful than your will. When you surrender, you let go of whatever is stubbornly holding you in the place you presently are, and flow with the current of the river of life that wants to take you to something greater.*[97]

---

[97] De Angelis, Barbara. *Passion*. Dell Publishing. New York. 1999. Kindle. Location 292. Page 32.

This definition of surrender is still missing something in that it does not tell us to what we are surrendering. We are surrendering to the power of our intentions and our vision to draw us forward in accordance with what we are trying to create. Surrendering in this way is the final ego sacrifice. The ego that is stuck in duality and self-importance wants to do and to control. It prefers the drama to the stillness. It can hide there. But the ego rooted in basic goodness is surrendered to wisdom and to whatever will be most useful and effective in bringing about the fulfillment of vision. It is surrendered to the ways of the Crone and to the stillness that brings life's messages.

Surrender is the final preparation for the nuptials that lie ahead. The decision to let go and to allow the current of intention to carry us forward is the vehicle that transports us to the threshold of a new world; a world founded in the new mythology of basic goodness, thriving, and blossoming potential. Therefore, this seems like a crucial place to expand the concept of basic goodness beyond the surface definitions we have been working with so far.

If you have been paying close attention, you have probably picked up on a few words that are key to the concept: gentleness, tenderness, open-heartedness, presence, discernment, neutrality... These are all essential descriptors. But at its heart, basic goodness is a very simple concept. It is self appreciation. It involves being gentle towards ourselves and it involves having real sympathy for what we have been through. It is the foundation of everything. Here is what Chogyam Trungpa had to say:

> *A great deal of chaos in the world occurs because people don't appreciate themselves. Having never developed sympathy or gentleness towards themselves, they cannot experience harmony or peace within themselves, and therefore, what they project to others is also inharmonious and confused. Instead of appreciating our lives, we often take our existence for granted or we find it depressing and burdensome.*

Basic goodness is, in the first instance, self love plain and simple. It is not some kind of self aggrandizement. It is not romantic love that happens with our feelings. This is self love as a practice. We practice being gentle and kind with ourselves.

The practice of self love is the doorway to marriage with the Maiden Tsar. Surrender brought Ivan to the threshold, now he must find the Maiden Tsar through the passageway of self love. If Ivan cannot be still and silent on the wall and appreciate himself enough to finally hear the messages of the phenomenal world, he will never bring his dreams to fruition. The doorway to an integrated, productive life does not open through self immolation (though the road that leads to its threshold is often a painful one). It opens through meditation, surrender, and self acceptance.

This whole journey has been about coming to know and love all of who we are with complete neutrality so that we can receive life's messages from a perspective of neutrality also.

At this point, I think it is worth considering the Inanna story in light of this concept of neutrality. Imagine what it would feel like if you had gone missing and instead of mourning you, your husband was out looting your bank account and running up your credit cards with reckless abandon. Imagine for a moment that you came out of a coma and discovered this very scene. Can you touch the kind of raw anguish you would feel? This is radically different from Ivan's story.

In Ivan's story, he disappointed the Maiden Tsar. He fell asleep while she waited in anticipation for their nuptials. The message that she no longer loves him, while painful, is to be expected. It is also useful. The Maiden Tsar has not betrayed Ivan, and beyond that, Ivan has received a clear message. He now knows were he stands.

Dumuzi has also delivered a strong message. He revealed himself and his intentions. Dumuzi appears to be an intimate predator who was waiting to advance himself in his wife's absence. At the very least, there has been a betrayal of the marital trust and intimacy they once shared as young lovers. This kind of treachery demands a powerful response, and Inanna gave one. It was primal, instinctual, and harsh enough to get the job done. It is important that we are able to spot a betrayal when one occurs and that we not get lost in the idea that everything deserves an empathic, kind response. No! Sometimes the answer is swift, powerful, fierce action expressly designed to put an end to the betrayal. Sometimes you just need to cut off the tutor's head as an act of pure self love.

Inanna, like Ivan, received a message. It was one that cried out for balancing action. The action She took served a profound purpose. Here is what Diane Wolkstein wrote about Dumuzi's descent in the book, *Inanna, Queen of Heaven and Earth: Her Stories and Hymns from Sumer*:

> *The Sumerians extolled the king who was wise and compassionate as well as powerful....It was Inanna's visit to the underworld that opened the Queen of Heaven's vision to her own vulnerability. If Dumuzi is to be a truly 'great' king in the ways extolled by the poets of Sumer, he too must journey to the feared place, to the Great Unknown. He too must meet Ereshkigal. Inanna's curse topples Dumuzi from his fixed position and forces him to face the dark, demanding aspects of his wife, as well as the uncontrollable, inexplicable, irrational mystery of death in the kingdom of Erishkigal.*[98]

Had Inanna never come into Her own wisdom, knowing, and wholeness, She could never have challenged Her husband to do the same. While it is pointless to tailor our actions

---

[98] Wolkstein, Diane and Samual Noah Kramer. *Inanna: Queen of Heaven and Earth*. Harper & Row. New York. 1983. Print. Pages 162-163.

around an attempt to control someone else's awakening, sometimes our fierceness in the service of self love is exactly what is needed to open someone else to their highest potential.

If you are ready to develop the practices of stillness and self love, go to www.rebeckaeggers.com to find out how you can get connected to Rebecka and The Passion Path. The Passion Path is the path of the Passionate Warrior and of whole-hearted, purposeful, and skillful living.

The Birth of the Passionate Warrior ∞ The Marriage of Love & War

*I am the weaver.
On my loom,
opposites unite,
a tapestry
of day and night.
In my hands,
twilight.*

∞

Rebecka Eggers

How might the concepts of self love and neutrality, as developed in the previous chapter, apply to the Babylonian creation myth?

It largely depends on how you look at the story. If you focus on the actions of Tiamat and Apsu as a psychological or spiritual call to ritual death within the Babylonian consciousness, the junior gods represent the failure to heed that call. If, instead, you focus on the murderous rampage as a deep violation of the parent-child bond, the story begs for a primal, clear, and swift action to end the betrayal and neutralize the threat.

Either way what ultimately happened in the Babylonian myth was not as Robert Bly described when he contemplated Ivan's actions against the tutor. Marduk's behavior was actually sneaky, the antithesis of Ivan's swift, impartial movements. Likewise, it ran contrary to the primal solution in the Inanna story. Marduk's ascent was not clean or primal. It was rooted in self aggrandizement and grandiosity. It was rooted in his own desire for control. Marduk represents war without love, but beyond that, he symbolizes the the warrior disintegrated into soldier. The soldier owes his/her allegiance only to the commander. S/he is not committed to any cause beyond him/herself and the fight s/he is paid to enter

When I think of Marduk and his grandiosity, I am reminded of Dumuzi seated on his throne. I see him there in all his arrogance, grateful for the chance to ascend, to take advantage of his wife's absence. In early Sumerian literature, Dumuzi was not originally a god. He was the earthly king married to Inanna, the Queen of Heaven and Earth. He was not meant to rule over her, but to reign with her. She gave him his throne and was the source of his status as a god.

Before her descent, Inanna was the embodiment of love but not war. When Inanna returned from the underworld, things reflected this imbalance between love and war. Dumuzi had taken over and revealed a shocking level of disregard and lack of affection for his wife. The story is explicit. He did not mourn her absence.

Inanna immediately chose him to take her place in the underworld, and rightfully so. Dumuzi absconded. A band of demons chased him down. Just as they apprehended him, the story took an interesting turn. His sister, Geshtinanna, intervened. As the story ended, they had struck an accord. Dumuzi and his sister would each spend six months of the year in the underworld.

I love this story. This moment is akin to Ivan's decision to cut off the tutor's head. But the reckoning for Inanna takes place after her descent. Until she is able to incorporate the lessons of death, she is unable to see the reality of her marital situation and her husband's opportunistic leanings. She is unable to be present to what is. When she returns she is in a righteous fury. She commends her husband to death. For a moment, Inanna makes a polar shift from love to war. But compassion intervenes in the form of Dumuzi's sister. Dumuzi must, for certain, face himself as Inanna has faced Herself. He must know Erishkigal's grief. Perhaps as Ivan did, he must come to know it as his own and to give voice to it. But Dumuzi does not actually have to die.

There is more! Inanna too experiences another level of refinement. The meeting between Inanna and Geshtinanna is as transformative for her as was the meeting between Inanna and Ereshkigal. Here is what Diane Wolstein had to say on the subject:

> *But now, having returned from the underworld charged with her own dark, ruthless powers, the widowed Inanna grieves because she pushed her way through and destroyed the bridegroom and husband she loves....*
>
> *...Once Inanna was also Dumuzi's 'sister.' They nourished and comforted each other; they delighted in each other; they shared each other's days and nights. When Inanna and Geshtinnana meet on the streets of Uruk, the two sides of the feminine, passion and compassion, willfulness and feeling—meet. But mourning and suffering have subdued Inanna's raging passion; and Geshtinanna's words awaken her nurturing, compassionate side.*

Regardless, however you look at the story, this is not about asserting control as Marduk did. This is an entirely different archetypal adventure. This is about balance. It is about the integration of passion, power, compassion, and wisdom. All the characters are transformed and urged towards their highest manifestations.

Recall what Walter Wink said about the sacrifice being offered as though it were real. I think of Dumuzi as the ego ascended before its time, before it is ready. Inanna, finally whole, finally in touch with all of who she is, returned and offered him in sacrifice. Inanna sacrificed him like she meant it. But compassion intervened and restored the balance.

In the end, Dumuzi too will rise and partner with his lady. The journey will not destroy him. It will season him, finally making him ready for the union that has already taken place. Romantic love is transformed into something more stable. The physical, "I desire" has become soul desire. The fractured feminine has come into a place of unity. The masculine ego has been brought into alignment.

If we relate all of this to the Genesis story for greater context, we gain important insights. In Inanna's rise and the subsequent events, Eve (who some think was another version of Inanna) has finally transcended Her shift into duality. You could say that she has uneaten the apple or perhaps she has finally eaten the whole damn thing. In any case, Adam will surely manifest this newly reintegrated way of being. In the terminology of Tibetan, Tantric Buddhism, he will bring forth the wisdom of the non-dual feminine in the form of skillful action.

Interestingly, in the Genesis story, once Adam ate the apple, God informed him of the consequences of his choice as follows:

> *To Adam he said, 'Because you listened to what your wife said and ate from the tree about which I gave you the order, 'You are not to eat from it,' the ground is cursed on your account; you will work hard to eat from it as long as you live. It will produce thorns and thistles for you, and you will eat field plants. You will eat bread by the sweat of your forehead till you return to the ground — for you were taken out of it: you are dust, and you will return to dust.' Genesis 3:17-19, The Complete Jewish Bible*

In plain English: from the moment of the "fall", Adam would have difficulty with his doing. It would yield only thorns and thistles and Adam would eat bread produced by the sweat of his forehead. Adam would no longer have access to the non-dual feminine being that would allow him to reap the fruit of his efforts, at least not with ease. Life would be hard. He would struggle.

This is similar to the "curse" placed on Eve. After the fall, she no longer had the benefit of the masculine aligned with her being. God informed her that she would have pain in child birth (in manifesting) and that she would long for her husband (the masculine vehicle for manifestation), and that he would rule over her.

Something radical shifted in the Garden of Eden. The feminine being lost its status as the source of doing. It would no longer be easy for Eve to manifest her creations. Doing took the place of being in a new, hierarchical structure. Doing gained ascendency and began to rule over the feminine. In the old, unified consciousness, being and doing were one process. Feminine and masculine were undifferentiated. Adam and Eve had no sense of the polarity and the duality that came from eating the apple. This duality lacked awareness and experience.

If we look at the Eden story as the journey of a single person, it reveals a profound division in the psyche. Adam, representative of the ego, will now rule over Eve who was once the psychological point of wholeness from which doing sprang forth.

But eating the apple is also a step towards maturity. It reflects the differentiation that is necessary for the maturation process to come to full fruition. Recall that this new unity consciousness we are cultivating contains differentiation. It is not like the puddle of undifferentiated unity that Adam and Eve experienced in the Garden. It is more like a passionate tango. Opposites are present, we are aware of them, but they are working together in harmony; they are bound together in an indestructible unity and that unity has been revealed and brought into equilibrium. Rather than seeing a fractured image of ourselves, and of our lives, we are able to see the entire picture in the form of a unified whole. We are able to work effectively with what is from a place of clarity and natural harmony.

Inanna's story provides a glimpse into the wholeness that awaits at the end of the journey and the Genesis story gives us a hint as to the ease of creation and manifestation that can become a reality when the feminine duality finally gives way to a profound, mature unity. Effort, finally rooted in being has the potential to bear fruit with ease. Beyond this, the maturation gained during the journey has revealed a wise quality in the feminine. The challenges and experiences of the journey season both masculine and feminine.

This journey to wholeness is what has the potential to bring together activism (doing) and spirituality (being). It also has the potential to heal a key conceptual division that has, in large measure, held activism and spirituality apart, namely, the division between love and war. Walter Wink addressed this division with reference to the Christian church as follows:

> *Those who have devoted their lives to the political side of social struggle may be mystified and even a bit uneasy about talk of changing the spirituality of the Powers as an integral part of resistance. They have seen all too many Christians limit their efforts to perfunctory prayers for the general betterment of humanity...A recent study of the mainline denominations in the United States reveals that 78 percent of adult church members never spend any time promoting social justice. It is important to*

stress that the issue is not either/or but both/and: The effort to change the structural arrangements must also include changing the spiritual gestalt that may survive our structural changes and undermine their efficacy...What the church can do best, though it does so all too seldom, is to delegitimate an unjust system and to create a spiritual counterclimate.[99]

You could easily apply his words to most of the modern spiritual movements in which naval gazing, feel-good personal development, and enjoyable associations have supplanted any real challenge to the status quo of our lives and our world. In other words, the focus on love (being/feeling) to the exclusion of war (doing/commitment to transpersonal cause) has made these movements far less effective. Beyond that, even the focus on being and feeling, or inner consciousness, has lacked the dimension and depth that would bring about revolutionary change on a personal and collective level because even though spiritual movements have emphasized inner change, many of these movements have failed to truly affect consciousness. This is evident because real inner change always manifests in external changes and consistent action.

Put another way, many spiritual movements are concerned more with the soul than with creating the kind of world community that would support the blossoming of soul potential. They are also distracted from developing

---

[99] Wink, Walter. *Engaging the Powers: Discernment and Resistance in a World of Domination.* Minneapolis. Fortress Press. 1992. Kindle. Location 2413.

potential by the need to sell their brand of spirituality to would be adherents. The end result is a spirituality that is more concerned with identification and conformity than with concrete change. Love that does not find embodiment within the world is wildly ineffective as an agent of change because, just as Walter Wink observed regarding the demonic, love cannot function unless it is concretized within persons and institutions that act.

Further, I think most activist movements are not really aimed at the transformation of consciousness. As Wink notes, the very idea probably creates a sense of uneasiness. As a result, activism has become an attempt to change the outer structures of the Powers by resistance or by force; it has become war devoid of love. As Wink says, it is not either/or, it is both/and. The world we are living in no longer affords us the time for or the luxury of remaining in our silos. The time to make a difference in the world is now. We must begin by erasing the division between love and war, and thereby, between being and doing.

This fault line between love and war not only makes us less effective. It is a key structural support for the Domination System. Somehow, in the present age, we have gotten the impression that love is the antidote to war. This is actually part of what is escalating the dysfunctional doing of the Domination System. Accordingly, if we want to create effective lives that exist outside the Domination System, we must see love and war united. The myth of Inanna provides important clues for what this might look like.

As was common in ancient times, the myth of Inanna was later carried over from Sumer to Babylon. She became Ishtar, the goddess of love and war. As we have already discovered, Her journey into the underworld is about creating wholeness within the feminine. It is about bringing together the Goddess of Light and the Goddess of Darkness. The completion of this task is actually reflected in the compassion displayed by Dumuzi's sister.

The love aspect of Ishtar represents the idealized feminine. In this aspect, She is the Goddess of Light. In Her war aspect, She is the Dark Goddess. In holding these two aspects, Ishtar is Erishkigal and Inanna united. I believe the key manifestation of this unity is compassionate, skillful action.

Compassion is radically different from the kind of polarized and disembodied "love" that we often see in, for instance, new age spirituality, or even in the Christian church. This kind of "love" has a naïve and enabling quality to it because it contains such large gaps in awareness. Further, it is incomplete because it is so often impacted by the kind of magical thinking that keeps us flying high in the ethers. It is rife with denial.

Love needs an element of war in order to express as compassion. I know this seems counterintuitive. We have all grown so accustomed to thinking of war as horror and violence. But, as explained in the first chapter of this book, what we are talking about here is an archetypal quality, not the kind of warfare we are accustomed to witnessing. We are talking about war as a way of being that exists outside the Domination System. The warrior archetype brings important qualities that are essential to our effectiveness as human beings.

One key element of the warrior archetype is emotional detachment. Without this element, "love" leans towards pity. We feel sorry for others or for ourselves. This is not at all the same as the kind of self acceptance that is rooted in basic goodness. Pity motivates us to indulgence. We ask less of ourselves than we are capable of offering. We do for others what they can and should do for themselves. We look the other way when someone is climbing onto the throne of our lives or onto the throne of the world. Love without war is endlessly accessible to others and holds no one and nothing accountable. It contains no structure.

Similarly, war without love is harsh, cold, unfeeling, completely detached. It is pure logic, the kind of logic that holds passion in its grips and believes that order can and should be imposed over chaos by brute force. War without love is what tempts us to refuse what the Baba Yaga is asking in a self defeating attempt to outrun death. It is the hallmark of the Domination System because it is void of any sense of interconnectedness. War without love cannot see that if I win and you lose, we have both lost important opportunities to create something more powerful and supportive for us both. It operates without mercy. War without love can never manifest as the kind of inspired, skillful action that creates something new. Even at its highest, war without love becomes so detached and so devoted to transpersonal cause, that it operates without human context. It becomes robotic.

The marriage of love and war yields compassion, clarity, decisiveness, and commitment. But there is also an element of passion and aliveness. This comes from the dynamic, aggressive quality of the warrior. According to Robert Moore and Douglas Gillette, "Aggressiveness is a stance towards life that rouses, energizes, and motivates." [100] Without this quality, love remains passive. It is the warrior archetype that inspires the masculine to action.

The marriage of love and war is the essence of the Passionate Warrior. Once we have achieved this marriage, we realize we didn't sacrifice the ego at all. Just as Geshtinanna extended compassion to Dumuzi, we begin to show real compassion for ourselves and for the world around us. Within the marriage of love and war, the ego is allowed to live in harmony with our newfound wisdom and unity. We are united within ourselves. From the unity of love and war comes wise, compassionate, skillful, passionate action.

---

[100] Moore, Robert and Douglas Gillette. *King, Warrior, Magician, Lover: Rediscovering the Archetypes of the Mature Masculine.* HarperOne. New York. Print. Page 79.

All of this sheds new light on the Babylonian mythology. Maybe the ascendance of Marduk is just what happened when Eve bit the apple, or while the collective feminine has been to visit Erishkigal. It does not really matter. What matters is that the feminine in each of us finally find the path of descent and that She rise.

Likewise, it matters that the masculine finally find its way into the crucible of Baba Yaga and into to the still point. Both journeys are needed. The feminine emergence of wisdom will mean absolutely nothing if the masculine, the earthy vessel, is not available to connect with that wisdom and to carry it into the world. We must make the sacrifice and we must make it as though it will mean the end of us, and then, in compassion, we must gaze tenderly upon ourselves at last achieving a sense of our own wholeness and our own basic goodness. Finally, with great energy and passion, we must then leap into life and into wholehearted living.

All of this is confirmed for us beautifully at the end of Ivan's story.

In the lead up to the much anticipated marriage between Ivan and his betrothed, we learn that the Crone's daughter knows where The Maiden Tsar's love is. Even better, the Crone is going to throw a party for the Maiden Tsar. Just as Dumuzi escaped death in the underworld by the compassion of his sister, Ivan doesn't literally have to sacrifice his life to get to the Maiden Tsar. She is going to come to him. As Marion Woodman observed, "Ivan does not have to cross the eternal ocean to find his true essence. He does not literally have to die to find the happily ever after of the fairy tale." Ivan just has to find the Maiden Tsar's love. If you will permit me to cross the myths at this point, Ivan must locate Geshtinanna's compassion and bring it to her.

So, where is The Maiden Tsar's love? Apparently, on this side of the ocean (where the Crone lives) there is an oak tree...Here is how the story explains the location of the Maiden Tsar's love:

> *On this side of the ocean there stands an oak; in the oak there is a coffer; in the coffer there is a hare; in the hare, there is a duck; in the duck there is an egg; and in the egg lies the Maiden Tsar's love.*[101]

How marvelously confusing! We could spend forever unpacking this. I think it is enough to understand what Marion Woodman concluded and to put a little context around it. She determined that, "All these last images suggest the divine within the human, and the eternal feminine pattern that moves from life into death into rebirth."[102] Woodman also said something else that is really important. Ivan's time with Baba Yaga "initiated him into the dark side of the feminine; now he will initiate the eternal feminine into life."[103] She

---

[101] Quoted from: Bly, Robert and Marion Woodman. *The Maiden King: The Reunion of Masculine and Feminine.* Henry Holt Company. New York. 1998. Print. Page 124.

[102] Bly, Robert and Marion Woodman. *The Maiden King: The Reunion of Masculine and Feminine.* Henry Holt Company. New York. 1998. Print. Page 214.

[103] Bly, Robert and Marion Woodman. *The Maiden King: The Reunion of Masculine and Feminine.* Henry Holt Company. New York. 1998. Print. Page 214.

concludes that in order to do this, Ivan must experience these symbols within himself. He must understand that life, death, and rebirth exist within him. Here is what Woodman had to say about the journey:

> *The Journey Ivan is about to make will open his soul to...non-duality—that most precious of mysteries that is already there for us to see, hear, smell, touch when we return to the mighty oak that is the axis of our life, our connection between earth and heaven. There we find the treasure that we buried when we left childhood vision behind. In that place, contradictions are robbed of their power to polarize. Instead, they carry, as a Zen koan carries, the spark of oneness best articulated by silence—the daffodil laughing in the spring sun.*
>
> *And so Ivan goes to that oak tree, and in the oak, he finds the coffer. Now, the coffer can be anything from a treasure box to a coffin. In this place of paradox, it is both. In the tree of life it holds that part of Ivan that was buried alive when his goddess mother wasn't there to love him anymore and his god father left him in the care of the tutor. All his dreams of perfection of she who could not love him are in that coffin, and his memories of the goddess who disappeared on the golden boat. And the man in himself who died with her when she left, and died again when he heard she*

did not love him anymore. His soul buried in that box is not dead.[104]

In that box there is life, a living hare, a symbol of fertility. In the hare there is a duck, which Woodman likens to the need to learn how to be in the conscious and the unconscious, on water (unconscious) and land (conscious), and in the air (refined consciousness).

All of this made me think of Babylon and the difficult circumstances in the Fertile Crescent. It made me think of Marduk and the fear of the mother who is either dead or treacherous. There was someone missing from the Babylonian creation story. There was no mention of a presence like that of the Maiden Tsar. There were no images of idealized femininity that might have drawn the story towards awakening and integration. Tiamat was presented alone as she moved out of nurturance and into the shadow of Babylonian consciousness. Was the idealized feminine there all along in the background?

There are hints that she was if you place the myth in the context of the yearly rites performed by the Babylonians. Recall that, at the beginning of the Babylonian myth, we find a peaceful co-creative process as Tiamat (salt water/chaos) and Apsu (fresh water) come together as mates and produce children. But soon after this act of peaceful co-creation, chaos emerges (in Babylon and within the Babylonian consciousness) in the form of the murderous parents. Marduk

---

[104] Bly, Robert and Marion Woodman. *The Maiden King: The Reunion of Masculine and Feminine.* Henry Holt Company. New York. 1998. Print. Pages 215-216.

arises to create order out of chaos by brute force. This consolidated power in the king as the servant of Marduk.

In the context of the annual rites performed in Babylon, Marduk's victory of order over chaos was only one small part of what took place. Each year, when the land was moving from fertility to rest, the king, like Ivan and his visit to the Baba Yaga, went through a ritual death. This represented the descent into the primordial chaos (Tiamat). Then, as the fertility returned to the land with the turn of the seasons, the god was revived, liberated, and released as the people celebrated his victory over the chaos inherent in the barren months. At this time, they ritually enthroned the king once more. Balance was finally restored with the sacred marriage rites that the Babylonians believed would revive all the life-giving forces in nature and humanity. Finally, death came again to the narrative as the richness and fertility of the land again began to give way to the chaos of infertility.[105]

Despite the preservation of union and balance in the Babylonian rites, something was shifting in Babylon. The Babylonian Creation myth focuses on imposing order over both the feminine and the chaos of nature by domination and force rather than by serving as the organizing principle that brings formlessness into form in the way that the union of Apsu with Tiamat had once done. What seems true is that Babylon stood on the edge of a transformation in

---

[105] Wink, Walter. *Engaging the Powers: Discernment and Resistance in a World of Domination.* Minneapolis. Fortress Press. 1992. Kindle. Location

human consciousness that was beginning to prize masculine supremacy and strength over balance and co-creation. The old rites that celebrated the life giving quality of the masculine and feminine in balance remained in tact as a part of a larger narrative that featured the masculine god as the hero subduing the feminine and the associated chaos. Nonetheless, like a hologram, the truth remained visible. The story ultimately progressed from the pure potential and chaos of the feminine to order, and then towards balance and union. Finally, the year resolved in death as the cycles came and went.

What does all of this amount to? It provides a clue as to what is to come if we choose to move beyond the egoic masculine that controls chaos, but resolves none of the underlying issues. It tells us what is possible if we are willing to do the work necessary to move towards a balanced union of the masculine and the feminine: the rich, the luscious, the fertile and the creative. It is in this place of resolution and balance that we are finally able to create something nourishing and pleasurable. From this place of integration, we are finally able to address the challenges we face. Force and control give way to pleasure and co-creation. Life is affirmed. Death is honored. In fact, in every creative cycle, there comes a point at which destruction is necessary in order to allow creation to advance.

Woodman points to this kind of resolution in her analysis regarding the symbolism of the duck. That symbolism seems to hold the key to masculine/ego transformation. Recall my earlier suggestion that Ivan must have glimpsed, in the Maiden Tsar, an idealized version of his own basic goodness or of God within him. With the appearance of the duck, the folk tale seems to have moved beyond the idealized to the concrete.

Marion Woodman noted that Ivan has, up until now, held two images of the feminine:

> *one, an ethereal maiden too high up on a pedestal to be real; the other, the shadow, counterpart, the devouring mother. The transcendent function, represented by the duck would connect heaven and earth—bringing both the love of the swan maiden and the lust of the Baba Yaga into human form, creating one integrated human being.*[106]

This is where horror (war) and beauty (love) are both transformed and revealed in their authentic forms. Horror is the unconscious, buried, unexpressed human anguish blowing out sideways all over the world and the corresponding need to lock down control. Once witnessed and expressed, this unconscious agony becomes the swirling eddy of chaotic potential from which we can manifest real beauty rooted in human compassion, love, and soul desire.

The Passionate Warrior is finally born from the horror transformed into pure passion and potential. Real beauty is

---

[106] Bly, Robert and Marion Woodman. *The Maiden King: The Reunion of Masculine and Feminine.* Henry Holt Company. New York. 1998. Print. Page 218.

human potential made manifest through our capacity to care for one another, to live passionately, and to bring the wise desires that Spirit has placed in our hearts to full fruition in our lives, individually, and collectively.

And what of the egg that Ivan finds inside the duck? According to Marion Woodman, the egg is "the eternal gem of life."

> *In Egypt, it was related to the red sun of the morning (the resurrection), it's golden yolk the sun, the wheel of fire, and by extension, the firebird.*[107]

The Crone will serve the egg to the Maiden Tsar at the party, and as the story concludes, the Maiden Tsar will "at once" conceive "a passionate love for Ivan."[108]

I love the way Marion Woodman explained this! I love Marion Woodman for her eloquence and wisdom!

> *The love of the Maiden Tsar lies hidden in the egg, which Ivan will take back, and which she will eat. There is a sweetness in this coming together of energies, a sweetness we often find in dreams. Here is masculinity concentrated on returning the precious egg to his feminine, and the feminine ingesting, with her own love, the golden orb (yolk) of her masculine*

---

[107] Bly, Robert and Marion Woodman. *The Maiden King: The Reunion of Masculine and Feminine.* Henry Holt Company. New York. 1998. Print. Page 223.

[108] Bly, Robert and Marion Woodman. *The Maiden King: The Reunion of Masculine and Feminine.* Henry Holt Company. New York. 1998. Print. Page 218.

spirit. In that union, the masculine is coming to consciousness through the feminine and the feminine is coming to consciousness through the masculine. In the egg lie all the new possibilities of their new relationship.[109]

This is what was missing in the Babylonian creation story when we considered it in isolation. There seemed to be no interdependence between masculine and feminine in the story at all. There was only subjugation. What a stark contrast there is between the Babylonian creation story and the story of Inanna where compassion intervenes and masculine and feminine come into a beautiful harmony, a kind of harmony that mirrors the seasons of the year. In fact, the Babylonian creation myth even stands in stark contrast to the fullness of the Babylonian rituals that ultimately seemed to carry humanity from chaos through birth, ego separation and control, and ultimately to union.

Again, Babylon is a mirror for us. Will we use the disruption in the world to choose the journey towards wholeness? Or will we allow power over and against to proliferate unchecked until we lose all contact with beauty and with the kind of human potential that lies buried in the tree of life that still stands on the other side of Baba Yaga's crucible? It is waiting there for us, somewhere between here

---

[109] Bly, Robert and Marion Woodman. *The Maiden King: The Reunion of Masculine and Feminine.* Henry Holt Company. New York. 1998. Print. Page 218.

and the shores of eternity. Marion Woodman explained the choice we face as follows:

> *The Maiden Tsar as an androgynous figure can be understood as the whole person having within himself/herself the source of his/her own integrity.*
>
> *...The androgyne is still in the unconscious, but it is there and ready to be born. Whether the masses will do the work necessary to bring it to birth or whether it will drop again into unconsciousness until someone else comes along to carry the projection is the question.*[110]

In other words, androgynous wholeness, the integration of the Light and the Dark Goddess archetypes and the ultimate expression of the integrated Divine Feminine by the Divine Masculine is the essence of the internal locus of control we chose to embody the moment we agreed to see ourselves as warriors rather than victims. It is the source from which springs our genuine sense of our own intrinsic worth and from which the practice of compassion (the unity of love and war brought to manifestation through skillful action) becomes our new normal. This inner androgyny is the source of the internally held self concept that allows us to expand beyond the habitual reactions and command performances of the Domination System, and ultimately to liberate our passion

---

[110] Bly, Robert and Marion Woodman. *The Maiden King: The Reunion of Masculine and Feminine.* Henry Holt Company. New York. 1998. Print. Page 221.

and our life force energy from it. The Passionate Warrior is the embodiment of the androgynous Maiden Tsar.

If you are ready for the marriage of love and war that will finally bring you to the point of integration and wholeness, go to www.rebeckaeggers.com to find out how you can get connected to Rebecka and The Passion Path. The Passion Path is the path of the Passionate Warrior and of whole-hearted, purposeful, and skillful living.

The Birth of the Passionate Warrior ∞ Passion Path Activism

Great Spirit, loving Earth Mother, give me your eyes to see and your ears to hear. Make me a witness not just of the tragedies, but to love unfolding in me and around me. Release me into the joy and the hope of spilling over. Amen. ∞ Rebecka Eggers, April, 2010.

I wrote those words just before my first trip to Chiapas. I knew then that I needed to see more than the tragedy that certainly awaited me. I needed to experience the joy and the hope of spilling over, somehow, someday. I needed to see love and happiness unfolding.

I had no idea what was waiting for me the day I walked past the familiar hum of the jet engines and took my seat on the flight that would carry me into the heart of Mexico. At that time, it took all the courage I could muster to simply get on the plane. I was strengthened by a vision I had at that time. I just kept seeing a tunnel of light open up over Chiapas. I had no way to know it then. But that was the light of my heart calling me home; calling me into a whole new way of being and into the fulfillment of my passion and my purpose. What I also did not know is that the light was as seductive for me as the Maiden Tsar was for Ivan. It didn't lead me into the sparkling light of pleasure and enjoyment, at least not right away. Where it took me was into the core of my darkness, and from this core emanates my freedom, my power, my passion, and even my compassion. There is no such thing as light that is not born in the darkness.

This reality of light born of darkness is magnificently represented in the formation of stars. Stars form from tiny particles floating in clouds of dust and gas. A disturbance (like a comet) enters the cold darkness that is already ripe with the material, the potential of light. The particles begin to collide forming clumps that grow over time. The clumps gain more and more mass and become more and more subject to the pull of gravity. They eventually form the core of a soon to be star. This core grows denser and hotter, until it collapses and eventually begins to produce a thermonuclear reaction.[111]

When I got on that first plane, I became like the particles in the darkness. My experiences in Chiapas were the catalyst that allowed me to ignite my own soul.

But let me back up a little.

---

[111] http://abyss.uoregon.edu/~js/ast122/lectures/lec13.html

I confess. I have a lot in common with Ivan and with Inanna. I was born in the relative privilege of the United States to a conventional merchant's family, and yet I was mistreated in important ways. Like Inanna, in many ways, my privilege and my spiritual journey had also left key gaps in my awareness. My sexuality remained, for all the sexual abuse I suffered, like hers: romanticized and undiscerning. There were things I had never been asked to look at and things I had chosen to suppress within myself. In many ways, I had spent my life flying too high to really be touched. I was avoiding the reality of my own pain and the reality of life outside the boundaries of my carefully constructed life and my pristinely appointed home.

When I decided to take that first trip to Chiapas, I was, in effect, deciding to surrender my right to look away; to escape; to fly so high into the heavens that I never had to face earth again. But I was also calling for beauty. I was asking for the beauty that comes through after you have willingly, and in many ways, not so willingly, chosen to see and to be changed by the experience of seeing.

This is the bedrock of Passion Path Activism: the love and the joy of spilling over that comes from the seasoning we gain in the descent, the discernment developed in the rising, and the equanimity developed in the still point. Passion Path activism is the crescendo of all this work.

This book is about liberating our full capacity for joy and passion, and above all, our capacity to love and to act compassionately, decisively, and wisely when action is required. It is also about learning when stillness is the wisest course.

Passion Path activism comes from love and joy as much as it may have started in anguish and aggressive resistance. In fact, it integrates the two. Passion Path activism is not born of love and nor is it born of war. It is born of the unity of love and war.

This book is so much more than words and electronic "paper." First, it is the offering of my heart to the world. It is the best I have to offer on one of the most painful things we will ever face: the loss of our autonomy and our gifts in the quagmire of control and victimization. In this sense, this book is an exodus. I wanted to name the "tyrant," describe it, and provide a means of dying out from under its control. But more than that, I wanted to inspire you to find the courage to finally enter the land of milk and honey; your promised land. This book isn't just about getting free. It is about living fully in a new reality. In short, my goal is to transition my readers from one state of consciousness, from one state of being, to another.

None of this will mean anything though, if all we accomplish is a momentary shift in the way we experience the world. If we settle for this, we will find ourselves, like the Israelites who fled captivity in Egypt, lapsing back into the servile will. And like them, we will be doomed to wander around in the desert for an interminable period of time waiting for all the doubters to die. For this reason, this book is more than an exodus. It is meant to create a marriage *between being and doing*. You might say that the proof is in the doing.

I think it is instructive that the reason the Israelites were not able to immediately enter the promised land is because, as the Bible says, the Israelites sent out spies to determine what they were up against. The spies returned to report that there were giants in the land. The relevant scripture actually says, in Numbers 13:33, "And there we saw the giants, the sons of Anak, *which come* of the giants: and we were in our own sight as grasshoppers, and so we were in their sight."

This is so important. We can choose to see the things we face as the giants in the land and we can choose to see ourselves as grasshoppers by comparison. In so doing, we inspire others to see us as grasshoppers (victims) too. We lay the foundation for a lifetime of identifying ourselves as underdogs and victims of circumstance.

The choice is ours. We can let our fear and our low impressions of ourselves deter us or we can put our faith in a new vision and in this new way of being. We can put our faith in wisdom, basic goodness, and our new identities as Passionate Warriors.

If our new identities are real and stable because we have integrated the still point and the wisdom of the Crone, we will be able to move boldly into a new kind of creative, inspired action. We will find the egg inside the duck inside the hare and bring it and all it stands for to fruition in the world around us.

If there is no action beyond flight, then we can safely assume that there has been a change in geography only. Like me, the Israelites in the Jewish mythology left the site of their captivity, but they could not leave the captors that had infiltrated their own minds. They literally wandered in the desert until every last person from the era of captivity had died. It took a whole new generation to accomplish what Moses set out to do.

Up until now, this journey has been about the death of something old and limiting and about the birth of The Passionate Warrior. But in reality, crossing the threshold from victim to warrior is really only the first step. Becoming a true seer is the final outcome. A seer is one who sees reality as it is. Which, interestingly, entails coming to the realization that there is no fixed reality. There is only the reality that flows from a way of being.

When you cross the threshold from victim to Passionate Warrior, you are crossing from one way of being to the other and from one way of seeing to another. You are crossing over from the grasshopper way of being to the Passionate Warrior way of being. Very simply put, Passionate Warriors have different habits and perceptions than victims do!

Carlos Castaneda captured this very thing in *The Fire From Within*. He relayed the following lesson given to him by his teacher, don Juan Matus:

> *He repeated that the warriors' way, the shift of the assemblage point is everything. The old seers absolutely failed to realize this truth. They thought the movement of the point was like a marker that determined their positions on a scale of worth. They never conceived that it was that very position which determined what they perceived.*[112]

What Castaneda is referring to should not be confused with positive thinking or a mere mental shift in perspective. I won't discount the benefits of positive thinking and paradigm shifts. But what we are talking about here is a wholesale shift from one way of being to another, from one level of awareness to another. When we experience this kind of change, it is solidified or verified through action. Here is what Castaneda shared on this subject:

> *[Don Juan] said that realizations are of two kinds. One is just a pep talk, great outbursts of emotion and nothing more. The other is the product of a shift in the assemblage point; it is not coupled with an emotional outburst, but with action. The emotional realizations*

---

[112] Castaneda, Carlos. *The Fire From Within*. Washington Square Press. New York. 1984. Print. Page 195.

> *come years later after warriors have solidified, by usage, the new position of their assemblage points.[113]*

In other words, a true shift in your way of being naturally manifests in a burst of action. It begins with clear intention to see what is and the will to make whatever inner changes are required in order to shift from one way of being and one way of perceiving to another. But it does not end there. It ends with outward expression!

The real name of the "chaos" that the Domination System seeks to control is freedom and human creativity. Creativity arises out of the chaos of infinite possibility. This unlimited human potential is contained in the emptiness, the silence, and the mutability (fluidity) of the human psyche liberated from self-importance (shame and pride) and reunited.

Freedom and potential well up from the inner emptiness and the silence in the form of passion asking for expression and purpose asking to be fulfilled. It comes out of the stillness like fireworks erupting against the darkness of the night sky. Passion and purpose emanate from the shift in the assemblage point that allows us to expand beyond the victim mentality of the Domination System and into the reality of the Passionate Warrior.

We will know that we have shifted into the Passionate Warrior's way of being once our passion and our purpose

---

[113] Castaneda, Carlos. *The Fire From Within*. Washington Square Press. New York. 1984. Print. Page 199.

move from impulse to a different brand of action. This new brand of action will emanate from wisdom and neutrality. It will be characterized by a certain kind of decisiveness and precision. Passionate Warriors are concerned with the cultivation of human potential and the exaltation of human freedom and dignity. Their actions reflect this focus.

In short, it is not enough to have the seed of human passion and potential. We must plant it and cultivate it. The passionate cultivation of human creativity and potential stands in stark contrast to the myth of redemptive violence which casts humans as savages and servants of a murderous, self interested, power hungry god. The myth of redemptive violence is based upon Marduk having co-opted the creative capacity of the feminine, subjected it to his will, and single handedly constructed a world of violence and savagery from the remains of the fallen mother god. This is exactly what the Domination System does. Human creativity, and in particular, the power of the feminine, is subjected to the control of the system by force and is then deployed in furtherance of the system's own self serving ends.

Many people are beginning to feel the tension between the Domination System and a life of freedom and passionate creativity. There is a great deal of anger rising up. Many people are devoting themselves to fighting the oppression. Still others have devoted their lives to making the oppression visible.

What I am very clearly saying, is that the time has come for a new approach. The effects of the Domination System are fast becoming visible to anyone with eyes to see. Beyond that, clear perception of the Domination System alone is not enough to complete the transformation. More is needed. Walter Wink addressed this as follows:

> *Vision heals. Mere awareness of the state from which we are fallen is not enough to effect systemic change, but it is an indispensable precondition. Apocalyptic (unveiling) is always a protest against domination. Liberation from negative socialization and internalized oppression is a never-completed task in discernment of spirits. To exercise this discernment, we need eyes that see the invisible. To break the spell of delusion, we need a vision of God's domination-free order, and a way to implement it.*[114]

He makes a very important point. The process of discerning the system and overthrowing its effects are never-completed tasks. If we stall out at awareness all will have been for naught. We need a new vision and we need a means of implementing it.

Similarly, the fight against the Domination System is born of the system itself, and therefore, cannot offer a solution. The answer is not in the blind ambition of the Domination System which leads us into an even less sighted opposition. This is that old foot fault into survival again: fight, flight, or freeze. There are, of course, circumstances so heinous

---

[114] Wink, Walter. *Engaging the Powers: Discernment and Resistance in a World of Domination.* Minneapolis. Fortress Press. 1992. Kindle. Location 1548.

that they really do force us into resisting with all the strength we can muster. There are times when the right answer is to survive or to stop a violation. I will talk more about that in the next chapter. But most of the time, a life of resistance is a life of missed opportunity. This is both a matter of energy following focus and a matter of practical reality. There are only so many hours in the day.

Furthermore, change wrought by force is generally shallow. It takes tremendous energy to hold an unwilling person (or institution) in a new energetic pattern. If we tried, we would find ourselves constantly at odds with the basic will of the Powers and of individual people still caught in the delusion of the Domination System. This is why the Israelites had to leave Egypt. They did not remain to fight for their rights. They left to bring forth their vision of the promised land. In other words, when we enter into resistance, we must be prepared to continue until either whatever we are resisting has been toppled or destroyed, we have managed our escape, or we are dead. Otherwise, nothing will really change. So, when we enter into resistance, not only are we determining our focus, we are entering into a battle to the death.

In order to understand the magnitude of what it means to resist an entire system, recall that the Powers are an expression of collective will in the form of institutions like governments, corporations, religious organizations etc. Yet, at the same time, they have taken on momentum. The existing Powers are self perpetuating and they generally outlive the individual people who serve them. As a matter of reality, subjugating the Powers would require a very large scale operation. This is why Walter Wink is so adamant that we must not stop at addressing the outer structure of the Powers. We must usher in a change in the collective consciousness that is being expressed through the Powers.

Our work is not, therefore, to force the existing Powers to correspond to our will. Our task is to see the Powers redeemed through intrinsic change (which will come from a critical mass shift in the collective consciousness expressed through the Powers) rather than through coercion.

Chogyam Trungpa addressed this issue in Shambala: The Sacred Path of the Warrior as follows:

> *While everyone has a responsibility to help the world, we can create additional chaos if we try to impose our ideas or help upon others. Many people have theories about what the world needs. Some people think that the world needs communism; some people think that the world needs democracy; some people think technology will save the world; some people think that technology will destroy the world. The Shambala teachings are not based on converting the world to another theory. The premise of Shambala is that, in order to establish an enlightened society for others,*

> *we need to discover what we inherently have to offer the world.*[115]

This same principle applies to activist and other organizations that have traditionally been oriented towards defeating or resisting the Powers. The organizations would do very well to begin by assessing what they "inherently have to offer the world." What is it that is asking to spill over, to literally overtake the walls of the organization like a river overflowing its banks?

Just as individuals must die to the influences of the Powers, these anti-establishment organizations must find a way to extract themselves from the system and begin a new creative endeavor.

But how?

The path of intrinsic change is rooted in The World of the Red Sun Morning. It is rooted in basic goodness, passionate living, partnership, and in the celebration of life. From the perspective of this new vision, activism will be oriented towards releasing human passion and potential. It will not be oriented towards the destruction or domination of the Powers. Further, a new focus on fostering human creativity and the development of human potential weakens the Domination System in a natural and organic way. Finally, it carries with it a key advantage.

---

[115] Trungpa, Chogyam. *Shambhala: The Sacred Path of the Warrior.* Shambhala Publications, Inc. Boston. 1984. Kindle. Location 314.

Active creativity does not suffer from the drawbacks of active opposition. It is the passion-filled antidote to the Domination System and its progeny. Active creativity has great potential to create a critical mass change in the collective consciousness, a change that favors the celebration of life over a battle against death. In fact, it accepts death as a natural part of any cycle.

Active creativity provides an attractive and effective alternative to the Domination System. It has the potential to destroy the system by attrition rather than by opposition. Further, when active creativity comes in contact with those agents of the system that would otherwise enforce its ethos, active creativity exposes the system for what it is and challenges its ability to impose hierarchies and/or to shame those of lower position within the hierarchies.

If you stop for a moment and think about what I just said, you will realize it is truly an important point. The Domination System is not like Egypt was for the Jews. We can't simply leave it and then work on our consciousness on our way to the land of milk and honey. The Domination System is everywhere. By virtue of this, we are being forced to transform in place. This makes good sense. My own story as well as the story of the Israelites proved that a change of geography alone is not enough to create intrinsic change. In any case, because we are being called to transform in the midst of the system, we are likely to encounter elements of the system from time to time, especially as we are transitioning our consciousness.

These encounters are challenges that can offer us the chance to develop new skills while also breaking the momentum of entrenched patterns.

Jesus actually provided some excellent examples of this. He lived as an alternative to the Domination System. He was in the system. But he was not of it. Therefore, he was incredibly adept at creatively exposing it for what it was and at breaking its momentum. In fact, the entire story of the crucifixion and the resurrection stands as an example of his creative approach.[116]

Jesus also taught his followers how to be in the Domination System but not of it. He taught them how to expel its influence and then how to act in accordance with their inner liberty.

For instance, in Luke 6:29, Jesus admonished his followers, "But if anyone strikes you on the right cheek, turn the other also…" Walter Wink explained the creativity of this approach as follows:

> *Christians have, on the whole, simply ignored this teaching. It has seemed impractical, masochistic, suicidal—an invitation to bullies and spouse beaters to wipe up the floor with their supine Christian victims. Some who have tried to follow Jesus' words have understood it to mean nonresistance: let the oppressor perpetrate evil unopposed…*

[116] http://rebeckaeggers.com/a-heart-cracked-open/

Cowardice is scarcely the term one associates with Jesus. Either he failed to make himself clear, or we have misunderstood him…

…'If anyone strikes you on the right cheek, turn the other also.' Why the right cheek? A blow by the right fist in the right-handed world would land on the left cheek of the opponent. An open handed slap would also strike the left cheek. To hit the right cheek would require using the left hand, but in that society the left hand was used only for unclean tasks. Even to gesture with the left hand at Qumran carried the penalty of ten days' penance. The only way one could naturally strike the right cheek with the right hand would be with the back of the hand. We are dealing here with insult, not a fistfight. The intention is clearly not to injure but to humiliate, to put someone in his or her place. One normally did not strike a peer thus, and if one did, the fine was exorbitant…

A backhand slap was the usual way of admonishing inferiors. Masters backhanded slaves; husbands, wives; parents, children; men, women; Romans, Jews. We have here a set of unequal relations, in each of which retaliation would invite retribution. The only normal response would be cowering in submission.

Part of the confusion surrounding these sayings arise from the failure to ask who Jesus' audience was... [They were] victims...

Why then does he counsel these already humiliated people to turn the other cheek? Because the action robs the oppressor of the power to humiliate. The person who turns the other cheek is saying, in effect, 'Try again. Your first blow failed to achieve its intended effect. I deny you the power to humiliate me. I am a human being just like you. Your status does not alter that fact. You cannot demean me.'

Such a response would create enormous difficulties for the striker. Purely logistically, how would he hit the other cheek now turned to him? He cannot backhand it with his right hand...If he hits with a fist, he makes the other his equal, acknowledging him as peer. But the point of the backhand is to reinforce institutionalized inequality...In that world of honor and shaming, [the tyrant] has been rendered impotent to instill shame in a subordinate...As Gandhi taught, 'The first principle of nonviolent action is that of noncooperation with everything humiliating.'[117]

In other words, our transformation from victim to warrior takes place in the midst of the Domination System as we

---

[117] Wink, Walter. *Engaging the Powers: Discernment and Resistance in a World of Domination.* Minneapolis. Fortress Press. 1992. Kindle. Location 2507-2529

learn to (i) create alternatives to it and (ii) refuse to succumb to its normal mode of operation. As a part of doing this, we learn how to enter into noncooperation with that which is meant to humiliate while actively focusing our attention on what we are trying to create. One way to cease cooperating with behavior that is meant to humiliate is to die to its impact. In this way, we gain the ability to choose our response as a matter of strategy, not as a matter of reaction.

If you think about it, this two-pronged approach makes infinite sense because, to be honest, fighting the Powers is a bit of a losing proposition in many cases. At the very least, it is extremely uncomfortable and stressful work. Further, as already noted, if you fight the Powers without fostering a shift in the collective consciousness first, you may even be courting death. This does not mean we should approach our situation passively. But we should approach the situation creatively rather than following the incentives and taking up the tools of the Domination System itself.

One way of doing this is to filter everything through the lens of purpose, mission, and vision. In their book, *Conscious Capitalism*, John Mackey and Raj Sisodia have defined purpose, mission, and vision as follows:

> *Purpose refers to the kind of difference you're trying to make in the world, mission is the core strategy that must be undertaken to fulfill that purpose, and vision is a vivid, imaginative conception or view of*

how the world will look once your purpose has been largely realized.[118]

If we define our purpose as the destruction of Monsanto, for instance, we have taken on a giant and oriented our purpose around destruction rather than creation. But if we define our purpose as creating a readily available supply of non-GMO products at a price that is accessible to the greatest numbers of consumers, we have not only oriented our mission around creative goals, we have also engaged Monsanto in its own territory (in the marketplace where it is most vulnerable to competition) and in a language it understands (profits). This mission might include a huge amount of education on the dangers of GMO foods, partnering with organizations like Whole Foods, lobbying for legal changes etc. We might have to find ways of exposing Monsanto that make it awkward for it to proceed as usual. But Monsanto is not the central focus of anything!

Also, when we filter everything through the lens of the Passionate Warrior, we are no longer bound to the Domination System at all. It no longer offends us. We see it for what it is: a way of being that made sense at a particular level of development and from a particular perspective. We understand that evil is born quite naturally from the myth of redemptive violence, and especially from the components

---

[118] Mackey, John and Raj Sisodia. *Conscious Capitalism: Liberating the Heroic Spirit of Business*. Harvard Business Review Press. Boston. 2013. Print. Page 47

of that myth that enshrine exploitation and domination as necessary components of a false security.

We may at times still determine that it is necessary to disempower and expose the system through creative noncooperation, but we do not do so for the sake of resistance alone. If we choose to take an action that is aimed specifically at disempowering the Domination System such as turning the other cheek, we do it with an eye towards our end goal. We focus on the way we would like the world to look when our purpose has been fulfilled (i.e., when our vision has come to pass). We do it from a place of freedom and not from a place of routine or by way of rote responses.

In another of Carlos Castaneda's books, *Journey to Ixtlan*, his teacher, don Juan addressed this issue in the context of learning to be a hunter (which is another word for warrior). Here is a passage from the book:

> *'I don't care how you feel,' he said. 'In order to be a hunter you must disrupt the routines of your life. You have done well in hunting. You have learned quickly and now you can see you are like your prey, easy to predict.'*[119]

When you come in contact with the hostile elements of the Domination System, if you are in the mode of a hunter (or a warrior), the system becomes your prey. You must know

---

[119] Castaneda, Carlos. *Journey to Ixtlan*. Washington Square Press. New York. 1972. Kindle. Location 1775. Page 75

the habits of the system. The Domination System is actually pretty easy to predict. Its habits are fairly well fixed.

If you continue with the routine actions of a victim, you cannot be a hunter/warrior. You will remain locked in place, prey to the system, it hierarchies, and its humiliations. The same is true if you wake up into a mere polar shift into dominance as this will lead you into a potentially unnecessary power struggle. By contrast, if you discard your routines and respond consciously and spontaneously, the system cannot function as it normally does.

But keep in mind, our aim is not really to engage the Domination System, though we will address its behavior when it becomes necessary or advisable to do so. Our focus is on the fulfillment of our vision. For this I have found an excellent example from Mayan mythology.

In Mayan mythology, Ixchel[120] is the goddess of the moon, midwifery, and weaving. At the beginning of Her story, Ixchel was absolutely infatuated with the sun god. She followed him around like a puppy trying desperately to gain his affections. Finally, the beauty of Her creativity (Her weaving) caught his eye. The two became lovers. But then the sun god became jealous, angry, and abusive. Ixchel left him.

---

[120] I came upon this story many years ago. I have been unable to verify its authenticity through any recognized source. The value of the story stands on its own and so, I relay it as it came to me. A summary of this version of the Ixchel mythology can be found here though no official citation was given by this website.: http://journeyingtothegoddess.wordpress.com/2012/05/07/goddess-ix-chel/

Like happens in so many stories of domestic abuse, the sun god persuaded Her to return. Nothing changed. In fact, things escalated. Ixchel did not stop to file a restraining order or liquidate their joint property. She made no effort to prove Her victim status or have him declared "wrong" in the court of public opinion. She did not start a resistance movement.

Ixchel said nothing at all. She simply turned Herself into a jaguar and made herself invisible to him. She then went off to the islands of Cozumel and Isla Mujeres – the Island of Women. There She served as a midwife, aiding women in the birthing process.

This is a wonderful model for a new kind of conscious activism and it confirms everything we have learned up until now. First of all, it was the product of Ixchel's talent, Her weaving, that first attracted the sun god. It was not Ixchel Herself. We can imagine that he wanted something of Her talent for himself. This is supported by what happened next. He began to abuse and control Her. Ixchel's response was typical. She ran. But Her heart was not in it. Something of the young woman who wanted the sun god's attentions so badly still remained. She was willing to trade Her dignity for another chance at finally gaining his affection.

The next time Ixchel left, the story offers clues that something else was afoot. This time She turned Herself into a jaguar. This reflects a crucial energetic shift. Though I sensed this, I knew nothing about what the symbolism of the jaguar really meant. So, I did what we do in this modern age. I Googled it. Here is what I found:

> *As for the mythology and legends, the jaguar was seen as a god in Peru, Mexico, and Guatemala, in pre-Columbian America. The Mayans, Aztecs, and Inca all worshiped the jaguar in some form…*

> *In Mayan mythology, the jaguar was seen as the ruler of the Underworld, and as such, a symbol of the night sun and darkness…*

> *The jaguar is representative of power, ferocity, and valor; he is the embodiment of aggressiveness. For some, the jaguar represents the power to face one's fears, or to confront one's enemies. However, they are also associated with vision, which means both their ability to see during the night and to look into the dark parts of the human heart. The jaguar often warns of disaster, he does not offer any reassurance. Along with physical vision, jaguars are also associated with prescience and the foreknowledge of things to come. Cats have binocular vision, meaning each eye can work by itself, which provides them with better depth perception. This gives more evidence to their connection with vision and foresight.*[121]

I am reminded of the moment when Ivan cut off the tutor's head. The jaguar seems to hold the same kind of clear,

---

[121] http://www.pure-spirit.com/more-animal-symbolism/306-jaguar-symbolism

straightforward aggression. Further, the jaguar is associated with the underworld. I am reminded also of Inanna's journey and of Ivan's time with Baba Yaga. By turning Herself into a jaguar, Ixchel invoked the transformation of the underworld journey and She invoked the warrior archetype. She also claimed new vision and the discernment that would allow Her to see the sun god for who and what he was.

The jaguar, in fact, contains elements of the Crone from Ivan's story. Marion Woodman said that "with no sentimentality and great love, [the Crone] takes the dreamer into a cave, a tunnel, or a grove and points Her finger at the scene that makes the core issue nakedly clear." The jaguar is both in touch with what is and with what is to come. I love this. By turning Herself into a jaguar, Ixchel was able to open to the truth of Her situation while also learning to hold a new vision of the future She wanted to create.

The second time Ixchel left, She didn't just make a lateral, geographic move. She made an inner shift that imbued Her geographic move with real significance. On the surface, it seems as though Ixchel could have solved Her problem with a mere change of residence. I sense this is not true. In this story, we are dealing with archetypes. The sun god strikes me as a kind of omnipresent, omnipotent power. The key to understanding the real nature of the shift Ixchel underwent is actually Her invisibility. Invisibility is a symbol for the transformation She underwent. By virtue of the inner transformation She experienced, Ixchel made Herself inaccessible to the archetype of the sun god. This freed Her up to pursue Her purpose.

Carlos Castaneda also addressed this in *Journey to Ixtlan*. What he described was a kind of hiding in plain sight. Here are some passages from the book:

> 'To be inaccessible means that you touch the world around you sparingly. You don't eat five quail; you eat one. You don't damage the plants just to make a barbeque pit. You don't expose yourself to the power of the wind unless it is mandatory…'

> …'I've told you already that to be inaccessible does not mean to hide or to be secretive.' He said calmly… 'A hunter deals intimately with his world and yet is inaccessible to that same world.'[122]

In other words, if we apply this to the context of dealing with the Domination System, we don't expose ourselves to it unless it is mandatory that we do so. This is what Ixchel was demonstrating. For what She wanted to accomplish in the world, She didn't need to expose Herself to the sun god. She didn't need to engage him. Her purpose did not require it. She dealt intimately with his world. That much is implied by the jaguar and by its connection to the underworld. But at the same time, She made Herself inaccessible to that same world.

---

[122] Castaneda, Carlos. *Journey to Ixtlan*. Washington Square Press. New York. 1972. Kindle. Location 1682. Page 70.

Ixchel died to the influence of the Domination System and She sacrificed Her victim mentality (presumably in the underworld). Once She entered the energetic space of the jaguar, the sun god simply could not see Her.

Interestingly, the story said She made Herself invisible to the sun god, and to him alone. In essence, She stopped empowering the Domination System. If you think back to the discussion of the power-dependence relationship, Ixchel overcame the typical foot fault of the "weak." According to, Elizabeth Janeway, "In the power-dependence relationship, what the weak bring to the bargain is the validation of the power of the powerful: its legitimacy."[123]

Ixchel stopped validating the sun god's power over Her in the same way that Jesus' admonition to turn the other cheek offered victims the opportunity to become warriors by reclaiming their human dignity. Ixchel rejected the dynamics of a power-dependence relationship. She chose to see Herself in a new way and to live according to a new reality.

When the tyrant is everywhere and exists with unlimited prerogatives, making yourself inaccessible to the tyrant is the most powerful thing you can do at the outset. But we should not stop there. Ixchel did not stop there!

Ixchel's shift was, in the end, about much more than becoming invisible to Her tormentor. Her shift was about

---

[123] Quoted in: Wink, Walter. *Engaging the Powers: Discernment and Resistance in a World of Domination.* Minneapolis. Fortress Press. 1992. Kindle. Location 1367.

becoming visible to the right people. At the same time, Ixchel made herself invisible (inaccessible) to the sun god, She made herself highly visible (accessible) to scads of people who were engaged in the creative endeavor of bringing forth new life. She became part of a life generating system rather than remaining negatively attached to the sun god. Ixchel gave up Her relationship to the Domination System and She eradicated the imprint of the system within Her. She then took on the role of being a midwife to the manifestation process.

This is what we are called to do. If we truly want to see the world changed, we have to change the world by extracting ourselves from the present system, fashioning an alternative, drawing people to it, and then finally, midwifing the elements of a brand new world. It is our job to create the Powers anew or to see them transformed through a change in consciousness. In this way, we will see them redeemed.

For instance, in the case of Monsanto, if we move beyond fighting the giant, we can begin the process of creating a truly sustainable global food system. This might include an element of resisting the proliferation of Monsanto's control over the global food system. But it would not stop there. It would actively incorporate the process of midwifing a brand new way of managing our food resources and our relationship to the planet. Any resistance would be oriented towards bringing that new vision to fruition and towards disempowering

Monsanto rather than merely attacking it. Who knows, some of Monsanto's scientists might even defect!

On the flip side, we don't necessarily have to oppose Monsanto at all. We can employ it for our own ends if doing so would ultimately support our vision and if Monsanto is willing to offer what is needed. But we should also be careful to discern whether Monsanto's interest in providing what is needed is genuine. We might consider whether it is coming from a change of consciousness, or, if, by contrast, it is riddled with booby traps. Regardless, in The World of the Red Sun Morning, we have no enemies. There are things we support, things that must be destroyed (like the tutor), things that can support us, things that give us joy, and things that don't. Which things are which depends in large part on the day and the mission. The key to knowing the difference? Discernment and curiosity. We don't make knee jerk reactions based on the old categories of victims and villains and good versus evil. We make decisions based on where we are going and what, in alignment with our core values, can actually take us there. We listen to the messages!

What all of this comes down to, in plain English, is that we have a choice. We can spend our lives trying to bend the Powers to our will or we can get to work creating a new world based on human dignity and the blossoming of human potential. Does this mean that our contribution to this transition from the Domination System to The World of the Red Sun Morning must be inherently political or that we must focus on remaking the institutions of government and industry. No it does not.

Ixchel is again a good example. Her very actions in terms of dedicating herself to supporting women in child birth and the creative arts symbolized a blow to the Domination System which devalues women and their contributions. Anything that stems from passion and purpose (rooted in wisdom) is inherently revolutionary.

Joseph Campbell very ably described the difference between our kind of revolution and the revolutions of the Domination System. Although I included this quote earlier in the book, it bears repeating. In *Pathways to Bliss,* Joseph Campbell said, "Revolution doesn't have to do with smashing something; it has to do with bringing something forth."[124]

And there you have it, the answer to my prayer. This revolution is about love and the joy of spilling over. It isn't blind to the tragedy. It simply overflows right in the big messy middle of it all. In actuality, it incorporates it. There can be no joy that does not also know sorrow. The trick is in integrating the two.

At the beginning of this book, I introduced the notion that the tyrannical global system is our ally in the awakening process. The awakening does not happen in spite of the system, but in response to it. These two things are happening

---

[124] Campbell, Joseph. *Pathways to Bliss: Mythologies and Personal Transformation.* Joseph Campbell Foundation. Novato. 2004. Print. Page 104.

in tandem. The global circumstances we face in combination with the acceleration of the Domination System have put us under the strain of death. Under the kind of pressure we are facing, we stand a very good chance of shifting the global assemblage point. The Domination System has reached a critical mass as have the resultant challenges facing this planet. We have two choices: Confront reality or allow our potential to lapse. In a sense, we are fortunate The Domination System has reached this critical juncture as it is forcing us to look at the context of our lives. Without the extreme pressure of the Domination System and its consequences, we might have been content to continue along the old trajectory and to live our lives in creeping misery. Burmese politician, activist, and Nobel laureate, Aung San Suu Kyi captured this concept beautifully as follows:

> *Sometimes I think that a parody of democracy could be more dangerous than a blatant dictatorship, because that gives people an opportunity to avoid doing anything about it.*

In other words, sometimes you have to face extreme circumstances before you are willing to see the truth of your situation and to undergo all that is required to bring about a real transformation.

Carlos Castaneda, in *The Fire From Within* relayed a story about his own transition. He talked about how don Juan told him he was going to throw himself off of a cliff and either the pressure of impending death would force him to assemble another world, or he would die the death of an ordinary man at the bottom of the cliff. Here is what Castaneda said:

> *Pablo, Nestor, and I didn't die at the bottom of the gorge—and neither did the other apprentices who jumped at an earlier time—because we never reached it; all of us, under the impact of such a tremendous and incomprehensible act as jumping to our deaths, moved our assemblage points and assembled other worlds.*
>
> *We know now that we were left to remember heightened awareness and to regain the totality of ourselves...*

We are, at this moment facing our deaths collectively and we are, at the same time, called to regain the totality of ourselves. We do not regain the totality by running from death or by merely escaping from the Domination System. We regain our totality by facing the reality of the jagged rocks awaiting us at the bottom of the cliff. Yet I am certain, if we choose it, more than death awaits us.

The original cover to this book contained an illustration which depicted the Passionate Warrior emerging from the waters of the unconscious and then rising like the phoenix from a banyan tree. The graphic artist who designed that original cover chose the image from pure instinct. In many ways, the banyan tree says more in its symbolism than I have said in these many pages.

A banyan is a fig that, according to Wikipedia "starts its life as an epiphyte (a plant growing on another plant) when its seeds germinate in the cracks and crevices on a host tree (or on structures like buildings and bridges)." Here is an excerpt from the Wikipedia article:

> *Like other fig species (which includes the common edible fig Ficus carica), banyans have unique fruit structures and are dependent on fig wasps for reproduction. The seeds of banyans are dispersed by fruit-eating birds. The seeds germinate and send down roots towards the ground, which may envelop part of the host tree or building structure, giving banyans the casual name of "strangler fig."*[125]

In the words of Albert Camus, "the only way to deal with an un-free world is to become so absolutely free that your very existence is an act of rebellion." In claiming his/her passion, freedom, and power, the Passionate Warrior becomes like the seed of the banyan tree germinating in the structures of the Domination System, putting down roots, and eventually, changing the very character and nature of the host.

It is no coincidence that the Banyan tree mysteriously made an appearance just as I was proofreading this chapter. It was none other than the leaves of the fig tree that Adam and Eve chose to cover themselves when they became aware

---

[125] http://en.wikipedia.org/wiki/Banyan.

of their nakedness; when they shifted into duality. What sweet symmetry.

> *"Now learn this lesson from the fig tree: As soon as its twigs get tender and its leaves come out, you know that summer is near. Even so, when you see all these things, you know that it is near, right at the door." Matthew 24:32&33, New International Version*

> *He told them this parable: "Look at the fig tree and all the trees. When they sprout leaves, you can see for yourselves and know that summer is near. Even so, when you see these things happening, you know that the kingdom of God is near. Luke 21: 29-31, New International Version*

Even in the "fall" the rise was at hand!

What once could not bear fruit will one day become like a fig tree offering ripe, sweet, nourishing, delight. What once was passionless will soon be overcome with soul desire and with the sweetness and the spilling over of summertime.

If you are ready to experience the joy of spilling over, go to www.rebeckaeggers.com to find out how you can get connected to Rebecka and The Passion Path. The Passion Path is the path of the Passionate Warrior and of wholehearted, purposeful, and skillful living.

The Birth of The Passionate Warrior ∞ Passion Path Destruction

> *I cannot teach you violence, as I do not myself believe in it. I can only teach you not to bow your heads before any one even at the cost of your life.* ∞ *Mahatma Gandhi*

> *It is better to be violent, if there is violence in our hearts, than to put on the cloak of nonviolence to cover impotence.* ∞ *Mahatma Gandhi*

Oh, how I didn't want to write this chapter. I really didn't. I even published this book without it. But it just kept nagging at me. Something felt incomplete. So, here I am.

I didn't want to write this chapter because when I sat down to write this book, I thought I was going to follow Walter Wink down the path of adopting non-violence as a way of life. For me, that meant giving up a whole host of things that were not physically violent, but were what you might consider unkind. When I began this endeavor, I was clinging pretty tightly to the idea of ahimsa. Ahimsa is a Sanskrit term that means "do not injure." The problem was that I seldom factored in the injuries I permitted in my own life. Writing this book forced me to think more critically about the meaning of compassion and about the relevance of ahimsa in my own life.

The truth about what happened around all of this is that I got to the part of Ivan's story where he cut off the tutor's head. When I attempted to deal with that aspect of *The Maiden Tsar* folktale, the question of violence versus nonviolence hit me like a ton of bricks. Here was a story that was primitive and raw in its simplicity. For the love of Ishtar, Robert Bly was even making the case for the resurrection of something animalistic, instinctual, and VIOLENT within our human nature. He called it a good thing. Beyond that, Ivan secured his freedom with one decisive blow. His captivity and servitude came to an abrupt end. This abrupt ending was also an astonishing new beginning.

I have wrestled with the question of violence versus nonviolence ever since. I did not land where I expected to land.

So, big inhale.

Long exhale.

Here we go...

Non-violence is a tactical choice, not a mandate. In the words of Burmese politician, activist, and Nobel laureate, Aung San Suu Kyi, we "do not hold to non-violence for moral reasons, but for political and practical reasons."

Polarizing into non-violence misses a key point: some things are not really worth preserving. In fact, some things just need to be destroyed or cleared out of the way.

I hear you. You were hoping we could shift immediately into a kinder, gentler reality and that we would not have to confront violence, our own or someone else's. I too remember the Chogyam Trungpa quote I included earlier in this book: "In the vision of the Great Eastern Sun, even criminals can be cultivated, encouraged to grow up." In principle, I agree with this. The problem is that there are many people and institutions in the world that are simply wedded to the Domination System. They have no desire to experience a shift in consciousness. Beyond that, they will destroy you if they can. Like Ivan's tutor, they intend to keep you bound.

I can't speak for Trungpa. But for me, there is a huge difference between an entire world, or even community, that is orientated towards the shared values of his Great Eastern Sun vision, and a world/community that is largely stuck in the Domination System. Even a world in transition from the Domination System presents issues. In a world oriented towards Trungpa's Great Eastern Sun vision, the greater collective consciousness would be oriented towards the blossoming of human potential and criminals would be aberrations. What we face now is a collective consciousness oriented towards exploitation, and in many cases, the suppression of human potential, which tends to multiply criminality. Further, even if we are able to achieve a grand scale shift in the collective consciousness, what we will face in the transition period is the reality of institutions and people who simply do not want to accept the changes. They will seek to hold the old power structures in place by whatever means available.

Beyond this reality, I have observed that non-violence often cloaks a kind of twisted empathy with the oppressor whereby concepts like ahimsa get applied in such a way that the well-being of the oppressor becomes an exaggerated consideration. As a result, we become unwilling to simply cut off the tutor's head. We mistake passivity for nonviolence. Accordingly, in the final analysis, if we are going to restrict ourselves to non-violent resistance, it should be for tactical reasons and the choice should be void of empathy for the oppressor. Further, when we choose non-violent actions for tactical reasons, our non-violence will naturally have a passionate, aggressive quality to it. It will represent a fierce challenge to the status quo.

On the flip side, if we are going to choose violence, we should be sure that we have not polarized into the fight of good against evil that alleviates our responsibility to look at ourselves and our participation in the Domination System. This distinction is inherent in Ivan's story. The violence, far from sparing Ivan from a confrontation with himself, was the point of entry into a journey of self awareness and integration. It was also a necessary step in terms of his mission to find the Maiden Tsar. Accordingly, the choice to resort to violence over non-violence should not be based upon the idea of eradicating some evil presence that abides in others. It should, instead, be based on a clean assessment of probabilities and purpose. This is about discerning what must be confronted and destroyed in order to protect life, limb, spirit, and mission. It should not be oriented towards holding the Powers or another person in an unwanted pattern of interaction, but rather towards clearing the path to freedom in the cleanest way possible. It might also be oriented towards self defense.

I hear the next question coming: What about seeing the Powers transformed? There are two ways to transform any structure. One is to tear it down and build it anew. The other is to remodel the existing structure. What is important is not the method that we choose for transforming the Powers, but that the transformation come from a critical mass shift in the collective consciousness. This will make the transformation complete as compared to simply imposing a new outer structure. When we are dealing with change through resistance, the key question is: what will give full effect to a shift in the personal or collective consciousness that has already taken place? If the change in consciousness has not yet taken place within the collective consciousness, resistance will be best directed at challenging the existing norms. This question brings us back to my original point: the choice between violence and non-violence is a tactical decision, not a moral one. The critical analysis to be undertaken, therefore, is one of impact. We are called upon to understand the greatest potentials and the greatest weaknesses of both violent and non-violent resistance as destructive and transformative forces.

The greatest impact that pure non-violent resistance generally has is to expose the true nature of the Powers or an individual oppressor and to highlight a new vision of what is possible. Both of these present such a challenge to the normal operation of the Domination System that non-violent resistance is rendered extremely dangerous. It is easy to focus on the success of people like Gandhi and overlook the reality of moments like the Tiananmen Square massacre. Those who undertake non-violent resistance are every bit the warriors as those who take up arms, perhaps even more so. Both courses of action are very likely to produce death. One involves death in combat and one involves a slaughter of the innocent. It is the very slaughter itself that often has transformative impact because it places the violent, ruthless oppressor in stark juxtaposition with the peaceful, non-violent resistor. The benefit is not for those who are in resistance, but for society. Non-violent resistance is a tool of awakening. By way of example, consider this story as relayed by Walter Wink:

> *Chai Ling was the Chinese student leader in Tiananmen Square when only five to ten thousand demonstrators were left, surrounded by the Red Army. She discovered that some students had*

machine guns. Calling them together, she told this story: a billion ants lived on a high mountain. A fire began at the base. It appeared that all billion would die. They made a ball, and rolled down the mountain through the fire to safety. But those on the surface died. We are the ones on the surface, she said; we must die for the people. So the students destroyed their weapons and sat down peacefully to wait for what seemed certain death. Perhaps as many as three thousand of them were killed. By refusing to use violence, they robbed the communist regime of its "mandate from heaven," guaranteeing its collapse—or transformation. 'The June 4 [1989] massacre was no more the end of communism in China than was the Amritsar massacre by Britain the end of India's freedom struggle,' predicts Richard Deats. 'Rather than the end, it may some day be remembered as the beginning.'[126]

We can draw a similar example from the early Christian martyrs. They refused to worship the emperor. Instead, they knelt and offered prayers to God on the emperor's behalf. Here again is Walter Wink's analysis:

This seemingly innocuous act was far more exasperating and revolutionary than outright rebellion would have been. Rebellion simply

---

[126] Wink, Walter. *Engaging the Powers: Discernment and Resistance in a World of Domination.* Minneapolis. Fortress Press. 1992. Kindle. Location 2071-2072.

> *acknowledges the absoluteness and ultimacy of the emperor's power, and attempts to seize it. Prayer denies it altogether by acknowledging a higher power. Rebellion would have focused solely on the physical institution and its current incumbents and attempted to displace them by an act of superior force. But prayer challenged the very spirituality of the empire itself...*
>
> *...Such sedition could not go unpunished. With rebels the solution was simple. No one challenged the state's right to execute rebels. They had bought into the power-game on the empire's terms and lost, and the rules of the game required their liquidation. The rebels themselves knew this before they started. But what happens when the state executes those who are praying for it? When Christians knelt down in the Colosseum to pray as the lions bore down on them, something sullied the audience's thirst for revenge... It was a contest of all the brute force of Rome against those who merely prayed. Who would have predicted that the tiny sect would win?[127]*

Of course, we also have to ask what it means to win. This relates back to the beginning of this book and my critique of Barack Obama's presidency. The tiny sect who prayed went on to become the state religion of Rome and later to form

---

[127] Wink, Walter. *Naming the Powers: The Language of Power in the New Testament.* Fortress Press. 1984. Kindle. Location 1265

the justification for the Witch Trials and the Inquisition. As a result, we must acknowledge the victory inherent (for Christians) in the survival of Christianity and its elevation. But we must also consider that the elevation of Christianity came at great cost to the core values contained in its original message. In any case, one thing is for sure: Having your revolution adopted by the very state (or institution) whose values it once opposed comes at a price in terms of the clarity and integrity of your message unless the state or other institution has experienced a shift in consciousness. In other words, you have to ask who is changing the consciousness of whom. As Wink noted:

> *The orthodox church, for its part, rigidly cleaved to materiality but soon found itself the darling of Constantine. Called on to legitimate the empire, the church abandoned much of its social critique. The Powers were soon divorced from political affairs and made into airy spirits that preyed only on individuals.*[128]

And that, my friends, is the rest of the story.

Of course, this reality persists today in the United States as the religious right has become the champion of the ugliest excesses of the capitalist oligarchy. There is a long history between Christianity and the most violent, dominating, exploitative regimes on the planet. It is not surprising to

---

[128] Wink, Walter. *Naming the Powers: The Language of Power in the New Testament.* Fortress Press. 1984. Kindle. Location 1288.

me that the Christian right has risen in power and visibility at exactly the moment when the United States has ceased to honor democratic principles; at the exact moment when it has, in fact, become a ruthless oligarchy backed up by the hands of the tyrannical national security state. Therefore, as a matter of clarification, note that I have cited Walter Wink's work extensively in this book not because he is a Christian, but because he is a seer. Here is what he had to say about the national security state and Christianity:

> *By divine right the state has the power to order its citizens to sacrifice their lives to maintain the privileges enjoyed by the few. By divine decree it utilizes violence to cleanse the world of evil opponents who resist the nation's sway. Wealth and prosperity are the right of those who rule in such a state. And the name of God—any god, the Christian God included—can be invoked as having specially blessed and favored the supremacy of the chosen nation and its ruling caste.*[129]

In terms of violent revolution, the material above highlights its greatest tactical weaknesses. First, no one really challenges the right of the state to execute rebels, especially on the battle field. For this reason, violent rebellion does little to expose the true consciousness of the state or its willingness to massacre its own in the name of security and the proliferation

---

[129] Wink, Walter. *Engaging the Powers: Discernment and Resistance in a World of Domination*. Minneapolis. Fortress Press. 1992. Kindle. Location 418.

of the state and its agenda. Further, it carries with it a risk that those who seek to overturn the corrupt state will only wind up imposing their own agenda on an unwilling bureaucracy and its citizenry. For violent revolution to be effective, it must arise as a result of a critical shift in mass consciousness. It must have as its aim the removal of the last vestiges of a stubborn regime. Even still there is a significant risk that the revolution will, itself, replicate the values of the Domination System. All of that said, if you can cut off the tutor's head cleanly, and effectively, there is no moral reason to spare him.

Violence as self defense is another matter to be considered. When I think of this kind of violence, I am immediately drawn to a passage from the book called *The Way of the Peaceful Warrior*. The passage is as follows:

> *...A large dark shape emerged from the mist. My half-forgotten dream flashed in my mind but vanished as I saw another shape, the a third: three men...The third approached us and drew a stiletto from his worn leather jacket. I felt my pulse pounding through my temples.*
>
> *'Give me your money,' he commanded.*
>
> *Not thinking clearly, I stepped toward him, reaching for my wallet, and stumbled forward.*
>
> *He was startled and rushed towards me, slashing with his knife. Socrates, moving faster than I had*

ever seen before, caught the man's wrist, whirled around and threw him into the street, just as another thug lunged for me; Socrates had kicked his legs out from under him with a lightening sweep. Before the third attacker could even move, Soc was upon him, taking him down with a wristlock and a sweeping motion of his arm. He sat down on the man and said, 'Don't you think you ought to consider nonviolence.'

One of the men started to get up when Socrates let out a powerful shout and the man fell backward. By then the leader had picked himself out of the street, found his knife, and was limping furiously towards Socrates. Socrates stood up, lifted the man he'd been sitting on, and threw him towards the knifeman, yelling, 'Catch!' They tumbled to the concrete; then, in a wild rage, all three came screaming at us in a last desperate assault.

The next few minutes were blurred. I remember being pushed by Socrates and falling. Then it was quiet, except for a moan. Socrates stood still, then shook his arms loose and took a deep breath. He threw the knives into the sewer...

...He turned to the three men stretched out on the pavement, knelt, and felt their pulses... Only then did I realize he was doing his best to heal them![130]

---

[130] Millman, Dan. *The Way of the Peaceful Warrior.* Novato. H.J. Kramer. 1980, 1984, Revised Edition, 2000. Kindle. Page 128. Location 2201-2217.

For me this passage embodies a very important truth. Nothing we are talking about here is based on hate or even anger (though our feelings of hate or anger might alert us to the need for action of some sort). It is based in the practical reality of what must be done. At its most basic level, it is about survival. At its highest level, it is about the kind of life you want to create and about the kind of things to which you are willing to consent. It is about the commitments you are willing to make and about what is needed to support those commitments.

The students in Tiananmen Square and the early Christian Martyrs died protecting their core principles and for the sake of exposing the inner spirit/structure of their respective empires. By contrast, violent revolutionaries often kill and die for the right and the ability to impose an agenda of their own. Those like Socrates and Ivan stand in stark contrast because they simply do what is necessary to refuse the agenda that others would otherwise succeed in imposing. In these cases, there is violence. Its aim is not, however, the subjugation of the other party, but rather, the wholehearted insistence on one's own freedom and bodily autonomy.

It is with these distinctions in mind that I now turn back to the Zapatista movement in southern Mexico…

In the early days of the Zapatista movement, I believe the Zapatistas intended to overthrow the Mexican government. Only they know for sure whether this is what they intended and only they know what they thought would fill the vacuum. It did not take long for this dream to die on the vine, so to speak. There were heavy casualties, particularly on the Zapatista side. Regardless, this was no ordinary armed insurrection, not by a long shot.

Perhaps the most remarkable fact about this rebellion is that the commander who led the siege on San Cristóbal de las Casas, the city where I am now sitting some 19 years later, was a woman, a major in the Zapatista National Liberation Army (the "EZLN"). Right from the start, the Zapatistas turned the values of the Domination System upside down and inside out as the subjugation of women is part and parcel of the Domination System. This distinction is undeniable, even if their original goal was to overthrow the Mexican state in what looked like a traditional rebel stance.

In an odd twist of fate, it was Marcos who garnered the spotlight, not the women. Here is what Marcos said about the moment when he first spoke to the press:

> *From that moment on, the impeccable military action of the taking of San Cristóbal de las Casas is blurred, and with it the fact that it was a woman—a rebel indigenous woman—who commanded the entire operation is erased.*[131]

---

[131] Ponce De Leon, Juana and Subcomandante Insurgente Marcos. "The Glass to See to the Other Side." *Our Word is Our Weapon, Selected Writings.* New York. Seven Stories Press. 2002. Kindle. Location 523.

It is important not to gloss over this history as it tells us we are not on the ordinary, everyday terrain of a garden variety rebellion. The presence of these women in top leadership positions is a crucial indicator that something original and fantastic was afoot from the first moments of the Zapatista rebellion. In fact, it was not Marcos who orchestrated the suppression of the significant role played by the women. It was the system itself, a fact that was explained as follows:

> *The federales' pride is deeply wounded: the Zapatistas have broken the blockade and, adding insult to injury, various municipalities have been taken by a unit headed by a woman. Much money is spent to keep this unacceptable event from the people.*[132]

The originality of the situation continued to emerge and has continued to do so for nearly 20 years now. On June 12, 1994, the Zapatistas addressed Mexican civil society. Among other statements, the Second Declaration of the Lacandon Jungle contained the following statements acknowledging the power of civil society and placing the Zapatista rebels beneath this power:

> *Civil society assumed the duty of preserving our country. It showed its disapproval of the massacre, and it obliged us to hold a dialogue with the government...*

---

[132] Ponce De Leon, Juana and Subcomandante Insurgente Marcos. "The Glass to See to the Other Side." *Our Word is Our Weapon, Selected Writings*. New York. Seven Stories Press. 2002. Kindle. Location 609.

...Our sovereignty resides in civil society. Only the people can altar or modify our form of government. It is to them that we address this Second Declaration of the Lacondan Jungle...

...We will continue to respect the cease-fire in order to permit civil society to organize in whatever forms they consider pertinent toward the goal of achieving a transition to democracy in our country...

...We reject the manipulation and the attempts to separate our just demands from the demands of the Mexican people. We are Mexicans, and we will not put aside our demands nor our arms until we have democracy, freedom, and justice for all.

...We call upon civil society to retake the protagonist's role that it first took up in order to stop the military phase of the war. We call upon civil society to organize itself to direct the peaceful efforts toward democracy, freedom, and justice. Democratic change is the only alternative to war.[133]

This communication accomplished three important things. First, it aligned the Zapatistas with Mexican civil society and placed the EZLN on the side of and at the disposal of both civil society and peaceful democratic

---

[133] Ponce De Leon, Juana and Subcomandante Insurgente Marcos. "The Glass to See to the Other Side." *Our Word is Our Weapon, Selected Writings*. New York. Seven Stories Press. 2002. Kindle. Location 1288-1315.

processes. Second, it acknowledged the supremacy of Mexican civil society in the process of directing democratic change. Third, it announced the claim of the Zapatistas on their Mexican heritage. When combined with other communications such as the following dated March 1, 1994, this marked a tremendous shift in the Zapatista strategy away from conquering Mexico and towards engaging civil society in the process of advocating for a broader dream of a truly free, inclusive, and democratic Mexico:

> *To the Mexican people*
>
> *To the people and governments of the world:*
>
> *IN OUR DREAMS we have seen another world, an honest world, a world decidedly more fair than the one in which we now live. We saw that in this world there was no need for armies; peace, justice and liberty were so common that no one talked about them as far-off concepts, but as things such as bread, birds, air, water…And so we started to move forward to attain this dream, make it come and sit down at our tables, light our homes, grow in our cornfields, fill the hearts of our children, wipe our sweat, heal our history. And it was for all. This is what we want. Nothing more, nothing less.*

> *Now we follow our path toward our true heart to ask it what we must do. We will return to our mountains to speak in our own tongue and in our own time.*[134]

This particular statement was a predictor of things to come. After many long years and many attempts to negotiate with the Mexican government to no avail, the Zapatistas cut off their dialogue with what they call the "bad government" and set about the task of establishing their own, autonomous communities. This year the Zapatistas celebrated 10 years of autonomous self rule. In a 2001 interview with Gloria Muñoz, Major Infantry Insurgent Moses explained the decision as follows:

> *The dialogue with the government didn't work but it enriched us, because we met more people and it gave us more ideas. After the "Color of the Earth march" in 2001 we said that with or without a law we were going to build our government the way we wanted.*[135]

The Zapatistas did indeed return to their mountains, and they turned towards their hearts. Having gained enough territory and enough credibility with the world community and Mexican civil society to sustain their movement, after nearly ten years of struggle, the Zapatistas let go of resistance and revolution as their primary goal. With the taste of

---

[134] Ponce De Leon, Juana and Subcomandante Insurgente Marcos. "The Glass to See to the Other Side." *Our Word is Our Weapon, Selected Writings*. New York. Seven Stories Press. 2002. Kindle. Location 763-775.

[135] http://roarmag.org/2013/08/escuelita-zapatista-10-year-autonomy/

freedom in their mouths, they set about the task of creating their dream. Now the Zapatistas describe their governing style as one that emanates from the bottom up. They speak of a government that rules by obeying.

I find in this story all the evidence I need that sometimes the right move is to simply cut off the tutor's head and sometimes the answer is to defend yourself with all the strength you have. The Zapatistas say they are the "race who must die in order to live."[136] This reminds me of what Walter Wink had to say about dying to the influence of the Domination System. Whether they accomplished it by the actual sacrifice of life in service of something new, which did occur, or by having metaphorically died to the mandates of a system that allows the exploitation of the many by the few, one thing is for sure: The Zapatistas somehow managed to come in contact with their own intrinsic worth and thereby to connect with and to fulfill the desires of their own hearts.

Let these words from a recent article by Raúl Zibechi really sink into your soul; really take it in:

> *In a December 30 [2012] communiqué, Subcomandante Marcos assured that 'over the years we have gotten stronger, and we have significantly improved our living conditions. Our standard of living is higher than those of indigenous communities*

---

[136] Ponce De Leon, Juana and Subcomandante Insurgente Marcos. "The Glass to See to the Other Side." *Our Word is Our Weapon, Selected Writings.* New York. Seven Stories Press. 2002. Kindle. Location 539.

> *who receive handouts from the government and waste them on alcohol and other useless things.' He adds that, unlike what happens in communities linked to the PRI, in Zapatista communities 'women are not sold as merchandise,' and that 'indigenous PRI members go to our hospitals, clinics and laboratories because there isn't any medicine, equipment, doctors or qualified personnel in those run by the government.'*
>
> *'We don't have difficulties anymore,' says Julian [a campesino], sitting on a rustic wood stool in his tin roofed house with wooden walls and an earthen floor...*
>
> *...All things considered, he's right when he says that the worst is behind them — the hacendado's whip, humiliation, hunger, violence, and the rape of daughters. On January 1, 1994, the hacendados fled, and the capangas ran behind them.*[137]

Many of the tactics adopted by the Zapatistas remind me of those used by another revered activist: Martin Luther King, Jr. For the sake of comparison and to lay the foundation for the remarks that follow, I include here key passages from Martin Luther King, Jr.'s "I Have a Dream Speech:"

> *I say to you today, my friends, so even though we face the difficulties of today and tomorrow, I still have a*

---

[137] http://roarmag.org/2013/09/raul-zibechi-escuelita-zapatista-autonomy/

dream. It is a dream deeply rooted in the American dream.

I have a dream that one day this nation will rise up and live out the true meaning of its creed: "We hold these truths to be self-evident: that all men are created equal."

I have a dream that one day on the red hills of Georgia the sons of former slaves and the sons of former slave owners will be able to sit down together at the table of brotherhood.

I have a dream that one day even the state of Mississippi, a state sweltering with the heat of injustice, sweltering with the heat of oppression, will be transformed into an oasis of freedom and justice.

I have a dream that my four little children will one day live in a nation where they will not be judged by the color of their skin but by the content of their character.

I have a dream today.

I have a dream that one day, down in Alabama, with its vicious racists, with its governor having his lips dripping with the words of interposition and nullification; one day right there in Alabama, little black boys and black girls will be able to join hands *with little white boys and white girls as sisters and brothers.*

I have a dream today.

I have a dream that one day every valley shall be exalted, every hill and mountain shall be made low, the rough places will be made plain, and the crooked places will be made straight, and the glory of the Lord shall be revealed, and all flesh shall see it together.

Martin Luther King, Jr.'s genius was that he staked a claim to the American dream, and like the Zapatistas, attempted to make his dream a common aspiration for a more inclusive, freer society. He challenged a nation to repent and he made huge inroads into changing the collective consciousness. As Walter Wink noted, "he resolutely refused to treat racism as a political issue only; he insisted that it be seen also as a moral and spiritual sickness…He called upon a nation to repent, and significant numbers did."[138] Yet, his final fate was more like that of the early Christian martyrs and the Chinese students.

Martin Luther King, Jr. adhered very strictly to non-violence. Perhaps this was his best tactical decision for a host of reasons, not the least of which is that there was no way to cut off the tutor's head. What Martin Luther King, Jr. sought to confront was a systemic problem that could never

---

[138] Wink, Walter. *Naming the Powers: The Language of Power in the New Testament.* Fortress Press. 1984. Kindle. Location 1517.

have been resolved by the mere taking of territory. There was no road to freedom save the collective transformation of American society. Nonetheless, though he articulated a new dream and made huge inroads towards seeing it fulfilled, he did not protect himself. Instead, he died making visible and challenging the true inner spirit of the Powers he sought to expose. His claim of right on a shared American dream and his successful critique of racism as a spiritual sickness largely died with him – at least in terms of how the movement evolved immediately thereafter. Soon after his death, the movement devolved from successfully challenging the concrete outer structures of the Powers while also addressing the collective consciousness of a nation into a battle between white power and black power.[139]

The Zapatistas, by contrast have sustained their movement for 20 years. Perhaps this is because they seemingly understand exactly what I outlined at the beginning of this chapter: Non-violence is a tactical decision, not a moral imperative. It seems that they understand when violence serves and when non-violence provides greater tactical advantages. The Zapatistas have never put down the guns that secure their territories nor have they ever ceased their battle for the hearts and minds of the world and of Mexican civil society. In this regard, they have managed to combine the best of four worlds: non-violent resistance; self protection; a sustained challenge to the collective consciousness of the

---

[139] Wink, Walter. *Naming the Powers: The Language of Power in the New Testament*. Fortress Press. 1984. Kindle. Location 1517.

world; and finally, the proactive articulation and fulfillment of their own dream.

The Zapatistas have always seen their dream as more than personal. They have invited the world to witness and to study their example. They have even invited others to support their dream and many nongovernmental organizations from all over the world have done so. They have invited everyone to become a Zapatista in his/her own way in his/her own land and life. Recently the Zapatistas hosted a school for activists. In an article about the school, the journalist captured this invitation and its limits perfectly as follows:

> 'What for?' some may ask. 'The Zapatista example is one that cannot be followed everywhere: we don't live in the jungles of Chiapas to create rebel armies and autonomous communities,' others say. You may have heard these arguments before, as have I. Well, the answer is simple: the Zapatistas never projected themselves as the one and only example to be followed. They have constructed a world in which they have realized **their own** vision of freedom and autonomy, and continue to fight for a world in which **other worlds are possible**.
>
> That's the world they invite us to experience. And, on the last day of the Escuelita, the Zapatistas will tell the students: 'the school is over, what are you still doing here? Go back to your lands!' After all, 'We didn't invite you in order to recruit you, train you,

> un-train you, program you, or, like they say, 'reset' you. We have opened a door and invited you to come in and see our house, to see what we have constructed with the help of people all over the world... The outcome of the Escuelita is not militancy, belonging, submission to command, nor fanaticism. What follows the Escuelita is something that you, and only you, can decide... and act upon."[140]

This is where the collective now gets reduced to the individual. These concepts and examples are meaningless if we cannot apply them in our own lives. Violence is a big word. It means, at least to me, more than just hand to hand combat. It can, for instance, also mean taking action that will intentionally and irrevocably alter the path of another person. Some people think of violence as a cruelty. When it is undertaken in a clean, clear, straightforward manner that is neither oriented towards domination nor motivated by hatred or revenge, violence can be clear communication and direct action in service of one's own well being. Often we think that if we are indirect, if we mince words or soften our message, we are being kind. I challenge you to question this and to consider that the most compassionate thing you can do is often also the most clear, most seemingly unkind thing. This establishes the boundaries. It lets everyone know where they stand. In drawing again from the Zapatistas, sometimes we must become the voice that takes up arms in order to be heard.

---

[140] http://roarmag.org/2013/08/escuelita-zapatista-10-year-autonomy/

Let us not, however, lose track of the most powerful message contained in the Zapatista story. Ultimately, what we are fighting for is the freedom and the means to pursue and fulfill our own dreams. The struggle that we undertake when we confront that which would destroy us (or even sap our resources and our potential) is the struggle for human dignity and the blossoming of human potential. Further, the Zapatistas did not ultimately destroy government, they redeemed it. They built an alternative system focused on the needs of the people. Therefore, the key lesson to be taken from this discussion does not center around the means of resisting, but rather around its purpose: to support the redemption of The Powers and the unfolding of our highest potential as individuals and as a species.

In order to take these lessons to heart, we need not cast the Zapatistas as the victim-heroes of this story and the Mexican government as the villain. The situation on the ground in Chiapas is a complicated one. There are no easy solutions nor are there bright lines drawn in the sands of time. Both sides are human. Both fall shockingly short of the ideal at times. Perhaps that is the point. The lessons we can take from this are, in their least developed state, about survival and about the tender points of hope that take shape on the ragged edge of nothing left to lose. At a more developed level, they are about making tactical and strategic decisions regarding what is needed in order to fulfill vision, purpose, and mission. None of this is neat. It certainly isn't pretty. But it is real.

If you are ready to risk destroying what needs to be destroyed in the service of your freedom and the unfolding of your potential, go to www.rebeckaeggers.com to find out how you can get connected to Rebecka and The Passion Path. The Passion Path is the path of the Passionate Warrior and of whole-hearted, purposeful, and skillful living.

The Birth of The Passionate Warrior ∞ Passion Path Redemption

> *If you look carefully, you might see the spark lighting the economic enlightenment's fuse: the global economy is reaching a decisive, defining moment. What powered prosperity in the twentieth century won't—and can't— power prosperity in the twenty-first.* ∞ Umair Haque

> *It appears that dignity is contagious...* ∞ Subcomandante Insurgente Marcos

Returning now to the symbolism of the banyan tree, I want to try to address what it means to be "like the seed of the banyan tree germinating in the structures of the Domination System, putting down roots, and eventually, changing the very character and nature of the host."

When I left corporate America, it was with a heavy heart and a sense of complete hopelessness. I recall asking a colleague where he thought the intersection was between social justice and capitalism. He assured me there wasn't one and that I should just give up searching for it. Another colleague told the story of how a well known corporate conglomerate has its back office functions so completely automated that it can quickly and easily move these operations to whichever country is offering the greatest sweetheart deal in terms of tax breaks etc. This is a fine thing if you are on the side of the winner—the global capitalist machine—and it is a terrible thing if you are among the "human resources" impacted by the whimsical decisions of people in far away places. In the long run, we all lose. In this inevitable race to the bottom there are winners today who will eventually join the ranks of the losers tomorrow. Umair Haque, author and economic advisor, has very aptly described what gives rise to this race to the bottom as follows:

> Conversely, you might ask, what about developing countries? You'd be right again. Though they aim for industrial era growth—despite all that is now apparent about its shortcomings—it is a hungry maw, and there isn't enough oil, copper, credit, employment, or export demand in the world for every nation to continue achieving prosperity that way. Doing so quickly deteriorates into a zero-sum game of beggar-

thy-neighbor, where growth in some countries is counterbalanced by stagnation in others.[141]

When the whole shebang of my corporate life blew up in my face, my heavy heart and my hopelessness led me to leave the United States and to establish a new home in Chiapas. I wanted nothing to do with a system as heartless and shortsighted as the one I just described. Even worse yet, I saw no hope for humanity, no silver lining, no way out. I certainly did not want to invest my time and talent in helping the system to proliferate.

When I moved to Chiapas, I was running from this zero-sum game Umair Haque described. It wasn't that I thought it did not exist in Chiapas. In knew it existed in its worst excesses here. It was that I thought I could disappear into the untamed mountains and somehow avoid engaging the system called industrial era capitalism. I thought I could be a voice for something new, and of course, I have become a voice for change. But when I came here, I had lost hope that capitalism could be redeemed. In a very real sense, I came here to drop out.

Recently, I found a ray of hope for capitalism and the economy, for myself, and for the world in Umair Haque's writing and in another book written by the CEO of Whole Foods Market. Both books epitomize what it means to be the

---

[141] Haque, Umair. *The New Capitalist Manifesto: Building Disruptively Better Business*. Harvard Business Review. Boston. 2011. Print. Page 5.

seed of change germinating in, and ultimately changing the very character of its host.

Before I begin this discussion, let me say that I recognize the inherent limitations of the system we are in, and even of the players who are beginning to change it – perhaps more than most. Nonetheless, this emerging body of work is worthy of consideration. It provides an explanation of what we are up against and articulates the kind of work that will need to be done in terms of redeeming the Powers. Better yet, it proves that our circumstance and existing market forces actually reward those who are learning to think beyond the boundaries of industrial age capitalism.

This is all truly hopeful news because the global community cannot function without an economy. Further, to destroy the one we have without creating a replacement would create hardship and death throughout the world. Finally, the corporate structures that are in place are global in their reach and in their infrastructures. If anyone has the power to make a huge and essential impact on the way we have been living, it is these global institutions of almost infinite reach.

Imagine, if you will, what might be possible if these Powers, these global corporate actors, got on board for a new kind of capitalism that is based on the notion that all stakeholders must be considered rather than simply following a mandate for the pure maximization of profits to one set of stakeholders (i.e., investors). What if they decided that their mandate included not just considering the impact on all stakeholders, but actually enriching them? What if the corporate mission became the creation of value for all stakeholders?

While you are contemplating the potential in such a radical shift, let me back up.

More than anything, what the Zapatistas stood up against is capitalism. Marcos has commented on this extensively. He has talked of the petroleum, farm products, minerals, natural gas, and indigenous work and wares that leave Chiapas in what he has described as something akin to a blood letting. Perhaps this quote captures the issue best:

> *Chiapas' experience of exploitation goes back for centuries. In past times, wood, fruits, animals, and men went to the metropolis through the veins of exploitation, just as they do today. Like the banana republics, but at the peak of neoliberalism and 'libertarian revolutions,' the Southeast continues to export raw materials, just as it did 500 years ago. It continues to import capitalism's principal product: death and misery.*[142]

It was my own fledgling understanding of capitalism and its impact that first brought me to Chiapas. Every morning when I woke up, I vowed to have a good day. But then, each

---

[142] Ponce De Leon, Juana and Subcomandante Insurgente Marcos. "The Glass to See to the Other Side." *Our Word is Our Weapon, Selected Writings*. New York. Seven Stories Press. 2002. Kindle. Page 25. Location 911.

day by 9 AM, I felt drained of all my hope and all my life force. I could not understand why. I had a competent and caring boss. I had all the money I could have desired. I had a house, vacations, two closets full of clothes...I was a woman sitting at the top of a ladder most people never climb. Without spoiling the story contained in the Epilogue, suffice it to say that when I encountered the Zapatista story, I came to Chiapas looking for answers about my own life. I found them in spades.

Until recently, I knew what I had observed. I understood why I felt defeated each day by 9 AM. It is because industrial era capitalism extracts being and it means to do so. What I could not do was explain this phenomenon in a coherent way and begin to address it, at least intellectually. In his book, *The New Capitalist Manifesto: Building a Disruptively Better Business*, Umair Haque explained it perfectly. Here is what he said:

> *Imagine two worlds: The first is a **big** world of abundant resources and raw materials, an **empty** world where demand is infrequent and easily satisfied, and a **stable** world where disasters are infrequent and weak. The second is a **tiny** world, emptying of raw resources, a **crowded** world where demand is always hungry, and a **fragile** world, where contagion of every kind can flow across the globe in a matter of minutes, days, or weeks. A big, empty, stable world is like a vast, placid, untouched*

game reserve. But a tiny, crowded, and fragile world is like an ark. Industrial era capitalism was built for a big, empty, stable world. But at the dawn of the twenty-first century, the world is more like an ark—tiny, fragile, and crowded.

*Consuming, borrowing, and utilizing are the engines of prosperity in a big, empty, stable world, but the engines of crisis in a tiny, fragile, and crowded one. Three defining characteristics of what I call the industrial era's 'dumb' growth, the last several decades have been their culmination. They've been an era of growth driven by the global **poor subsidizing the rich** to fuel the **overconsumption** of an array of more and more ephemeral goods and services dependent on steeply **diminishing returns economics**, where the natural world, communities, and society are marginalized…*[143]

Haque went on to describe something he calls, *"deep debt"* as follows:

*What I call **deep debt** is the harm institutionalized by the cornerstones of industrial era capitalism. It can be conceived of as a debt owed to people, communities, society, the natural world, or future generations. Debt is simply shifted costs and borrowed benefits, from an economic point of view… Though industrial*

---

[143] Haque, Umair. *The New Capitalist Manifesto: Building Disruptively Better Business.* Harvard Business Review. Boston. 2011. Print. Pages 6-7.

era capitalism's debt is often invisible and uncounted, it must be settled or repaid for prosperity to expand...

...That's why, while capitalism is unquestionably responsible for prosperity, industrial age capitalism is also inextricably linked to crisis...

*...Think of the crisis **behind** today's crises...all are underpinned first by a great imbalance that undercounts costs and overcounts benefits...More and more people are beginning to sense that the mounting unsustainability crisis is interconnected—symptoms of a larger global system that is out of balance...*

*In the great imbalance, industrial era capitalism's cornerstones institutionalize what economists call negative externalities—or negative impacts excluded from market prices—making them systemic, and on the flip side, deinstitutionalize or limit positive externalities—benefits not included in market prices. Its institutions produce **too much economic destruction for too little creation**. That's what the great imbalance means.*[144]

Put another way, and at the risk of sounding repetitive: industrial era capitalism extracts being and it means to do so. It is the perfect symbol of the Domination System. Just

---

[144] Haque, Umair. *The New Capitalist Manifesto: Building Disruptively Better Business*. Harvard Business Review. Boston. 2011. Pages 13-15.

like the system itself, it made sense in one kind of world, and according to one set of values and perceptions. It made sense in a big, empty, stable world. But it no longer makes sense. Industrial era capitalism will destroy us all or else create a permanent underclass of slave labor in order to sustain the imbalance. This approach makes no sense in a world that Haque rightfully described as an ark.

The Zapatistas have been pointing out this imbalance for years. They did not put it in terms of externalized costs, but Marcos very aptly described the imbalance in August of 1992 as follows:

> *A handful of businesses, one of which is the Mexican state, take all the wealth out of Chiapas and in exchange leave behind their mortal and pestilent mark: in 1989 these businesses took 1,222,669,000,000 pesos from Chiapas and only left behind 616,340,000,000 pesos worth of credit and public works. More than 600,000,000,000 went to the belly of the beast...*
>
> *One million indigenous people live in these lands and share a disorienting nightmare with mestizos and latinos: their only option, five hundred years after the "Meeting of Two Worlds," is to die of poverty and repression.*[145]

---

[145] Ponce De Leon, Juana and Subcomandante Insurgente Marcos. "The Glass to See to the Other Side." *Our Word is Our Weapon, Selected Writings*. New York. Seven Stories Press. 2002. Kindle. Pages 22-26. Location 855-911.

For decades, the developed world exported the values of poverty and repression. Now the Western democracies are finding out exactly how the machine they created works. It has no alliances and it is no respecter of nations or persons. What was done to the third world in the name of progress is coming home and it has no intentions of sparing the countrymen and women of those who spawned the beast.

When it comes to the Powers, none is so powerful or destructive at this moment in history, as the global capitalist machine. If we do not succeed in shifting the collective consciousness around the great imbalances that Umair Haque and the Zapatistas have highlighted, there will not be much left of us, our human potential, or this earth. The built-in methodology of industrial era capitalism is the externalization of costs and the raping, looting, and pillaging of raw materials and human potential.

Fortunately, a transformation is underway!

In their book *Conscious Capitalism: Liberating the Heroic Spirit of Business*, John Mackey (Co-Ceo of Whole Foods Market) and Raj Sisodia have articulated an alternative. Like Umair Haque, they began by expressing the "Unintended Consequences of Low-Consciousness Business" as follows:

> *When businesspeople operate with a low level of consciousness about the purpose and impact of business, they engage in trade-off thinking that creates many harmful, unintended consequences. Such businesses*

view their purpose as profit maximization and treat all participants in the system as a means to an end. This approach may succeed in creating material prosperity in the short term, but the resultant price tag of long-term systemic problems is increasingly unacceptable and unaffordable.[146]

They went on to challenge the genesis of this mentality, namely the notion that maximizing profits for investors should be the sole organizing principle of business. They said, "We need to recapture the narrative and restore its true essence: that the purpose of business is to improve our lives and create value for stakeholders."[147] They continued noting that, "Free-enterprise capitalism must be grounded in an ethical system based on value creation for all stakeholders. Money is one measure of value, but it is certainly not the only measure."[148]

The following quote sums up the transformation of consciousness that they are advocating:

We humans can choose to exist at the caterpillar level, consuming all we can, taking as much as possible from the world and giving little back. We are also capable of evolving to a degree that is no less dramatic than

---

[146] Mackey, John and Raj Sisodia. *Conscious Capitalism: Liberating the Heroic Spirit of Business*. Harvard Business Review Press. Boston. 2013. Print. Page 17.

[147] Mackey, John and Raj Sisodia. *Conscious Capitalism: Liberating the Heroic Spirit of Business*. Harvard Business Review Press. Boston. 2013. Print. Page 20.

[148] Mackey, John and Raj Sisodia. *Conscious Capitalism: Liberating the Heroic Spirit of Business*. Harvard Business Review Press. Boston. 2013. Print. Page 22.

what happens to a caterpillar, transforming ourselves into beings who create value for others and help make the world more beautiful. The same is true of corporations. They too can exist at a caterpillar level, where they strive only to maximize their own profits, extracting resources from nature and from human beings to do so. Or they can reinvent themselves as agents of creation and collaboration, magnificent entities capable of cross-pollinating human potentials in ways that nothing else can, creating multiple kinds of value for everyone they touch.[149]

Similarly, Umair Haque has articulated the two fundamental axioms of this transformative shift within capitalism as follows:

> *The first axiom is about minimization: through the act of exchange, an **organization cannot**, by action or inaction, **allow** people, communities, society, the natural world or future generations to come to economic harm.*
>
> *Conversely, the second axiom is about maximization: the fundamental challenge facing countries, companies, and economies in the twenty-first century is creating more value of higher **quality**, not just low-quality of a higher **quantity**. Think of it as **reconceiving value creation**: not merely creating*

---

[149] Mackey, John and Raj Sisodia. *Conscious Capitalism: Liberating the Heroic Spirit of Business*. Harvard Business Review Press. Boston. 2013. Print. Page 26.

larger amounts of thin, inconsequential value, but learning to create a value of greater worth.[150]

Both of these books went on to articulate the means for achieving this new vision of capitalism. I am not going to take you through that analysis. I couldn't do it justice in a brief synopsis. Further, it is not necessary that I do so. The important take away from this discussion is not really about the nuts and bolts of how modern businesses are achieving this transformation (as some are, at least in part). It is about the changes that are taking place in the mythology that governs capitalism in the twenty-first century.

A shift is underway within the corporate structure from the mythology of the Domination System to a new mythology of empowerment, creativity, and greater inclusion. Accordingly, some of the most impactful Passionate Warriors on the planet are those who are well positioned within the corporate culture to usher in this new point of intersection between social justice and global capitalism. Further, this is a perfect example of why it is important to place our emphasis on the transformation of the collective consciousness so that we can see the Powers transformed either through the creation of parallel systems or through a radical change in the narrative adopted by existing systems. This proves out Walter Wink's assertion that some of the most important work

---

[150] Haque, Umair. *The New Capitalist Manifesto: Building Disruptively Better Business*. Harvard Business Review. Boston. 2011. Print. Pages 25-26.

involves a challenge to the inner structure or consciousness of the Powers.

Don't get me wrong. I think this whole idea of transforming capitalism would be a losing venture but for one key fact: Changing the mythology governing capitalism is economically profitable. Here is what Umair Haque reported regarding the performance of what he called the "constructive capitalists":

> *But while the equity markets stagnated, the stock prices of constructive capitalists held ground, gained ground—and sometimes, skyrocketed...That's the power of twenty-first century economics at work: during the most stagnant decade in financial history, a difference in returns of 300 percent.*[151]

Industrial era capitalism is dead whether its proponents know it or not. It is a self limiting system because it uses and destroys resources, communities, and people as though they were infinite. The real question is whether we will continue as we have been until there is nothing left to salvage or whether we will role up our sleeves and do the work necessary to usher in a new era that is both sustainable and aimed at creating real value for everyone.

What I am saying is that there is no need to make a polar flip to a system where those who have resources become slaves

---

[151] Haque, Umair. *The New Capitalist Manifesto: Building Disruptively Better Business*. Harvard Business Review. Boston. 2011. Print. Page 32.

to those who are in need. We are not talking about a socialist utopia here or even class warfare. We are talking about is a system that measures the externalized costs for what they are: an indicator of destruction rather than construction. It turns out there is more profit to be had in genuine value creation and sustainability than there is in looting and pillaging. Who would have ever guessed?

What I am saying is that an us-versus-them mentality is neither useful nor transformative in a situation in which, like the one we are facing, a solution cannot be fashioned through the separation of factions. Further, us-versus-them is the motto of industrial age capitalists. It is an us-and-them mentality that will ultimately achieve the most impressive changes as the global capitalist machine is deeply entrenched in the same way race relations presented a national challenge during the American Civil Rights Movement. It is a true partnership between capitalism (or at least economic leaders) and the world that has the greatest potential to bring about the fastest and most viable change

This is incredibly instructive because, there are so many people who are invested in the idea that we should simply destroy all that we have built and start from scratch or that the redistribution of wealth will solve our problems. This is a dangerous and foolhardy line of thought not because what we have built is admirable or because wealth is equally distributed now, but because it is uninformed and it is based on a faulty premise. I am not saying that the imbalance in wealth created under the current system will not need to be addressed or that we do not need to build parallel and innovative economic systems. I am saying a redistribution of wealth and/or the destruction of our present economic system do not address the much needed shift in mythology and consciousness. Further, they may overlook key opportunities for collaboration

In short, before we resort to violent and/or non-violent resistance and/or destruction, we must first, last, and always ask ourselves where we want to go and what role those we have considered destroying might actually play in the transition if only we can mount a successful challenge to their mythology. Martin Luther King, Jr. understood this. This is why he staked a claim to his and his people's rightful participation in a shared and transformed American dream. The Zapatistas understood this as well. That is why the dreams they articulated were not theirs alone, but the dreams for and of a more just world for everyone where true democracy flourishes in the support of human dignity and potential.

At this moment in history, we are called upon by our deteriorating circumstances to move beyond the critique of capitalism and the Domination System; we are called upon to stake a common claim to the benefits of a new kind of economy and to insist that all stakeholders be recognized, considered, and enriched by it regardless of its form. But there is more. We are also being summoned to the table. We are being asked to participate in the creation of something powerful, compelling, and sustainable. Like the Zapatistas, we must begin by creating these things in our own lives, and then we must also constantly invite others to join us in doing so on a collective level.

This is the ultimate aim of The Passion Path: to activate your freedom, ignite your passion, and evoke your power so that you can fully invest in the fulfillment of your greatest human potential and fully participate in and contribute to the fulfillment of the shared dream: a society that invests in creating the infrastructure to support the full blossoming of human potential. This shared dream involves the transformation and reinvention of the Powers, including the economy and the global economic actors that control the economy.

It is with this in mind that I now choose to go forth in service of The Passion Path and as the agent of change I once committed to become. I claim in this moment my own individual freedom, passion, and power so that I might, in the words of Albert Camus, become so absolutely free that my very existence is an act of rebellion; that I might become so absolutely passionate, so absolutely powerful, and so absolutely fulfilled that my very existence denies the Domination System in principle, and thereby, threatens it in its entirety simply by standing in stark contrast to it. But I won't stop here. I am ready to get my hands dirty in the process of seeing the Powers transformed and reinvented; I am ready to do my part in supporting their shift from agents and enforcers of the Domination System to the structural supports of a society whose greatest aim is to bring to fruition our humanity and our individual and shared potential. As agents and enforcers of the Domination System, the Powers are top down enforcers. As structural supports of society, the Powers are more like the foundational, bottom up government of the Zapatistas.

If you think this bottom-up idea can't work in economic terms, I offer three key examples from Umair Haque's work. Threadless, a t-shirt manufacturer who has run circles around traditional retailers, like Old Navy and The Gap, offers its customers the chance to vote on which designs it manufactures. The customers decide the next trend and Threadless manufactures it in real time. Similarly, Lego now allows people to upload their own designs. Lego then manufactures what the Lego enthusiasts actually desire. Finally, Fair Trade, which offers small growers a chance to organize and bargain collectively with large entities, like Starbucks, receives a premium for its products. The Fair Trade members then decide how to use the premium for maximum results in their local communities. Here is what Umair Haque relayed regarding each of these examples:

> Now if you're thinking, '...but it's just a T-shirt company,' think again. Here's why what Threadless is doing matters to you. That radical new approach to managing T-shirt production has yielded growth and profitability in an industry almost entirely bereft of it. Yesterday's giants—Gap, Tommy Hilfiger, and

Nautica—have spent the last decade struggling with a long, slow, seemingly irreversible slide into decline…Threadless…built a business worth, by my informal estimate, more than $100 million, growing by leaps and bounds, already enjoying industry-leading margins, slowly, but surely wrestling market power from them…Threadless churns out innovative new T-shirts day after day, while Gap struggles to eke out a dozen barely interesting ones per season…

Lego Factory doesn't just minimize Lego's costs. It minimizes customers' losses as well. The same bricks are turned into designs that match individual customer preferences more efficiently. Because I am getting exactly the Lego set I want, fewer resources are wasted…Lego is creating thick value in toys—achieving loss advantage—through a value cycle that is spun by demand, which radically reconceives toy design and production.

Here's a richer example. Usually buyers for powerful, developed countries decide for suppliers in weak, developing countries what they need most, such as new dormitories, new roads, new uniforms. Fair Trade creates room for a negotiated premium between powerful retailers, like Starbucks, and relatively *weak producers, like coffee farmers...Under Fair Trade, the weaker party has the right to dissent.*[152]

The shift that is represented in this chapter must move beyond rhetoric and partial implementation if we want to have a future together on this planet. This new version of capitalism and the economy, like our transition to Passionate Warriors is essential. We are not the first civilization to face the challenging times we are confronting now. Sumer, the source of the Inanna mythology, like Babylon, found its home in the Fertile Crescent. It is also considered the cradle of civilization because it was in Sumer that the first great urban centers came into being. In this sense, as the source of our common beginning as organized societies, Sumer offers us a cautionary tale as follows:

> *In the course of centuries, Sumer became a 'sick society' with deplorable failings and distressing shortcomings: it yearned for peace and was constantly at war; it professed such ideals as justice, equity, and compassion, but abounded in injustice, inequality, and oppression; materialistic and short-sighted, it unbalanced the ecology essential to its economy; it was afflicted by a generation gap between parents and children, and between teachers and students. And so Sumer came to a cruel, tragic end, one melancholy Sumerian bard bitterly laments: Law and order*

---

[152] Haque, Umair. *The New Capitalist Manifesto: Building Disruptively Better Business*. Harvard Business Review. Boston. 2011. Print. Pages 62, 68, 72, 86

ceased to exist; cities, houses, stalls and sheepfolds were destroyed; fields and steppes grew nothing but weeds and 'wailing plants.' The mother cared not for her children, nor the father for his spouse, and nursemaids chanted no lullabies at the crib. No one trod the highways and the roads; the cities were ravaged and their people were killed by the mace or died of famine. Finally, over the land fell a calamity 'undescribable and unknown to man.[153]'

If you are ready to work for the transformation of the Powers and for a society organized around adding value for all stakeholders, go to www.rebeckaeggers.com to find out how you can get connected to Rebecka and The Passion Path. The Passion Path is the path of the Passionate Warrior and of whole-hearted, purposeful, and skillful living.

---

[153] Wolkstein, Diane and Samual Noah Kramer. *Inanna: Queen of Heaven and Earth*. Harper & Row. New York. 1983. Print. Page 126.

Part 3
∞
Coming Alive

Flight

I breathe in the moist air,
My lungs fill with the thickness of summertime.
I am bathing in the silver light of a moon,
So round and full,
Like the curves of my hips.
And God is moving upon the deep tonight.
My womb,
Once a barren wasteland of regret,
Is quickened by the light.
I come bearing joy,
From the weaving of a new life
And of destinies making space to unite.

The stillness of the night envelopes me,
I breathe out delight in heaping buckets full,
Meld into the sacred silence,
And the celebration song of every sound.
My bones are soaking in ecstasy.
Sweet Spirit,
You have given me over to flight.

And yet, I am like a flower,
Low to the ground,
Sensitive and alive.
I open
To dawn's early morning light,
A soliloquy of love.
Its audience?
The impending night.

©Rebecka Eggers, 2009

Coming Alive! ∞ The Warrior's Ma'at

Ride your horse along the edge of the sword,
Hide yourself in the middle of the flames,
Blossoms of the fruit tree will bloom in the fire,
The sun rises in the evening. [154] ∞ Zen Koan

I promised you a journey that would take us to the other side of the looking glass. Along the way, we learned to move beyond the fun house mirrors and into a world made up of the transparency of glass; we found our glass to break. We are now through the looking glass and nearing the end of our journey together, which I hope is really just a new beginning.

Our looking glass journey concerned our ability to see and to know. It called upon us to see things clearly and then to shift our way of being. This shift in our way of being utterly changed our manner of seeing. This journey

---

[154] Quoted in: Woodman, Marion and Elinor Dickson. *Dancing in the Flames: The Dark Goddess in the Transformation of Consciousness.* Shambhala Publications. Boston. 1997. Print. Page 175.

challenged us also to a new way of doing rooted solidly in the feminine ground of wisdom. It urged us to restore the natural father and its active, masculine ordering principle. This ordering principle turns ego or doing into a vessel. This vessel, in turn, brings feminine wisdom and potential to life. Our Journey also inspired us to reclaim the natural mother in our own consciousness as the root source of self acceptance and our sense of intrinsic worth. We also began to imagine, that instead of fighting against chaos, we could draw what we desire from the swirling eddies of its unbounded potential.

We began with a world ordered by masculine, top down, hierarchical structures and we ended with a world that finds its ground in bottom up structural support of democracy and the wisdom principles of the feminine. What originated in the imposition of masculine control now has its beginnings in feminine wisdom and chaos. What was aimed at the aggrandizement of those at the top of the hierarchy has transformed into a cooperative, collaborative venture aimed at advancing the potential of all concerned. What was imposed from without is now sourced from within.

As an organizing principle of our journey, we left behind the values of what Chogyam Trungpa called the setting sun world for the values of what I defined as The World of the Red Sun Morning, an amalgamation of several principles and concepts from many traditions, including what Chogyam Trungpa called the vision of the Great Eastern Sun. We even found the point of intersection between this Buddhist master's analogy and the one articulated by indigenous rebel leader, Subcomandante Insurgente Marcos: "To the west, the sun is like a rock, shattering the glass pane of the morning…"

Like the ballerina in the display window with whom we started our adventure, we came in contact with something truly original, truly revolutionary, a gift that cleanses, if you will, and it set us free from the uncomfortable immobility of our little music boxes. The alarms are ringing uselessly, and we are no longer in the display window.

Now we arrive on this momentous occasion at the very end of this book. These last, but not final, chapters of our journey begin with a Zen koan that captures the multifaceted nature of the journey we have been on. This has been a journey of reversals. In fact, just as you might expect from a journey to the other side of something that by its nature holds our backward image, we have turned the whole narrative of our lives inside out and upside down. This Zen koan reverses even our reversals.

The essence of the journey into the The World of the Red Sun Morning is that we, in accordance with Chogyam Trungpa's vision of the Great Eastern Sun, relinquished our fear of dying and our dramatic, damaging, and exhausting efforts to ward off death. In fact, this fearful effort to ward of death, as we discovered, is what so empowers those, who, like Marduk in the Babylonian mythology, would offer us security in exchange for our freedom and submission. The fear of death is the root of the Domination System. So, we replaced this cult of fear with a genuine celebration of life and of human potential, and rightfully so. We reoriented ourselves towards birth, life, potential, and the rising sun.

Yet, there is something about our language and metaphors that has bothered me right from the start. A journey that was all about not polarizing into extremes like dominated/dominator and light/darkness, has all been largely expressed through a mythological framework that had us rising into a world oriented towards the birth of the sun and towards life. I know now what the issue is. So long as we express our journey in this way, we are, in some odd manner, still tied to the Domination System and its fear of death. We are tied to its duality.

We have been talking about a journey that approximates a spiral in the language of a linear trajectory that takes us through darkness and death and ultimately back to the light as though the ultimate goal is to confront, overcome, and move beyond the darkness and death. Of course, we talked in terms of integrating the Dark Goddess and the Light Goddess. But the discussion was not explicit enough for my taste. It failed to fully express that our journey has been, at least in part, about reclaiming darkness and death and harnessing the power of both.

I feel the need now to make our relationship to death and darkness explicit and also to complete the circle by drawing our conversation squarely back to the topic of order and its relationship to chaos. There is good reason for this! Just like the Powers cannot simply be destroyed lest we lose our ability to express the common will, we cannot toss order out with Marduk. As we move away from top-down, exploitative order, we need an explicit example of a new kind of order, a kind of order that supports. This kind of order is foundational. You could call it wisdom, and yet it is more than that. Regardless, it is essential. Therefore, we can't afford to speak in general terms only.

We also cannot avoid the reality of death, which is always stalking us, and reminding us that time is precious and ever marching forward. We cannot eschew the truth that in every cycle there is a death and that one day death will claim us. We must not ignore the reality of darkness either or even, as many people habitually do, continue to think of it as synonymous with evil. We are, instead, compelled to make order, death, dying, and darkness our partners in a life fully lived.

We must go forward in life with the full awareness of death and of the sun which recedes each evening to reveal the darkness. This darkness is penetrated by the rising sun each morning. Darkness is the original state. Light is something that enters the darkness and illuminates it. It is the energy that brings potential to life. Yet, light, as we discovered earlier in this book, is born of that which already exists in the darkness. We cannot separate the two. In reality, light is born of and cradled in the vast expanse of the Universe's womb-like dark space. It is the same with life and death. We must learn to see that they form what amounts to a contiguous whole that is bound together by the ultimate transformation inherent in dying. In fact, this has been a book about dying to one world and coming alive to another. Our journey has taken place in the space between our old lives and the ones we will soon create.

The Zen koan at the beginning of this chapter recognizes this reality and it highlights the beginning that is inherent in every ending. "The sun rises in the evening," Each sunset contains within it the reality and the expectation of the next sunrise. Further, if we look more closely at the Marcos quote, we realize not just the truth of this statement, but something more: There is an east in every west. If you are west of me, you are east of something else. That is the nature of living on a globe. There is an indestructible unity.

This indestructible unity is, in fact, the very premise of The Passion Path and of this book. When we choose to claim our freedom, our passion, and our power, we are also impacting the system in which we live and the people with whom we associate; we are relinquishing the relationship patterns of the Domination System and replacing them with something more compelling. This notion of an indestructible unity acknowledges that we are always impacting one another and the broader circumstances in which our lives unfold. This is also the meaning of the banyan tree. We change ourselves, we put down roots, and we change the very nature and character of that which contains us.

With all of this in mind, I now reverse our reversals and take up the subject of order as the foundation of a life lived to its full potential. This concept of order is, for the Passionate Warrior, contained in what Robert Moore and Douglas Gillette called "the Warrior's Dharma, Ma'at, or Tao, a spiritual or psychological path through life." [155] Accordingly, I am going to talk about this principle of order with reference to the Egyptian Goddess Ma'at.

The introduction of Ma'at into our journey represents a further reversal of our original mirror image because our journey has been, up until now, largely about achieving the freedom of a rebirth. It is not really natural to think of freedom and order as comfortable bedfellows. You will soon see that they are. Further, we previously talked about orienting our lives towards life and towards the rising sun. But Ma'at inhabits death's domain. So, now we are going to talk about death as a defining principle in our lives. We are going to explore the reality that life finds its guiding principles and structural supports not in the fear of death, but in its relationship to it. Just as light is born in the darkness, a rich, full, and powerful life finds its root in our awareness of death and willingness to embrace destruction as a necessary creative and transformative force. Put another way, the process of dying is the ultimate transformation and it is one we will all

---

[155] Moore, Robert and Douglas Gillette. *King, Warrior, Magician, Lover: Rediscovering the Archetypes of the Mature Masculine.* Harper Collins. New York. 1991. Print. Page 79.

undergo first ritually, if we choose it, and later as an actual transition to whatever comes at the end of this life.

It is our ability to let things die that ultimately empowers those things we choose to cultivate. Likewise, it is our awareness that we will all die that infuses our choices with a sense of urgency and significance. Ma'at is relevant, at least in part, because it was She who attended Egypt's dead as they made the transition from life to death and from creating a life to accounting for the lives they had created. She also has much to teach us about what it takes to create an authentic and meaningful life.

The material I am about to introduce regarding Ma'at is less scholarly than it is a representation of my own relationship to Ma'at and of my own willingness to allow Her and Her mythology to change me in profound ways. The following discussion is based upon the experience of having invoked Her and of having engaged Her. It is the hard won understanding that came from living through the things that immediately followed the invocation.

It was Ma'at who first brought me into awareness of the global context of oppression in which my life as a privileged corporate executive played out. It was She who brought my own traumas to the surface of my life for the purpose of awareness and healing. Ma'at is what drew me to the mountains of southern Mexico. What ensued was a series of escalating experiences that ultimately put me in unmistakable contact with my own experiences of violation and exploitation and with my sense of justice, personal and collective. She has been a key inspiration for this book which is founded on ideals of justice. It is justice that demands we place our emphasis on bringing human potential to fruition.

Ma'at is the genesis of everything I have become. I say this, because knowing Her destroyed both life as I knew it and my then existing sense of myself as a woman and as a person. Step by step, my interactions with Her stripped away the lies and illusions and introduced me to my own essential worth. Together we unearthed my authentic sense of myself and ultimately, my freedom.

Once invoked, Ma'at is an exacting task master. She is merciless and yet filled with compassion. As you will see, Her aim is for us to live a fruitful and enjoyable life on a personal and communal level. She constantly exhorts us to reveal ourselves and to insist on a life that is more than we ever thought we could create.

Perhaps the best way I can introduce you to Her is with the following quote:

> *Maat touches all concerns in life: survival, independence, family situations, love, hate, jealousy, fear, illness, death, eternity, loneliness, purpose, and choices. There is no situation that cannot be improved with an infusion of truth, even though the process is often painful.*

No one comes to Maat without a profound dissatisfaction with ordinary answers, conventional wisdom, the traditional institutions of society and one's own thoughts. The essence of initiation lies beyond all naturally-occurring means of realization, ant yet, once attained, seems plainly obvious.[156]

This quote captures the essence of what we are doing here. When we have had enough of the stock answers, of our own despoiling/egocentricity, and of a world organized around domination and exploitation, we choose the path of the Passionate Warrior and we invoke Ma'at; we invoke a kind of truth that emanates from outside our existing consciousness and yet, from within ourselves. We ask to be remade. We become truth.

When we talk about invoking Ma'at, we are not so much talking about invoking truth as compared to falsehood so much as we are asking that clarity take the place of opacity. When we claim Ma'at as our inner consciousness, we are calling upon Her to strip away that which obscures the essence of who we are; we are asking Her to strip away our opaqueness. When we call upon Her, we are asking that She brush every aspect of our lives with the power inherent in Her famous feather of truth and that She initiate us into a new way of being. The idea is to learn what is true for us once the traumas, illusions, wounds, and chains of the past have been

---

[156] Nema. *Maat Magick: A Guide to Self-Initiation.* Samuel Weiser. York Beach 1995. Print. Page 8.

burned off. With Ma'at, we are revealing our authenticity and our full potential as human beings and communities.

It is said of Ma'at that She was both revered as a goddess and as a principle or function of the universe to be embodied by the Pharaoh and also by the Egyptian people. "To the Egyptian mind, Ma'at bound all things together in an indestructible unity: the universe, the natural world, the state, and the individual were all seen as parts of the wider order generated by Ma'at."[157] Interestingly, Ma'at was Egypt's answer to the complex needs of a diverse society. "Maat as a principle was formed to meet the complex needs of the emergent Egyptian state that embraced diverse peoples with conflicting interests."[158] Like Marduk, Ma'at arose for the purpose of addressing chaos but with an eye towards achieving an overall equilibrium as explained in the following quote:

> *The significance of Maat developed to the point that it embraced all aspects of existence, including the basic equilibrium of the universe, the relationship between constituent parts, the cycle of the seasons, heavenly movements, religious observations and fair dealings, honesty and truthfulness in social interactions.*
>
> *The ancient Egyptians had a deep conviction of an underlying holiness and unity within the universe.*

---

[157] http://en.wikipedia.org/wiki/Maat.
[158] http://en.wikipedia.org/wiki/Maat.

> *Cosmic harmony was achieved by correct public and ritual life. Any disturbance in cosmic harmony could have consequences for the individual as well as the state. An impious King could bring about famine or blasphemy blindness to an individual. In opposition to the right order expressed in the concept of Maat is the concept of **Isfet**: chaos, lies and violence.*[159]

Ma'at was the Egyptian goddess of truth, justice, and cosmic consciousness. In stark contrast to the ethics of the Domination System and the Babylonian creation myth, She existed in the Egyptian consciousness for the express purpose of recognizing and holding the unity and interconnectedness of all things as well as for the purpose of drawing together a diverse collection of people into a common society. I recognize that Egypt is not a perfect example of anything as it was heavily stratified and its survival depended upon everyone occupying his/her place. What we are looking for is not a perfect representation of Ma'at expressed in Egyptian culture as one likely does not exist. Accordingly, what we are concerned with here is an expression of what might be considered the core essence of The Passionate Warrior's guiding principles, his or her, "Ma'at." Put another way, the concepts are brilliant and they stand on their own. When we invoke Ma'at, we are evoking an already existing connection

---

[159] Moore, Robert and Douglas Gillette. *King, Warrior, Magician, Lover: Rediscovering the Archetypes of the Mature Masculine.* Harper Collins. New York. 1991. Print. Page 79.

with the cosmos and with the innate kind of equilibrium and justice that already exists within us.

Ma'at is the order that forms the structural supports of the Passionate Warrior's life and his/her associations. This is the kind of order that allows things to flourish. Of course, because Ma'at is that which binds everything into an indestructible unity, She must, necessarily include within herself Her own opposite, the Isfet, the chaos, lies, and violence. This is not the war of one against the other (or Marduk against Tiamat), but rather the relationship between order and chaos. As we saw in the story of Ivan and his tutor, sometimes it is violence and chaos that set us free. But, of even more interest is the reality that Ma'at stands for the principles that bring order out of chaos in a society and/or individual life founded on unity and interconnectedness. Ma'at is the Passionate Warrior's strongest ally in the creative process.

This truth of Ma'at as the structural support of Egyptian society, and indeed, of the Passionate Warrior's life, is born out in Ma'at's role as the goddess of the Duat. The Duat is the Egyptian underworld. In the Duat, the souls or hearts of the dead were weighed against Ma'at's feather of truth. If the heart was lighter than Her feather of truth, the dead person was allowed to move on to paradise. If not, his/her heart was eaten by the goddess/demon Ammit. The heart was symbolic of the soul or the essence of the person.

Recall, that as a scientific fact, destruction is rather a fallacy. In the words of Albert Einstein, "energy cannot be created or destroyed, it can only be changed from one form to another." And so it was when Ammit devoured the heart. "Once Ammit swallowed the heart, the soul was believed to become restless forever; this was called 'to die a second time'."[160]

What did it mean to become restless forever? I believe this was about giving effect to what the person had been in life. Restless energy is energy that has never found its place. In some sense, it is ungrounded. It is in perpetual motion. You get the sense that this heavy heart was a product of a life that was never fully lived, a life that never found within its perpetual motion, the ability to order its potential into the kind of life that produces a light or joyful heart. The heavy heart is an unsatisfied heart; it is a heart that never embodied Ma'at. The result is less like the concept of punishment and more like the cosmic outcome of a life that was, for the simple reason of wasted opportunity or outright destructiveness, never brought to fruition.

We do not often apply this kind of exacting standard. We have been trained to think in terms of grey areas and to look for the explanation that would make someone's heavy heart somehow explicable by circumstances, and therefore, not their responsibility. We believe in a series of "second chances" that will never come to an end. Ma'at does not show leniency.

---

[160] http://en.wikipedia.org/wiki/Ammit

Subjectivity is not a part of Her make-up. There is a clear standard and the standard is applied. Ma'at is concerned here with the sum total of who someone has chosen to become and what they chose to make of their lives. She is an excellent antidote for the kind of subjectivity that never calls upon us to make firm commitments or to radically execute around a clear vision.

The heart is symbolic. A light heart is associated with purity and a heavy heart with impurity. Pure means, among other things: unmixed with any other matter; free from what vitiates, weakens, or pollutes; containing nothing that does not properly belong; free from moral fault or guilt; and having exactly the talents or skills needed for a particular role.[161] In other words, a person possessed a light heart if s/he chose Ma'at as the core of his/her consciousness. A person who eschewed Her had a heavy heart. The truth and justice were not in them. They had not found balance or come into any kind of equilibrium with themselves and the world around them.

The image of the heavy heart laid out on the scales of justice has much to teach us about the Passionate Warriors consciousness. It is a consciousness that has learned the lessons of death and finality, and conversely, of life and commitment. Far from fearing death or even the kind of reckoning symbolized by the weighing of the heart, the Passionate Warrior is inspired by these things towards living

---

[161] http://www.merriam-webster.com/dictionary/pure

life with gusto. It is the Passionate Warrior's aim to arrive at death's door with a heart that is light, mirthful, and fulfilled. A light heart is an unrepentant heart, a heart without remorse. This is not to be confused with the enforced positivity that has become popular in New Age circles. This is the joy that springs from a consciousness that is imbued with Ma'at and a life oriented towards the fulfillment of potential on a personal and collective level. Enforced positivity is about papering over a mountain of hurt and distress by brute force. It controls but does not resolve. By contrast, to have an unrepentant or remorseless heart in this context means to have lived a life for which you do not feel the need to repent. This is about bringing life to fruition.

Ma'at is also the source of the Passionate Warrior's wakefulness. The Passionate Warrior is keenly aware of what it cost him/her to live in the Domination System. But the Passionate Warrior does not live a life oriented around warding off the experience of the Domination System. Instead, his/her life is lived according to the balanced principles of order that give full support to a fruitful individual and communal experience.

Along these same lines, when the Passionate Warrior embodies Ma'at consciousness, s/he has Ma'at's impartial and decisive nature. S/he is willing to destroy what needs to be destroyed and to relinquish what needs to be relinquished. This is not about malice, but rather, about releasing the energy that was once trapped by things that do not serve the Passionate Warrior's purpose and mission or his/her joyfulness. It is the Ma'at consciousness of the Passionate Warrior that holds the exacting standards and the discernment that tell him/her what is supportive of a fully developed, fully expressed life and what is not. Ma'at is the source of the Passionate Warrior's protection. She is also the source of his/her commitment. The purpose of destroying one thing is to make space for another. If something is sapping the Passionate Warrior's energy, s/he cuts it loose quickly. On the flipside, the Passionate Warrior is careful to always invest fully in the cultivation of his/her purpose and fulfillment.

With Ma'at as his/her consciousness, the Passionate Warrior addresses the the heart of things. The Passionate Warrior knows how to see and to address dysfunction at its root. It was not the body that Ammit devoured in the Duat. It was the soul/consciousness of the person. As we learned from Walter Wink, we do not struggle against the outer structure of the Powers, another person, or even ourselves. Ma'at calls upon the Passionate Warrior to address the core consciousness and root of whatever he/she is confronting. Ma'at also teaches the Passionate Warrior to place Ma'at's wisdom and order at the core his/her creations.

Recall that Ma'at is also the order that binds the universe into an indestructible unity. She is the order that supports our unfolding. She and Her exacting standards are exactly the tools that allow us to pull order out of chaos in service of our own blossoming. In this sense, Ma'at is also very dark.

That which contains everything has a richness to it. This is the richness and power of the color black which contains within it all other colors. It reminds me of the power and the energy hidden away in a lump of coal. Ma'at is like the darkness from which stars are born. She calls upon the Passionate Warrior to integrate him/herself and to become androgynous and total.

Ma'at is also that which distinguishes the warrior from the soldier. Ma'at is the source of our commitment to what Douglas and Gillette called a "transpersonal cause." In plain English, Ma'at is the part of us that knows our dreams. We can, when She becomes our consciousness, discern that which will draw use closer to the fulfillment of our purpose from that which will draw us closer to our own destruction. Ma'at is in intimate communication with the mission we have accepted. She holds the clarity and deep devotion with which we have committed to our purpose. Ma'at calls upon us to fulfill our potential with commitment and exacting standards. She is the foundation of the discipline that emanates from wisdom and purpose.

Ma'at recognizes the indestructible unity of the community and the individual. She was that which operated in the Egyptian consciousness as the glue of civilization. Just as Ma'at is the foundation of a rich and powerful life, She is also the structural support for a rich and powerful communal experience. Ma'at calls upon the Passionate Warrior to participate in and support intentional communities who have as their aim the fulfillment of human potential and the cultivation of human dignity. This requires that, while we do not forget what it cost us to live by the ethos of the Domination System, we move beyond a distaste for its lifelessness. Ma'at calls upon us to develop a whole new orientation towards the joy, pleasure, and potential of being together. It is telling that one of the most popular and widely revered deities in Egypt was Hathor, the goddess of joy.[162]

Ma'at shows us that a society organized around joy requires that the individual participants surrender their freedom, but not to someone whose aim is control and self aggrandizement. In Egypt, notions of justice bound the Pharoah as much as, if not more than they did the commoner. The kind of society Ma'at supports is a society in which we surrender some of our freedoms to one another in a social compact designed to support the greatest unfolding for all involved. With our commitment to Ma'at and to each other, all sorts of new possibilities open up. This type of surrender is not about controlling one another, but is more akin to making agreements that uphold our common commitment to one another.

If the Egyptians, and indeed, Eastern spirituality in general, lost track of something, it was the freedom and potential of the individual as an individual. Nonetheless, what we gain from interacting with Ma'at is extremely valuable. She has much to teach us as we work our way out of a situation that prized individual gain through domination

---

[162] http://en.wikipedia.org/wiki/Hathor

and exploitation and into a situation of communal thriving. As individuals and communities, we will be well served to embody Ma'at and Her concepts of justice, equilibrium, and interconnectedness as the structural supports of our unfoldment.

Does Ma'at have to express as She did in Egypt. No! We can make Her our own. What matters is that we understand Her purpose: to bring together a diverse group of people (or diverse aspects of the individual) into a functional whole. What is lost in Ma'at as a result of Her stark objectivity is counterbalanced in the Passionate Warrior by his/her passion. Recall that the Passionate Warrior is the unity of love and war. Ma'at is the consciousness of the warrior archetype. She is not the sum total of the Passionate Warrior. She is the foundation of an ecstatic and meaningful experience of life.

In conclusion, we cannot build an ecstatic experience until we know what to cultivate and what to destroy. Ma'at allows us to bring ownership and finality to both our YES and our NO. The heart is either heavier or lighter than our feather of truth. It was Ma'at that Inanna integrated during Her time with Erishkigal. Interestingly, it was Ma'at at work when Geshtinanna intervened to spare Dumuzi the finality of death. Balance and justice were at the heart of the Inanna mythology.

Ma'at is also the source of our stillness. It was Ma'at that Ivan was integrating when the Crone pinned him to the wall. Ma'at is the source of our equanimity. She allows us to hear and receive the messages life is providing with neutrality and to use them to fuel a satisfying life.

Sometimes the messages we receive indicate that we must be still and wait, and sometimes they indicate that it is time to remove Dumuzi from his throne. Ma'at is the Passionate Warrior's wisdom. It is the wisdom of Ma'at or Ma'at consciousness that binds everything (especially our being and our doing) together in an indestructible unity. It is She to whom the ego, now transformed, pays its allegiance in service of our passion. She brings into our lives that which justice implies: balance. This is as true of individuals, as it is of societies. Balance is the foundation from which our passion is lived and our thriving unleashed. It is not an enforced harmony. It is a dynamic equilibrium that embraces all the cycles of life. Ma'at represents an absolute covenant with balance and with individual and societal unity and interconnectedness. She is clear, and unwavering. She is also detached. Perhaps Douglas and Gillette summed it up best as follows:

> *If we are accessing the Warrior appropriately, we will be energetic, decisive, courageous, enduring, persevering, and loyal to some greater good beyond our own personal gain.*[163]

---

[163] Moore, Robert and Douglas Gillette. *King, Warrior, Magician, Lover: Rediscovering the Archetypes of the Mature Masculine.* Harper Collins. New York. 1991. Print. Page 95.

They go on to conclude that if the warrior archetype works in tandem with other archetypal forms, the warrior will take on other characteristics as well. The summarize this as follows:

> *If we are accessing the Warrior in the right way, we will, at the same time that we are "detached," be warm, compassionate, appreciative, and generative. We will care for ourselves and others. We will fight good fights in order to make the world a better and more fulfilling place for everyone and everything. Our war making will be for the creation of the new, the just, and the free.*[164]

In line with what Douglas and Gillette have said, if Ma'at is the core consciousness of the Passionate Warrior and the source of his/her equanimity, detachment and even compassion, passion is the Passionate Warrior's way of expressing in the world. The Passionate Warrior lives an ecstatic, integrated life of purpose and commitment with immense passion and skill. Ma'at is the order, discipline, detachment, equanimity, and clarity that allows the Passionate Warrior to bring the ecstatic experience to life.

---

[164] Moore, Robert and Douglas Gillette. *King, Warrior, Magician, Lover: Rediscovering the Archetypes of the Mature Masculine.* Harper Collins. New York. 1991. Print. Page 95.

If you are ready to invoke Ma'at, go to www.rebeckaeggers.com to to find out how you can get connected to Rebecka and The Passion Path. The Passion Path is the path of the Passionate Warrior and of whole-hearted, purposeful, and skillful living.

Coming Alive! ∞ Passion

How many miles to Babylon,
Three score miles and ten.
Can I get there by candlelight?
Yes, and back again!
If your heals be nimble and light,
You can get there by candlelight.
∞ Traditional

You cannot deny what has been missing in this our modern world. You cannot escape what disappeared, no, what was mercilessly snuffed out by the advance of Christendom and other monotheistic and patriarchal religions.

She was nearly laid to rest. It matters not what you call Her, Inanna, Ishtar, Venus, Aphrodite, Shakti or, as Peter Grey, the author of *The Red Goddess*, has called Her, "Babalon."[165] What matters is that you see Her and that you know Her as an essential part of who you are. She and Her consort,

---

[165] Grey, Peter. *The Red Goddess*. Scarlet Imprint. 2007. Print.

represented masculine and feminine in balance within the individual and within society. They represented passion and its fruits. They were the repositories of a lush and fertile world within human consciousness.

We cannot go forward without Her. We also cannot go forward without Him. But in some sense, to evoke Her, is to invite Him. So, for now, I want to talk about what I know. I want to address the aspects of the Passionate Warrior that are contained within the one who came to me. Ishtar is inside of me. She is knocking around the edges of my being threatening to explode in a red hot fountain of lava. Can you feel her too? She is the life force building. She is what Marion Woodman called the "I desire" threatening to overtake everything in its wake. It was Her essence and ours that was trapped in the Domination System. Slowly but surely, patriarchy and its jealous monotheistic, male, gods have tried to vanquish Her during what has amounted to something like a centuries long snuff film; an homage to greed and predation. Perhaps Peter Grey captured it best as follows:

> *The three great religions of Marxism, Capitalism, and Christianity have failed to address the very real fact that we can consume ourselves to destruction. It is tempting to label this endless insatiable desire Babalon. In one sense it is. Neither Love nor War Goddesses act within limits. She wants, and will have, everything. Yet it is the philosophy of greed and separation from the natural order which has*

> *wrought this havoc. Both gross materiality and detached spirituality are to blame.*[166]

Indeed! As I have pointed out repeatedly in this book, activism and spirituality; the material outer structure and consciousness; life and death, cannot be dealt with separately. A spirituality that is not embodied is useless. Materiality that has no spiritual component is death dealing.

Ishtar, on the other hand, demands to be fully embodied. She has been raising in me the kind of desire that will possess this "everything" that Peter Grey is talking about. It is through Her that the "I desire" can be revived and ultimately fulfilled.

In a delicious amalgamation of mythologies, I now understand a vision that came to me years ago. In 2007, the detective assigned to my mother's case called to ask if I was sitting down. This was about 10 years after the my mother was murdered. His was not a voice I expected to hear nor was I prepared for the fact that he had arrested a suspect.

We were headed to trial in the spring of 2009. It was a complex situation that I do not feel the need to discuss. But it shook my life to the foundations yet again. I comforted myself with a vision that just kept coming to me. I saw red hot lava burst through this pie crust looking thing and land in my hand as a feather. A friend pointed out that this feather belonged to Ma'at. I had never heard of Her. But when I read

---

[166] Grey, Peter. *The Red Goddess*. Scarlet Imprint. 2007. Print. Page 223.

about Her, I assumed it was Her feather of truth come to comfort me, to tell me that justice would be done.

That day in court never came. Whether justice was served or not, I leave to some final reckoning that may never come. Either way, Ma'at was already with me. I went to Maine that spring where I encountered, quite by accident, the High Priestess of the Temple of Ma'at. I saw her flyer the weekend before the D.A. dropped all the charges. When I got home from Maine, after years of telling us how sure he was that he had the right man, the D.A. delivered that little bombshell and then simply rode off into the sunset. But he was no cowboy and that was no noble steed! I digress.

I went back to Maine that summer and looked up Ma'at's priestess. I sensed that she could help me recover somehow. She comforted me and sang my chakras back to life.

I did not know then of Ishtar (though Inanna preceded Ma'at in my goddess awareness). But I understand the red lava now. It will usher in my truth with all the force, power and passion contained in the Goddess of Love and War. This red lava will unleash the core truth of my desire like an explosion. Yet, somehow, that truth will land in my hand with the gentleness and the soft caresses of a feather. Incidentally, this reminds me of San Cristóbal in the spring when Semana Santa and its week long celebration of death and resurrection give way to a cleansing summer rain. Sweet peace in the wake of the storm!

In any case, up until I wrote this book, I had conceived of the Passion Path in a certain way. It was all I cared about. So, in this sense, it was my passion made manifest. But I tried to follow directions. I tried to bring it to term the way everyone else says you bring a personal growth businesses to fruition. Before long, I wasn't having very much fun.

Naturally, the Passion Path and my whole life are shifting yet again as this tag team of goddesses ushers me more deeply into the brilliant, red, rouge, of my desire. I can feel it pumping through me like the blood in my veins. It is changing everything! You see, the Passion Path cannot exist as a service I offer to the world separate and apart from the fulfillment of my own most compelling personal desires.

Yes, now I understand the red lava. What I saw in the spring of 2009 was the life force moving through me and revealing itself as the most authentic kind of truth: Passion insisting on expression. Passion fulfilled! This passion is demanding, counterculture, intense, and wildly subversive. It is the stuff of genuine satisfaction. It represents a hardcore challenge to the consciousness of craving that goes hand in hand with the kind of rampant consumption that can never get enough. This kind of truth represents a core challenge to the Domination System. The process of unleashing this truth isn't pretty, it isn't neat, it is certainly no respecter of the best laid plans, but it is real and it is the most beautiful thing I have ever dared to imagine.

So, now I invite you into the beauty. I ask you to empower it. I urge you to invoke the lava, to call Her up, and to open yourself to Her. More than that, I now place a shovel in your hands. There is work to be done. If you are willing, we will conclude our journey together with an excavation, Hers and ours. We will work by candlelight, of course. May our heals be nimble and light…

If this book has done its job, you are now catching a glimpse of your own zero point. You are not who you thought you were when this whole experiment started nor do you know who you really are. Whatever you used to think brought you joy no longer compels you. Whatever stories have driven you through all these years in the Domination System no longer mean anything. This is the sweet taste of freedom, yet you are terrified. What will fill the void left behind by your chains?

She will. You will. She is a part of you long forgotten. She was long ago buried, and not for safe keeping either. You recognize the seditious act of picking up the shovel. You understand its significance. It represents a treason against all you have ever known. Yet there is no turning back.

You have nothing but your intuition to tell you where to begin digging. For a moment, you think you see Her shadow in the flickering candlelight and that is where you drop your shovel. Inch by inch, relic by relic, you are now uncovering traces of Her, traces of you.

Her...

You have known Her already in the sweet, sparkly idealized version of your desire. It was She who seduced you into this journey with Her dazzling light. I know Her well. She was the light I kept seeing over Chiapas when I first found the courage to board the plane that brought me here in search of answers about my life. It was her sweet seduction that gave me the incentive and the courage to keep coming back and to keep confronting my life until I broke through to a new way of living.

You have known Her also as war. It was She who taught you how to fight for yourself. She blew apart your sense that aggression was a violation of ethics and that empathy for the oppressor was a command from the godhead. She taught you about your freedom and about doing what is necessary. She was there urging you to cut off the tutor's head. It was She who unleashed the demons that tore Dumuzi from his throne. In some sense, She is the inexplicable, unmistakable, invisible hand behind everything that brought you to this moment. She is not as nice as you thought She would be. You are not even a fraction as nice as you imagined you could be. She is the universal, timeless, feminine darkness. She is the lusty Baba Yaga and the dark, unrelenting death of Erishkigal. She is Ma'at. Don't you be fooled by the looks of Her. She assumes the form you most need to see. But within all that darkness, in the midst of all that death, beats the blood thirsty heart of the wild woman. She thirsts for your blood, your signature applied, in an unshakeable covenant with yourself, with Her.

Now that you have made that bond, it is Her in the form of a wild kind of love and ecstasy with whom you seek the most urgent of encounters. It is a rich kind of beauty that is calling you to dig in the dark of night by the sultry candlelight. You are unearthing the red rose of your passion. She is covered in thorns. But once the sweet, tantalizing scent of Her envelopes you, you will belong to Her, thorns and all.

As you begin to dig, a scene flashes across the night sky. A luscious Goddess appears: bountiful breasts, resplendent hips, naked body bejeweled and sparkling in the moonlight. She is seated on the back of a lion, riding bareback across the moon. You think you have been searching for Her. But all of a sudden you realize, She has been after you for years.

The Holy Whore has come for you.[167]

If you think this is about being sexy or merely about sexual desire, you are mistaken. This vision of the luscious goddess traversing the night sky is about having. She is about evoking your desire and your carnality. She has come to wake you up to yourself and your longings. She has come to restore the "I desire" that took a nose dive when your life force was trapped in the Domination System. This bodacious babe of a Goddess has come to restore your sense of the possible and

---

[167] In The Red Goddess, Peter Grey used the sentence, "The Holy Whore is coming for you." Credit where credit is due!

your investment in the here and now. Peter Grey captured this reality perfectly and so I cannot resist quoting him:

> *Babalon is ripe with sexual promise. She's all woman, revealing her physicality. This is a big change from the amorphous beard job Jehovah. This is a Goddess you can actually touch and feel. There's no vague promise of hereafter, Babalon is about direct hands on experience. To worship this Goddess is to make Love to Her, and revel in a world of the senses. Rather than denying the world, She asks us to Love it.*[168]

In other words, this Red Goddess, your passion made manifest, asks you to touch Her, to feel Her, to come alive to Her. She asks you to have what you want and to relish having it right here and now, in this world, in this moment. It is time to burn the conditioning that says satisfaction happens in the years when you are most keen to make the transition to death or else in the great hereafter. Are you willing to demand your counterculture, revolutionary, even treasonous stake in the dream that comes true in the present moment no matter what it costs you? She will settle for nothing less, and She has arrived.

Now that you have seen Her, you have a choice to make. This book and our journey together has brought you to yet another crossroads.

---

[168] Grey, Peter. *The Red Goddess*. Scarlet Imprint. 2007. Print. Page 21.

Are you giddy with the smell of Her perfume? Has something come alive in the sweet scent of roses and the wild gyrations of your candle lit night?

Then this is your time. This is why you have come all this way. If you pay attention, you will feel Her energy tickling your feet, lapping at your legs, tantalizing your loins. She is asking to come in. For the first time, tonight, you know yourself as the empty vessel you have worked all these years to become. There is nothing left of who you once were. There is only you standing here in the moonlight and the scent of your passion enveloping you. She is the red rose of your passion looking for its garden. She is the temptation of your desire asking to be fulfilled. She needs a vessel. Will you have Her? Will you become Her?

Then open!

It's time!

If you are ready to embody your passion, go to www.rebeckaeggers.com to find out how you can get connected to Rebecka and The Passion Path. The Passion Path is the path of the Passionate Warrior and of whole-hearted, purposeful, and skillful living.

Epilogue

I have only one thing left to say. There are those who will tell you that myth does not matter. They are wrong. Myth informs our way of being together. If you do not believe me, consider the way in which different mythologies led to whole different ways of inhabiting the world in early societies. In his book, *Myths to Live By,* Joseph Campbell made an incredibly astute observation about the development and impact of mythology. According to him, in the hunter gatherer societies, the mythology centered around animals as teachers and in rites, assumed the identities of the animals. Social ritual acknowledged the relationship between the hunters and the animals.

By contrast, in tropical jungle environments where the "spectacle of nature was predominantly of plants," human sacrifice was common. In these cultures, where plant life formed the center of mythology, sacrificial death meant knew life. Cutting away old growth gave way to new growth. As a result, certain young people were sacrificed just as they came to physical maturity in order to bring the constant renewal the tribe counted on for survival. The puberty rites involved actual killing.

The way we interpret the world around us determines how we relate to that world and to the people with whom we share it. If your only mythology says that you must either dominate or be dominated, that will inform everything. If your mythology says you can co-create and thrive together, that will inform your choices and your way of being in relationship. In discussing the power of rites, Joseph Campbell said something truly profound that sums up everything I have tried to demonstrate and create with this book through the power of myth. Here is what he said:

> *Myths are the mental supports of rites; rites the physical enactments of myths. By absorbing the myths of his social group and participating in its rites, the youngster is structured to accord with his social as well as natural environment, and turned from an amorphous nature product, prematurely born, into a defined and competent member of some specific, efficiently functioning social order.*[169]

What I have offered is a way out of the social order created by the rites and mythologies of the Domination System and a way into a new kind of social order with a whole new set of myths, rites, and relationships. The Passion

---

[169] Campbell, Joseph. *Myths to Live By*. Joseph Campbell Foundation. San Anselmo. 1972. Electronic Version, 2011. Kindle. Location 853. Page 43.

Path programs that I offer are about creating these things for ourselves with an eye towards sharing them with an ever increasing group of new initiates. These programs are the birth children of my own journey and of the shifts that have taken place in the mythology that undergirds my participation in this world.

At this point, it seems important to share some of my own personal story. I have alluded to the fact that I live in Chiapas, Mexico. I have shared very little about how I got there. Here is the story as recounted in an article that predates this book but which formed much of the inspiration for it:

I am personally, at this moment, surrounded by Zapatista rebel territories in Southern Mexico. I live in San Cristóbal de las Casas, Chiapas.

For a brief time in 1994, a mostly indigenous Mayan force rose up against the Mexican government in protest against NAFTA and in search of survival in the form of farm land. They initially took the city of San Cristóbal de las Casas and other major cities in Chiapas before finally retreating to what are now zones of autonomous self-rule. Their story profoundly changed my life.

My life in San Cristóbal is the byproduct of a powerful spiritual practice. Some years ago I began assuming a new spiritual name every New Year's Eve. Taking a new name is a powerful magical act. Don't change your name unless you want to change your life. Whiplash associated with sudden change is a possible hazard!

In 2009, I chose the name Ma'at. Ma'at is the Egyptian goddess of truth, justice, and cosmic consciousness. She made her presence known just before New Year's Eve.

On December the 29, 2009 a strange thing happened to me. I was standing in my bathroom at a posh resort called "Dreams" in Tulum, Mexico. I was looking in the mirror when suddenly my image of myself as a woman cracked for just a moment and I saw a whole person. All the things that usually leave a woman feeling *less than* and fragmented simply dissolved and disappeared for a fraction of a second. Then I heard a voice in my head very distinctly say, "He is near." I had no idea what that meant and I was certainly not accustomed to hearing voices. Two days later, on New Year's Eve, I walked into a bar in Tulum…

As I walked into the bar my eyes landed on the face of a man across the room. Our eyes locked and I knew that "he" had arrived. He began to tell me of the struggle in Chiapas and of his work with the Zapatista communities. He shared his story Mexican style – in between dances and in the shining light of romance. He spoke no English and my Spanish was almost as bad. But I heard what his heart was telling me and I understood just enough of the facts to know that I had to find out more.

Later that night, we made love on the beach under the full moon and then we said goodbye. The next morning, I boarded a plane to Massachusetts. I am sure he thought he would never see me again. He was wrong.

I went home and read everything about the Zapatistas that I could get my hands on. By April, I was on a plane to Chiapas and in search of answers. The questions I was asking were as personal as they were global in nature. It is the personal I am going to deal with here (as a predicate to dealing with the global).

I went to Chiapas in search of what I had termed "my authentic sense of self." I have experienced a wide variety of traumas in my life from severe sexual and physical abuse to the brutal murder of my mother and the ensuing police investigation.

My authentic sense of self was buried beneath a mountain of trauma. I think I might have seen it for the last time as I stood next to my mother's grave. She died challenging the status quo of her life and she died living her dream – but that is a whole other story. Suffice it to say that from my perspective, coloring inside the lines suddenly seemed like a very good idea.

When I went to Chiapas in 2010, I had no reason to believe in my own intrinsic worth and very little sense that I ever could. The only hope I had was contained in my memory of that one tiny moment when my mirror reflected my wholeness and in the sudden and shocking arrival of a man who knew about a group of indigenous rebels who seemed to have a part to play in making that memory a constant reality.

I didn't understand how or why, but based on my New Year's Eve experiences in Tulum, I knew that the Zapatistas held the key to my authentic sense of self. I knew I needed to find them. I didn't care what it cost me!

I had exactly one rather embarrassing conversation with the Zapatista Good Government Board in Oventik, Chiapas. My visit to Oventik was one of the most humbling days of my life. I went there thinking (as a successful, highly educated lawyer) I had something to offer the Zapatistas.

The moment I crossed over into rebel territory, I suddenly knew for certain that I didn't even understand my own plight well enough to help myself much less understand their situation enough to contribute meaningfully. I just began to softly weep. When I met the people on the Good Government Board, I was still crying. The best I could manage was to stammer something about how they had changed my life while wiping away my tears.

At the time I could never have put it into words. But the Zapatistas changed my life more by their example than by our brief interaction. They weren't even all that nice to me when I appeared before them as the crazy, crying gringa with nothing much to say. Clearly they had not read *Eat, Pray, Love*, ergo, I doubt they had a frame of reference for my pampered white girl awakening. From their perspective it looked like I was wasting their time.

Their example, on the other hand, altered the course of my life dramatically. The Mayans have been oppressed and marginalized for generations. In spite of it all, these indigenous rebels managed to find it within themselves to arrest their self definition from the hands of the dominant system. They undertook the most revolutionary of human acts. They found the courage to define themselves (rather than being defined by the gaze of another) and to invest their energy in creating the kind of world they want to occupy.

The Zapatistas withdrew from Mexico from within its own borders. They refused all government money and set up their own internal governments. They declared their right to freedom and self rule. The Zapatistas have created their own alternative way of life.

My encounter with the Zapatistas was the beginning of an emotional and spiritual breakdown that ultimately led me to leave behind my career as a successful and financially secure tax lawyer and head to Chiapas in search of my own alternative way of life.

That first trip to Chiapas was the beginning of the end of my ability to hold my personal traumas at bay. When I got home I started to cry and I just couldn't stop. I must have cried every pent up tear I had. I think I cried for 6 months.

Every day when I came home from work, I sat down to meditate and the tears would just begin to flow.

Not long after my trip to Oventik, my past began peeking around the corners of my present in the most uncomfortable ways. The man who had severely abused me when I was 16 contacted me after 20 years of silence and my employer began restructuring my department at work. To me, the environment at work began to feel very much like the police investigation and the murder. I couldn't tell who I could trust and I no longer knew how to function. I have to say, the situation at work was uncomfortable. But to be fair, this had more to do with the traumas that were surfacing in my life than with any actual events that unfolded with my employer.

In any case, all of my wounds got triggered at once. The barriers that separated my traumas from my everyday life ruptured like a dam that has seen a little too much rain. I collapsed. I was forced to stop and deal with the pain of my past.

My encounter with the Zapatistas and my subsequent breakdown were the beginning of my recovery. The lessons I learned from studying the Zapatista movement and the healing work that followed were indeed the key to finding my authentic sense of self.

Like the Zapatistas, and perhaps because of my exposure to their example, I have finally arrested my self definition from the traumas I experienced and from the hands of those who inflicted them.

I know who I am separate and apart from the gaze foisted upon me by the people who abused me and by those elements of society that have attempted to define me as a woman and a person. I found the courage to finally face my pain, and as a result, I have found my worth and my authentic sense of self. My mirror image reflection is 99.9% whole.

I have moved from being a victim to being a visionary![170]

∞

After writing this book, I will personally never be the same. In the spring of 2010, when I stepped off of a plane in Villahermosa, Tabasco and began my journey south in search of the Zapatista rebels and some hardcore answers about my life, I could never have imagined where my journey would take me. I never could have imagined the inner changes it would demand of me. It has been worth it. I hope you will join me.

If you are ready to begin your Passion Path Journey, go to www.rebeckaeggers.com to find out how you can get connected to Rebecka and The Passion Path. The Passion Path is the path of the Passionate Warrior and of wholehearted, purposeful, and skillful living.

---

[170] http://rebeckaeggers.com/beyond-the-wounded-warrior/.

About the Author

Rebecka Eggers, Freedom Activator and Passion Priestess, is trained as a Metaphysical Minister, a Co-Active Life Coach, and a Reiki Master. After spending the better part of 20 years studying to become and working as a transactional tax attorney, Rebecka had a spiritual awakening that changed the course of her life. She now lives in Southern Mexico where she is trailblazing The Passion Path.

Rebecka represents the best of two worlds that seldom intersect. She has all the grounded, practical skills her legal training provided. She also has what it takes to navigate in the celestial world of Spirit. She takes all the analytical and practical skills that made her successful as a transactional tax lawyer and combines them with the mystical and the sacred in order to provide her clients with an unparalleled opportunity for clarity, growth, and ultimately, freedom. Rebecka applies all of her analytical and spiritual gifts to initiate her clients into a powerful, purposeful, and passionate way of living.

If you are ready to create a rich and powerful life of purpose and passion, Rebecka is available to guide you in the process of claiming your freedom and your power so you can get on your Passion Path. Go to <u>www.rebeckaeggers.com</u> to learn more.

Additional Credits

The cover for Coming Alive! was created by artist and designer Charlotte Hayes, while typography, layout and additional graphics were provided by Jennifer Soucy. Together, Charlotte and Jennifer form the creative team at The Brand Box, a small marketing company in NC. They can be reached through their website at www.the-brand-box.com.

www.ingramcontent.com/pod-product-compliance
Lightning Source LLC
LaVergne TN
LVHW041606070426
835507LV00008B/152